Tony Lazzeri

ALSO BY PAUL VOTANO
AND FROM MCFARLAND

*Stand and Deliver:
A History of Pinch-Hitting* (2003)

*Late and Close:
A History of Relief Pitching* (2002)

Tony Lazzeri
A Baseball Biography

PAUL VOTANO

McFarland & Company, Inc., Publishers
Jefferson, North Carolina, and London

LIBRARY OF CONGRESS CATALOGUING-IN-PUBLICATION DATA

Votano, Paul, 1929–
    Tony Lazzeri : a baseball biography / Paul Votano.
    p.   cm.
    Includes bibliographical references and index.

    ISBN 0-7864-2014-6 (softcover : 50# alkaline paper)

    1. Lazzeri, Tony, 1903–1946. 2. Baseball players—
United States—Biography. 3. New York Yankees (Baseball
team). I. Title.
GV865.L34V68   2005
796.357'092—dc22   2005001972

British Library cataloguing data are available

©2005 Paul Votano. All rights reserved

No part of this book may be reproduced or transmitted in any form or by any means, electronic or mechanical, including photocopying or recording, or by any information storage and retrieval system, without permission in writing from the publisher.

On the front cover: Lazzeri as a member of the Salt Lake City Bees, 1925 (National Baseball Hall of Fame Library, Cooperstown, NY)

Manufactured in the United States of America

McFarland & Company, Inc., Publishers
  Box 611, Jefferson, North Carolina 28640
  www.mcfarlandpub.com

To Mom and Dad
who supported and encouraged me
every step of the way.

Acknowledgments

I would like to acknowledge some people who provided me not only with the wherewithal but also with the background information I needed to put this volume together.

My friend and neighbor, Chet Wargocki, was extremely helpful in providing me with pictures and excerpts about Tony Lazzeri from a number of the scores of baseball books in his library. I also wish to thank another neighbor, the distinguished baseball historian Bob Creamer, for his kind words and encouragement.

Then, too, I had a pleasant telephone conversation with Dario Lodigiani, Tony's fellow San Franciscan who played for "Poosh 'Em Up" when he managed the Toronto Maple Leafs.

Finally, I wish to commend Society for American Baseball Research members Larry Baldassaro, Ted Hathaway, Dick Beverage and John Infanger for the information they provided me that was relevant to Lazzeri and his extraordinary career.

Contents

Acknowledgments vii
Preface ix
Introduction 1

1. The Formative Years (1903–1924) 5
2. The Talk of Minor League Baseball (1925) 15
3. A Breakout Rookie Season (1926) 23
4. Murderers' Row (1927) 42
5. Back-to-Back Champions (1928) 67
6. Also-Rans (1929–1931) 83
7. Back on Top Again (1932) 103
8. Runners Up (1933–1935) 117
9. Return to Paradise (1936–1937) 131
10. The End Draws Near (1938–1943) 155
11. Retirement and the Final Exit (1944–1946) 169

Appendix A: Career Statistics 175
Appendix B: Career Highlights 179
Appendix C: Inscription on the Hall of Fame Plaque 184
Notes 185
Bibliography 191
Index 195

Preface

By an accident of fate, I was born too late to see Tony Lazzeri play major league baseball. By the time I had become a serious follower, "Poosh 'Em Up" had left the big leagues forever. My loss.

As a lifelong fan of the New York Yankees, Joe DiMaggio in particular, I would have loved nothing better than to have gone to Yankee Stadium to see the heroes of that rich tradition — Lazzeri, Babe Ruth, Lou Gehrig, DiMaggio, Frank Crosetti, Red Rolfe, Lefty Gomez, Red Ruffing — perform on the giant stage that is affectionately called "The Big Ballpark in the South Bronx."

I had heard of their exploits, of course, but other than DiMaggio and Crosetti, I was not fortunate enough to see them in action. And even those two, I had seen only at the tail ends of their careers.

However, I am thankful for the many books and articles that have included the accomplishments of the remarkable individual who was Tony Lazzeri. I was also able to talk to a handful of people still around who either knew him or of him. All in all, I was able to get more than just a passing glimpse of the man in my attempts to draw as complete a picture of him as would be humanly possible.

Regretfully, Tony Lazzeri lived in an era when information was not made available as abundantly as it is today. Couple that with Lazzeri's own reticence toward talking to the press as a matter of course. Unfortunately, what could have been a stockpile of data gathered when he was a prominent figure in the big leagues is somewhat limited.

Compare this situation with the millions of words that are available to all of us at this moment in time, when everything that can be dug up about the modern ball player, including what they had for breakfast, is instantly available. The Internet alone provides us with that and more at the flick of a key on one's personal computer.

Remember, too, that Tony Lazzeri was the product of an immigrant family who came to America from Italy shortly before the turn of the century and, consequently, did not accumulate much of anything that could be called a paper trail. Other than his father, none of the earlier generations of his family appear in the public records of the City of San Francisco, not his grandparents or even his mother.

Obviously anyone who may have known someone in the Lazzeri household has long since passed from the scene. Also many of the records that may have been available were lost in the terrible San Francisco earthquake and subsequent fires of 1906. Documentation on thousands upon thousands of families who were living at that time was completely gone.

Compound all of this with Tony's skillful ability to avoid coverage from the media other than the statistics he amassed on the baseball field, and it is little wonder that the reporting on his life and times is scant, especially compared to other stars of his era like Babe Ruth, Lou Gehrig and even, to an extent, Joe DiMaggio.

It has always amazed me that there was no biography written about Tony Lazzeri. I would have thought that his achievements on the major league baseball diamond alone would have cried out for one. The very fact that he accomplished all of what he did while suffering from epilepsy throughout his life adds an improbable exclamation point to his extraordinary career.

Perhaps the absence of material about the man may well have frightened off some would-be biographers. All the better for the first writer to chronicle the life of Tony Lazzeri, however cut short it may have been. Be that as it may, I could not be happier with the results of my digging around to discover whatever I could on "Poosh 'Em Up."

By all accounts, he was a complex individual. Even with his lack of a formal education — it was reduced by his own doing at the age of 15 — one could never consider Tony Lazzeri lacking smarts. As a matter of fact, his rise from the streets and playgrounds of San Francisco as well as his experience as a boilermaker at a tender age enabled him to develop a set of self-made standards and morals beyond reproach.

Nothing that I came across gave any hint of scandalous behavior.

When he set out to seek his fortune as a baseball player, everyone who came into contact with him was not only amazed by his obvious skills but also by his leadership qualities and his honesty and integrity. All were quick to recognize that the young man was wise beyond his years, setting an elevated tone that few among his peers possessed.

Even when he was with the Yankees, it was Lazzeri and not Ruth or Gehrig that most of his teammates looked up to for advice and counsel.

After all, it was Lazzeri who took Joe DiMaggio under his wing when he first came up to the Yankees and showed him exactly how to act and carry himself. And that was not just because he and Joe shared the same birthplace and heritage but because it was the thing to do when a player came up to the big club. When you compare the two of them, great similarities in their character and makeup are readily apparent.

Frank Crosetti and Lefty Gomez, among others, publicly asserted how much Lazzeri had shaped their careers and personal lives. When it became clear in 1937 that the Yankees were turning over their roster almost completely and that Tony Lazzeri was going to be among the first to go after that season, he trained Joe Gordon to become his successor without a whimper or complaint. The man just could not be any other way.

After Ted Williams ended his glorious career, he claimed that his Red Sox and not the Yankees would have won all those pennants and world championships had someone other than Phil Rizzuto been their shortstop. So too would the Yankees have lost some of their luster if someone other than Tony Lazzeri had been their second baseman during his 12 years with the "Bronx Bombers."

Why did it take so long for this man to be voted into the Hall of Fame? That question has been open to conjecture for many years. Many fingers have been pointed in the direction of several individuals who served on the old Veterans Committee and blocked Lazzeri's induction year after year. It is said that an anti–Yankee attitude existed on that committee; some believed there were just too many of them already in the hallowed Hall.

There has also been talk that one or two on that committee were prejudiced against him because of his Italian heritage. Who knows? It would serve no purpose to dwell on the possible reasons it took so long after his playing days ended for Lazzeri to be inducted into the Hall of Fame.

It took the work of a dedicated group of individuals from the Bay Area and some of his former teammates to spearhead a drive to insure his election at long last in 1991, over five decades after he played his last major league game.

I believe there is no point in devoting more than a passing mention to this apparent miscarriage of justice. The fact remains that Tony Lazzeri is enshrined in the Hall of Fame where he surely belongs with the other greats from major league baseball's glorious history.

Introduction

It is ironic that a Hall of Fame player who spent nearly his entire career with the all-time winningest franchise in baseball should be remembered first for notable failure. But ask the more casual among baseball fans to recall a single event in the career of Tony Lazzeri, they remember the time he struck out against Grover Cleveland Alexander in Game Seven of the 1926 World Series. It was a moment of hard luck — against one of the all-time great pitchers, whatever his age and condition — at the very beginning of a brilliant, otherwise successful career.

In as powerful a lineup as has ever been put together in major league baseball — the fabled 1927 Murderers' Row team — Lazzeri batted sixth behind Earle Combs, Mark Koenig, Babe Ruth, Lou Gehrig and Bob Meusel. He starred on that team as its best right-handed power hitter in a lineup of superstars, only a year after establishing a then-rookie record for home runs.

Lazzeri spent 12 years as the Yankees' regular second baseman until Joe Gordon replaced him following the 1937 season. Typifying the kind of individual he was, Lazzeri worked closely with Gordon, knowing full well that the youngster had been chosen by club management to take his job. As with Gordon, he was always available to take young players like Joe DiMaggio and Frank Crosetti under his wing when they entered the big leagues.

Lazzeri, in fact, would also give advice to any player who asked for it, be it a teammate or even an opponent. After his own illustrious playing career had ended, slugger Hank Greenberg commented to his biographer, Ira Berkow, "Certainly I took tips from a few players. One is Tony Lazzeri, who advised me to move up on the plate in order to follow the ball better and hit the outside pitches."[1]

As a defensive second baseman, Lazzeri possessed an excellent glove and a potent throwing arm. These qualities, coupled with his outstanding leadership and superior baseball instincts, make him truly one of the most complete second basemen to ever play the game.

While the sportswriters reporting on the Yankees in Lazzeri's day judged him to be temperamental and even sullen at times, his teammates saw him as a player who mixed in readily with them in the clubhouse give-and-take. "Taciturn" was an adjective often used by some reporters back then in their stories about the ball club. In point of fact, none of it played a role in his performances on the field.

During his storied career, "Poosh 'Em Up" batted over .300 five times, drove in over 100 runs in seven seasons and hit 187 home runs on the way to compiling a .292 overall batting average. He was also selected to appear in the first All-Star game ever played in Chicago in 1933.

Seldom before had second basemen on the major league level produced such offensive numbers. The keepers of the keystone sack were looked upon principally for their defense. Lazzeri joined Nap Lajoie, Eddie Collins, and Rogers Hornsby in a select group of second basemen who were among their teams' and leagues' best hitters.

His glove, throwing arm and good speed on the base paths all contributed to his outstanding success in the big leagues. He had tremendous instincts for the game, and there was no one during his era who could work the double steal better than Tony Lazzeri.

He was looked up to as the inspirational leader on Yankee teams that won six American League pennants and five world championships while he wore the pinstripes. These were ball clubs that included not only such immortals as Ruth, Gehrig, Combs and Meusel but also Bill Dickey, Waite Hoyt, Herb Pennock, Joe DiMaggio, Lefty Gomez and Red Ruffing, among other outstanding players.

In 2003, when the Yankees were celebrating the one hundredth anniversary of their founding, the *New York Daily News* had a panel of experts select the all-time Yankee team, position by position. Although Gordon, Willie Randolph, Bobby Richardson and Alfonso Soriano were high on their list of second basemen, Tony Lazzeri received the nod for best ever.

In his article "The Unknown Star" reporter John Harper of the *New York Daily News* identified "Poosh 'Em Up" as "surely the least celebrated, the least familiar to generations of fans."[2] No doubt it was the low profile he maintained through most of his playing days that contributed to the seeming lack of appreciation.

In 1925, the year before he joined the Yankees, Lazzeri hit 60 home runs for the Salt Lake City Bees of the Pacific Coast League to set a new organized baseball record, surpassing the 59 that Ruth had slugged in 1921. "Poosh 'Em Up" also banged out 222 hits and drove in 220 runs that season during the PCL's lengthy 197-game schedule. He was the talk of the entire professional baseball world in that incredible season and drew the attention of many major league scouts.

General Manager Ed Barrow, considered the architect of the Yankee dynasty, purchased Lazzeri that year for $50,000 for delivery in 1926. He later called Tony the "glue" that held the Yankee team together. "He was one of the greatest players I have ever known," Barrow wrote in his autobiography. "Lazzeri, though only a rookie himself, took over the leadership of the infield, guided Gehrig on his left and Koenig on his right, and remained a leader thereafter. He will always be one of the greatest in my book.

"Bridging the span between the first teams to win a championship for the Yankees, and the great teams which were to follow, he made his influence felt on the field and off. The help he gave in making Frankie Crosetti and Joe DiMaggio outstanding Yankees never can be overestimated."[3]

"Poosh 'Em Up" was celebrated by the thousands of Italian immigrants who began following baseball because of him. While other major league teams were hesitant to sign Italian-American ballplayers, the Yankees were not. With New York City home to the largest Italian immigrant community in the United States, players like Lazzeri, and later Crosetti and DiMaggio, fit very snugly into their innovative marketing plans.

Lazzeri was known as the "quiet man of the Yankees" for obvious reasons. But it was "Poosh 'Em Up" who became the first great Italian-American superstar in American professional sports, a full decade before Joe DiMaggio arrived in New York to inherit that mantle.

Born and raised in poverty in San Francisco, Lazzeri was a welder's son who learned his baseball on the playgrounds of the city. These were the same grounds that produced such other Hall of Famers as Lefty Gomez, Joe Cronin, George "Highpockets" Kelly, Harry Heilmann, Wally Berger, Chick Hafey, Billy Martin and Ernie Lombardi, among a host of other greats.

Lazzeri's reputation, even as a rookie, was that of a "ballplayer's ballplayer" who had the respect and admiration not only of his teammates but of opposing players as well. Columnist Arthur Daley of *The New York Times* called him "one of the most intelligent athletes ever to patrol the diamond."[4]

After his release from the Yankees following the 1937 season, Lazzeri signed with the Chicago Cubs and helped them win the 1938 National

League pennant, although they were swept by the Yankees in the World Series. He divided his final year in the big leagues with the other two New York teams at the time, the Giants and the Brooklyn Dodgers.

In addition to his fine batting average and home run totals, "Poosh 'Em Up" completed his tenure in the big leagues with 1,840 hits and 1,191 runs batted in. At the time of his retirement, he had established himself as the most powerful second baseman in major league history.

With his big league playing days behind him, Lazzeri tried his hand at managing. He had brief stints as the skipper of the Toronto franchise of the International League in 1939 and 1940, Portsmouth of the Piedmont League in 1942 and Wilkes-Barre of the Eastern League in 1943.

What might be most astonishing, considering what he accomplished on the diamond, was that Lazzeri suffered from epilepsy throughout his entire life. Fortunately, he never had an attack while on the field, and it obviously never affected his play. It is now believed that his epilepsy occasionally kept him aloof.

His premature death in 1946 at the age of only 42 was officially attributed to a heart attack. However, many believed that he had been stricken by an epileptic seizure in his home, fell down a flight of stairs and broke his neck. John Harper's article in the *Daily News* indicated that "it wasn't until he died that even those who knew Lazzeri found out how courageous he had been, playing his entire career while suffering from epilepsy."[5]

It took some 53 years after he played his final major league game, and 45 years following his death, for "Poosh 'Em Up" to gain election to the Hall of Fame. A petition-signing campaign initiated by a group of Lazzeri's friends and associates from his hometown of San Francisco helped bring about a new awareness of his outstanding accomplishments. Ultimately he was enshrined in Cooperstown in 1991 after being voted in by the Veterans Committee.

1

The Formative Years (1903–1924)

Anthony Michael Lazzeri first saw the light of day on December 6, 1903, in San Francisco, California. When he died in 1946 at the age of 42, he had no doubt packed more into his comparatively brief life than many whose plaques would also hang in the Major League Baseball Hall of Fame.

Raised in the hard-hitting Cow Hollow district of North Beach, the city's "Little Italy" section, Tony grew up in a part of San Francisco that carried an unvarnished history. As part of the old Barbary Coast, North Beach was a haven for the hundreds of thousands of Italian immigrants who began drifting in as far back as the 1860s. The neighborhood was known for its Mediterranean essence featuring an assortment of bakeries, gelato parlors and restaurants where pungent smells wafted through the air night and day. Happily, not much has changed there since then.

Tony Lazzeri's grandparents selected the area for their "home away from home" because its look reminded them of the old country, and it provided them with the only kind of housing they could afford. Before the Italians arrived, it was mostly the Irish, Mexicans, Spaniards, Australians and Chileans who had inhabited the neighborhood.

North Beach's main thoroughfare was and still is Grant Avenue, San Francisco's oldest street. One of the city's most recognizable and well-known landmarks is Coit Tower, located high atop Telegraph Hill and named after Lillie Hitchcock Coit. Madam Coit was a philanthropist who set aside funds in her will for a memorial to be built in honor of the volunteer firemen who had served the area in the 1850s and '60s. The Tower was built to resemble the nozzle of a fire hose and remains a "must-see" stop for visiting tourists to this day.

Other prominent landmarks in North Beach included two Roman

Catholic churches where Italian families in the community worshipped: the Church of Saints Peter and Paul, topped by a pair of majestic white towers, and St. Francis of Assisi Church that was dedicated as a shrine to St. Francis, the city's namesake.

At Tony Lazzeri's birth, San Francisco was a city just coming into it's own and slowly fulfilling its promise as the "Paris of the Pacific." A glance down Market Street revealed a lively city teeming with horseless carriages, cable cars and the best-dressed men and women to be found anywhere in the United States. With a population of 350,000 at the time, it ranked as the ninth largest city in the country. It was also the greatest port on the west coast, moving more goods than all the other ports from California to Oregon combined.

A copper dome topped its spanking-new City Hall that was bigger and more spectacular than even the capitol dome in Washington, D.C. The city's 800-room Palace Hotel was one of the largest luxury hotels in the world. And the newly completed Golden Gate Park represented one of the most elegant city sanctuaries in the country.

According to author Gary Brechin, the citizens of San Francisco were supremely optimistic at the turn of the century after having made complete recovery from the destructive depression of the late 1800s. "Everything was available in the way of vice and sin," he says. "And it prided itself on that as a matter of fact. It had wine; it had a strong Latin culture, especially in the North Beach area, its hills and its pastels next to the Golden Gate. And all this contributed to this bohemian Mediterranean quality which really was unlike any other city in America at that time."[1]

Author Daniel Bacon says that San Francisco led a charmed life as the 1900s began. "It was a city on the roll," says Bacon. "San Francisco's society was enjoying European opera singers, cordon bleu chefs. They were going to Delmonico's on Market Street and eating oysters and drinking champagne. It was a time of revelry and joy in the city."[2]

Then, as now, San Francisco represented an open invitation to immigrants and other exiles to make a new life for themselves amidst thousands of like-minded refugees. For some it was also the place that would lead them on to the mysterious Orient, while others viewed it as a city of doorways that opened up to surprises galore.

Despite all of its seeming opulence, North Beach, where the youthful Tony Lazzeri lived, could be a tough place to grow up. He and his friends had to learn how to defend themselves in order to survive on the sometimes volatile streets of the district. Being of Italian extraction didn't help their situation. As a matter of fact, their heritage was often the reason they were compelled to protect themselves physically.

1. The Formative Years (1903–1924)

From 1906 to 1915 nearly two million Italians immigrated to the United States. The previously established émigrés often treated the newly arrived immigrants as outcasts. At the time Italians were thought to be among the least desirable of all the immigrant groups that were drifting in from Europe, only slightly better than blacks. They were subjected to vicious stereotyping and prejudice, as they were considered greasy, hot-headed thieves on a par with gypsies, Slavs and other "unwashed" who were only suited for menial labor. The sportswriters that Tony Lazzeri was to encounter later in New York often referred to them as "fascists," "wops" and "dagos" up until the end of World War II.

It was not uncommon for Tony and his friends to be called such names as well as a few other even less complimentary labels. Consequently, he and his counterparts learned rather early on how to use their fists. No matter how famous Tony Lazzeri was to become, this aspect of his life was one that he would have to deal with throughout his entire being.

"I was a pretty tough kid," he told Harry T. Brundidge, a reporter for *The Sporting News* in an interview that appeared in the paper's December 11, 1930, edition. "The neighborhood wasn't one in which a boy was likely to grow up a sissy, for it was fight or get licked, and I never got licked."[3]

In fact, according to Leo Trachtenberg, the author of *The Wonder Team: The True Story of the Incomparable 1927 New York Yankees*, Tony was so good with his fists that he had contemplated becoming a professional boxer for a time.[4]

However, the young Lazzeri was drawn more and more to the playgrounds of the city. There was nothing that he would rather do than play baseball. The city's playgrounds were where he could be found every Sunday from dawn to dusk, playing his beloved game. It soon became apparent to everyone who saw him that Tony Lazzeri could hit and throw a baseball with even better skill and more ferocity than he could deliver a punch.

Baseball had come west during the Gold Rush and was played in the often-chilly weather that dominated the San Francisco sandlots. The city is where players first became known as "sandlotters." When the poem "Casey at the Bat" was published in a local newspaper, a new legend was born.

Apart from the natural desire for most youngsters to play the sport, it was also looked upon as a pastime that offered the promise of fulfilling a boy's dream of escaping the tawdry streets of the city into immortality. In many ways it was similar to the escape hatch that professional basketball symbolizes to urban kids in today's world.

In the same year that Tony Lazzeri was born — 1903 — San Francisco became home to the nation's first Japanese baseball team, the Fuji Club. However, Asians faced the same hostility that the Italians had to endure, perhaps more so.

Players of Japanese ancestry hoped that sharing a love of the game with their contemporaries in San Francisco would allow them to be respected and integrated. They truly believed that putting on a baseball uniform was akin to waving an American flag, that it would provide them with a connection to the country and specifically to the community. That same year, the first World Series ever took place when the Boston Pilgrims (now Red Sox)—featuring the immortal Cy Young—played the Pittsburgh Pirates. The Pilgrims were victorious, winning five of the eight games.

With no big league teams on the horizon west of St. Louis, it was the Pacific Coast League that beckoned to young men like Tony Lazzeri. And practically every waking moment of his formative years was spent on those very sandlots that spawned the likes of the DiMaggio brothers, Joe Cronin, Ernie Lombardi, Frank Crosetti and scores of other soon-to-be legends of the game.

The Pacific Coast League, comprised of teams in six cities from Seattle to Los Angeles, was established in 1903, the same year that Tony Lazzeri was born. However, it almost diappeared three years later following the disastrous San Francisco earthquake and fire. With most of the city in ruins, over 3,000 people dead and damage put at somewhere over a billion, the league was on the brink of total collapse.

In order to survive, the league needed San Francisco. Cal Ewing, owner of the Oakland franchise, who was helping the other financially strapped teams, offered money and the use of his ballpark to the city's Seals. With Ewing as their salvation, the league resumed its schedule by late May of 1906.

Tony Lazzeri was a mere toddler, barely three years of age, when the infamous earthquake and resultant fires ravaged San Francisco. His family along with other Italian immigrants were credited with helping to protect their neighborhood against the fires that swept through the city following the tremors. They cracked open barrels of their precious homemade red wine, soaked blankets with the stuff and covered the roofs of their homes. This procedure helped them stem the tide of the fires that raged following the worst earthquake in this country's history.

In that same decade after 1900, San Francisco also endured a bubonic plague that quarantined Chinatown, lethal labor violence, racism and extensive political corruption. Some in the city felt it was being punished because of its sinfulness, as sermons from the pulpits of many of its churches had proclaimed.

1. The Formative Years (1903–1924)

Tony Lazzeri as a toddler, long before he knew what a baseball was. (National Baseball Hall of Fame Library, Cooperstown, N.Y.)

But under the leadership of Mayor "Sunny Jim" Rolph, the city began a golden age of rebuilding and expansion. A new city hall was dedicated, as was an exposition auditorium in the civic center. World-renowned opera singer Luisa Tetrazzini came to San Francisco and performed for thousands on Market Street. In 1915 the first coast-to-coast telephone conversation took place when Alexander Graham Bell spoke from New York to Thomas Watson in San Francisco. These were but a handful of events that helped bring the city back from the depths of despair.

The city's most dramatic accomplishment in 1915, though, was the building of The Panama Pacific International Exposition on 635 acres of leased and reconstructed marshlands called Harbor View. The even reestablished San Francisco on the roster of prominent American cities at a time when the city desperately needed it. The fair was thrilling to behold with its magnificent depictions of the past, present and future. It even included the Liberty Bell that had been transported across the country from Philadelphia to be on display. Admission was only 50 cents for adults and 25 cents for children under 12.

The fair featured a 400-mile grand prix race with its star attraction the greatest automobile racer of his time, Barney Oldfield. A 435-foot tower of jewels with thousands of pieces of colored glass sparkled in the daylight sun. At night a device called "The Scintillator" that projected 48 beams of light through steam lighted the building. Finally, it boasted the Palace of Fine Arts, designed by the famed architect Bernard Maybeck, whose vision became a representation of San Francisco's rebirth.

It was evident early on that Tony Lazzeri was not destined to become a scholastic overachiever. He barely got through St. Theresa's parochial school in his neighborhood. His high school administrators and teachers suggested that it might be best for all concerned if Tony were to find something else to do with his life when they expelled him at the age of 15. He could not have agreed more with their assessment of his academic endeavors.

In that same interview with Harry T. Brundidge noted above, Lazzeri summed up that period in his life this way: "I voted all of them my thanks and good wishes."[5] The fighting, the running around and the baseball playing had left him little time for schoolwork, which was never all that high on his list of priorities anyway.

Thereupon Tony, in his mid-teens, joined his father as a boilermaker's helper. The hours in the plant were long and difficult but never enough to prevent him from playing ball on Sundays. In fact he was able to play baseball on the factory's team. It was evident that nothing would stop Tony Lazzeri from playing ball at any time when he was growing up.

1. The Formative Years (1903–1924)

"Poosh 'Em Up" as a dapper teenager growing up in the Cow Hollow district of San Francisco (National Baseball Hall of Fame Library, Cooperstown, N.Y.)

The local semi-pro team of which Tony was a member was called the Golden Gate Natives. "My pitching stood me in good stead at boiler making," he said half-jokingly in another 1930 interview. "I could toss a rivet with the best of them."[6] Those Sunday ball games were where he also met his future wife, Maye. She was the sister of a teammate and before long it was evident that the pair were made for each other. But not just yet. There were ball games to be played.

Like most immigrants, Tony's dad scoffed at his son's ball playing. The elder Lazzeri's rationale was that the only way for someone to succeed in this country was to work hard to put food on the table for the family. Tony had other ideas. He was one of those boys who had a dream and he was determined that his love of baseball and the skills that he possessed would lead him to far greener pastures than those which life in North Beach offered.

When Tony Lazzeri was growing into manhood, the city of San Francisco was relatively peaceful. However, some neighborhoods like Cow Hollow, where he lived in the West Coast's busiest port, were beginning to feel the effects of the extremely unpopular prohibition law of January 17, 1920. With probably more bars per square foot than any other city in America, San Francisco's alcohol consumption simply went underground and it remained the wettest city in the United States at the time. The result was that gangland violence erupted as smuggled liquor was being trucked in over the Golden Gate Bridge and onto the city's streets.

Just after Lazzeri turned seventeen, the city had its first bitter taste of the Roaring Twenties on December 5, 1920, when two police detectives were shot and killed by three members of the Howard Street Gang, a group of bootleggers operating out of a South-of-Market district warehouse. The killers were apprehended and jailed two days later by police in nearby Sonoma County. Emotions ran so high over the death of the two officers that an angry mob stormed the Santa Rosa Jail and, acting as vigilantes, lynched the three suspects forthwith.

Although this type of disruptive behavior was sprouting up all around him, it seemed to have no influence on Lazzeri, who made his way regularly to the playgrounds of San Francisco to play baseball. He continued to hone his skills while competing against the likes of Joe Cronin, Ernie Lombardi, Wally Berger and other future Hall of Famers who were growing up there around the same time.

In the book *The Great Rivalry*, written by Ed Linn, Cronin remembered how Tony would arrive late at the park after working almost all day in his father's grape press to make homemade wine, just like many other Italian immigrant families did. Cronin recalled that Lazzeri would immediately take over the game as both a pitcher and a slugger. "He'd come to the park around the seventh or eighth inning," Cronin recollected, "and always—always—hit a home run, strike everybody out and beat us."[7]

In Frank Graham's *The New York Yankees: An Informal History*, the author described the teenaged Lazzeri thusly: "He was tall, lean, square-shouldered, and, for all his comparatively slight build, exceedingly strong and durable. He had a face like those in the paintings of the Italian masters — olive-skinned, oval, with high-cheekbones and smoldering eyes. He spoke seldom, and, when he did his voice had an angry quality, although he was seldom angry."[8]

Throughout his career, Lazzeri carried the reputation of being standoffish and incommunicative with the press. Possibly a by-product of his hot temper as a youth, he was often sullen with reporters. One reporter went so far as to say: "Interviewing that guy is like mining coal with a nail file."[9]

The San Francisco Seals of the Pacific Coast League were tremendously successful in the 1920s. They won four PCL titles and attendance increased regularly. Even in the one season in which they finished last, the Seals recorded the highest attendance figures in the league.

Rec Park, which was their bandbox ballpark built in 1907, was pre-prohibition institution known as the "booze cage." During prohibition, although sales of beer and whiskey were prohibited, fans just brought their own into the games unimpeded. According to historian Daniel Bacon, "fans could pay 75 cents admission, and included with the price of the ticket was their choice of a ham and cheese sandwich, a shot of whisky or two beers. And needless to say it wasn't called the ham and cheese cage."[10]

But the game was the thing and players like Gus Suhr, Smead Jolley and the incomparable Lefty O'Doul helped to pack the house regularly. O'Doul was popular not only because he had once been the best hitter in the National League but because he was a local kid from a section of the city known as "Butcher Town."

The Seals' success only paved the way for Tony Lazzeri and others like him to follow their dreams. Although the hours at the boilermaker factory were long and difficult, Tony continued to play baseball religiously every Sunday. It wasn't long before a scout recommended him to former Red Sox outfielder Duffy Lewis. Then a player-manager for the Salt Lake City Bees of the Pacific Coast League, Lewis signed Lazzeri to a contract in 1922.

When the 18-year-old shortstop walked into the Bees training camp in Modesto, California, in 1922, it was evident to one and all that he was indeed a green kid. But it was also apparent to even the most experienced players that he had the physique and skills to be an exceptional ball player.

Tony batted only .192 for the club in 45 games that season while splitting his time between first and third base. Not only did he fail to hit, he played equally poorly in the field. It was obvious to all concerned that the young man was not quite ready for prime time.

The Bees felt he needed to play regularly and assigned him to Peoria of the Three-Eye League, where he was to start the 1923 season. Tony agreed but did not want to spend his time there alone. He talked Maye into marrying him. He went so far as to threaten to quit the game if she turned him down. She didn't and off they went to Peoria.

"I thought he was just teasing when he said he wanted to marry me and take me with him to Peoria," Maye said. "But when he said he wouldn't go unless I went with him, I knew he was serious. I wasn't sure he loved me, but I knew Tony loved baseball. I couldn't believe he was ready to give up baseball for me."[11]

Maye, who never remarried after Tony's death in 1946, said in 1992: "I still can't believe Tony is really gone. It's like he's on a very long road trip."[12]

Though Lazzeri loved baseball and wanted more than anything to succeed as a professional, he nearly did quit the game altogether midway through the 1923 season. Disgusted with his back-and-forth shifts between the Salt Lake City ball club and its affiliates, Tony decided to pack in his budding career when he was optioned to a team in the Eastern League.

He told the Bees' management of his decision and actually stayed out of uniform for about ten days. However, after sleeping on it for a while, he reconsidered. The ball club allowed him to remain in Salt Lake City for the balance of the season and he responded by playing shortstop and hitting a robust .354 in 39 games. However, the Bees still felt that he required more experience and ticketed him to start the 1924 season in Lincoln of the Western League.

Although he remained supremely optimistic that he would be able to make a success of his new profession, he kept his Boilermakers Union card not only during that season but throughout the length of his baseball career — just in case. Apparently in his heart of hears he wasn't all that sure his dream would materialize.

Tony started off like a house afire in Lincoln in the following season. In 82 games he banged out 28 home runs and hit .329. He also displayed his versatility by playing every position on the infield. His performance earned him a recall to Salt Lake City at mid-season, where he played in another 85 games at both shortstop and third base and smacked an additional 16 home runs while driving in 61 runs and batting a modest .283.

Lazzeri had made his point. He had played his way back to Utah so convincingly that both he and the Salt Lake City ball club were certain that they had found their starting shortstop for the upcoming season. Could a trip to the major leagues be far behind?

2

The Talk of Minor League Baseball (1925)

No one, least of all Tony Lazzeri himself, could have been prepared for what was to take place in 1925 when he reported to the Salt Lake City Bees for the start of the new season. The 21-year-old Lazzeri would go on to set a new organized baseball home run record that year and his name would be on everyone's lips. Furthermore, his exploits would provide him with a ticket to the big leagues to fulfill his still-young life's dream.

The former boilermaker joined a ball club that led the Pacific Coast League in hitting for two years and would do so again in 1925, thanks in large measure to Lazzeri's contributions. Bonneville Park, where the Bees played, did not hinder their league leading offense either.

The Bees played their home games at the highest altitude in the PCL and the ballpark's dimensions were smaller than all of the other parks. The right and left field lines were a decent 325 feet each, but the distance to dead center field was only 360 feet while the power alleys were short also. It was not uncommon for games there to wind up in double digits.

When Tony Lazzeri reported to the Bees in 1925, the manager, Oscar Vitt, had him playing shortstop and batting seventh in the lineup. Like Lazzeri, Vitt was a native of San Francisco. Originally headed for a career as an architect, he wanted to play baseball first. He was good enough to draw some offers but his father refused to give him his permission to play. However, after the earthquake and fires of 1906, his father changed his opinion and let Oscar sign on with Oakland of the California State League.

Vitt spent ten years in the major leagues, where played against immortals like Ty Cobb and Babe Ruth. Cobb once threatened to blow his head off for some sort of incident that brought the pair into conflict. Vitt himself was something of a character — a fighter, a storyteller and a practical joker who always seemed to have a smile on his face.

When he was hired to manage the Salt Lake City ball club, he became more intense and more successful. He was the man who was instrumental in convincing the owner of the Bees to sign Lazzeri when he was only 18 years old. He tutored the youth well during his association with the Bees.

Tony's name was spelled "Lazerre" in the newspapers throughout the 1925 season. One of the leading sportswriters in Salt Lake City was John C. Derks, who wrote for *The Salt Lake City Tribune* and was known to readers of the newspaper simply as JCD. Lazzeri's talents fascinated Derks ever since the ball club had signed him to a contract as an 18-year-old in 1922.

"He was green," said Derks, "but even experienced players could tell right off that the kid had it in him to make a ball player. He had the size, the hands, some speed, the aggressiveness and perhaps the best arm in baseball."[1]

When Bees owner H.W. Lane originally signed Lazzeri at Vitt's urging, he did it with an eye to the future, which was the reason he was brought along so slowly. It was his and Vitt's belief that the time Tony put in at Peoria and Lincoln was indeed well spent. Now was the time for the youngster to fulfill the promise they felt that Lazzeri had.

The Bees started off the 1925 season in a blaze of success, winning ten of their first eleven games, all of them at home. Lazzeri hit two home runs on April 16 in an 18–9 win over Portland, and then hit another one the next day as his team prevailed in a slugfest, 16–12. Two days later, he smacked a three-run homer off Charlie Root that helped win a game for the ball club. It was then that Vitt pushed him up to hit in the number five hole following Johnny Frederick and Lefty O'Doul and where he remained for the rest of the season.

While Lazzeri was making a name for himself in Salt Lake City and throughout the league, there was never a more devoted fan of his than Cesare Rinetti, who co-owned the Rotisserie Inn in downtown Salt Lake City with Francesco Capitolo. Rinetti appeared to adopt both Tony and his bride, Maye, and fed him "good Italian food to build him up."[2]

Rinetti was also a big baseball fan. One Saturday afternoon in late April when the Bees were hosting the Seattle Indians, Rinetti was in the stands cheering them on — specifically Lazzeri — as was JCD. Rinetti shouted out "Poosh 'Em Up, Tony" and the crowd joined in with the mantra. Lazzeri promptly deposited a home run over the center field fence and the crowd went wild. Tony added a double later in the game and wound up with three runs batted in as the Bees won easily, 12–3.

The next day, Derks wrote a headline to his game report story that read: "'Poosh Um Up, Tone,' Yella Da Fan, an' Tone She Poosh."[3] From that day on, Tony Lazzeri was known as "Poosh 'Em Up" to fans in Salt Lake City and everywhere that the remainder of his baseball career took him.

The following day in a doubleheader against the Indians, Tony only got one hit in five trips to the plate and a stolen base in the opener that the Bees won, 5–4. He blasted two triples in the nightcap though, which the Bees won by a score of 11–8. Derks' headline the next day was: "Tone She Poosh Um Down an' Den She Poosh Um Up." The subhead in smaller type read: "Lazerre's Great Work Afield and With Club Factors in Twin Win."[4]

Tony did not play well during the month of May, but he picked it up once again when the Bees began a home stand on June 10. In the next ten days, he hammered out six home runs to take the league lead with 17. He had his best day yet on June 28 against none other than his hometown San Francisco Seals. The Bees won it, 11–7, and Tony blasted three home runs and drove in eight runs. To make it all the more memorable, one ball was hit to left field, another to center field and the third one to right field. He added a triple for good measure.

Lazzeri now had poked 21 home runs to stay firmly in the league lead. Also, the team had come within six and a half games of the first place Seals. The following day before a huge crowd, Lazzeri hit still another homer, a three-run blast in the eighth inning, and a solo home run in the ninth, which disposed of an early Seals lead to win it for the Bees. The fans were so excited over the dramatic victory that they threw money at him as he circled the bases.

It was about this time that interest was beginning to surface in the major leagues about what this young man in Utah was doing. Word was now circulating that a few teams, notably the Yankees, Reds and Cubs, were eyeing Lazzeri. The Cubs, who had a working agreement with the Salt Lake City ball club, were nervous about Tony because they were told that he "took fits."[5]

Cincinnati Manager Jack Hendricks also passed on Lazzeri. Club owner Garry Herrmann wrote to Colonel Jacob Ruppert of the Yankees giving him the reasons why they had not purchased "Poosh 'Em Up."

Other influences were at work here as well. For example, the failure of some previous PCL so-called superstars entered into the decision for some clubs. Paul Strand, a former Salt Lake City Bee who had won six games as a 20-year-old pitcher for the 1914 "Miracle Braves," was one player who did not produce in the majors as an outfielder.

Connie Mack bought Strand for $100,00 after he hit 71 home runs for the Bees in 1923 and part of 1924. For the Athletics, he batted but .228 in 167 at-bats without a single homer in the remainder of the 1924 season. The A's sold him to the minor leagues for practically nothing after that unacceptable performance. The rap on Strand, among other things, was that the thin air in Salt Lake City had falsely inflated his home run statistics. There was no reason for them to believe that "Poosh 'Em Up's" home run power was in that same category.

Another Pacific Coast League bust was Jimmy O'Connell, for whom the Giants paid the enormous sum of $75,000 in 1922. O'Connell confessed to offering Phillies shortstop Heinie Sand $500 to throw a game in 1924. O'Connell claimed that Giants coach Cozy Dolan had talked him into making the offer to Sand. After Sand reported the attempted bribe, both O'Connell and Sand were banned from baseball for life.

Even Willie Kamm, yet another San Franciscan who was in the early stages of a 13-year big league career, was not considered any great shakes following a very successful run in the Pacific Coast League. Kamm had cost the White Sox over $70,000 and some felt that they had overpaid for the third baseman.

Perhaps even more significant in the thinking of some ball clubs was their reluctance to take on an Italian-American player. Prejudice existed among some of the teams, who felt Italians were hotheaded and excitable. Only a handful of them had played in the big leagues up until then and some preferred to keep it that way.

Some in the press had even resorted to describing Italians as "greasy and smelling of olive oil."[6] This was the kind of bigotry that a budding superstar like Lazzeri was facing as he tried to break through the barrier of prejudice that existed in the United States at this time.

The Yankees, on the other hand, under their president and general manager Ed Barrow, didn't hesitate to sign a player of Tony Lazzeri's abilities. As a marketing tool alone it was a wise investment. New York City was home to the largest Italian community in the country. One out of every seven New Yorkers was either Italian or of Italian ancestry in those days; the city had more than one million of them at the time.

Besides that, the city had already accepted a ballplayer of Italian extraction earlier. The player was named Ping Bodie, although he was born Francesco Stephano Pezzolo, also in San Francisco. His nickname came from the sound of his monstrous 52-ounce bat stinging a dead ball that was used when he was a young player.

Bodie spent four seasons in New York with the Giants, from 1918–1921, with modest results after playing for the White Sox and Athletics. For what

2. The Talk of Minor League Baseball (1925)

it was worth, the nine-year veteran, now out of the major leagues, had set a precedent in major league baseball, particularly in New York.

The Giants had tried to attract Jewish players from 1910 to 1930 in order to appeal to fans from the Polo Grounds' adjacent neighborhood, which was becoming increasingly populated by Jewish families. They had found a utility infielder, Andy Cohen, in the late 1920s, which cleared the way for the signing of other Jewish players. The Yankees, though, avoided bringing in Jewish players until 1930, when they purchased Jimmy Reese from the Pacific Coast League.

Despite what was being felt or not felt among major league baseball fans at the time, the "bible" of the game, *The Sporting News*, had recognized what was happening when it proclaimed in 1928: "Except the Ethiopian, the Mick, the Sheeney, the Wop, the Dutch and the Chink, the Cuban, the Indian, the Jap or the so-called Anglo-Saxon — his nationality is never a matter of moment if he can pitch, or hit, or field."[7] In other words, if you could play it didn't matter any longer what your nationality was.

Barrow felt that if a deal could be made for Lazzeri, it would give the Yankees a tremendous advantage over their opponents for the next decade at least. The acquisition would also increase their road appeal, where they received one-third of the gate. The club was the favorite of fans throughout the northeast region, especially in the Italian sections of Worcester, Providence and Boston.

Barrow sent Ed Holly, a Yankee scout, out to see Lazzeri. According to Barrow, Holly gave the Yankee general manager a glowing report on "Poosh 'Em Up's" capabilities. Holly also honestly reported on Lazzeri's epileptic condition.

Thereupon, Barrow dispatched Holly to San Francisco to check on the family's medical history while sending another scout, Paul Krichell, to Salt Lake City to see Lazzeri as well. He also asked Bob Connery, president of the Yankees' St. Paul farm club, to scout him also. Connery begged off, saying: "I've got my own club to think about." "You've got to go," Barrow, known for his explosive temper, demanded of Connery.[8]

All of the reports that came back on Lazzeri were excellent, including the fact that no other members of his family were affected by epilepsy. Also, the insurance company in which "Poosh 'Em Up" had a policy was willing to increase it. To be further on the safe side, the Yankees sent Tony to see a doctor, who assured them that he would not be handicapped in his ball playing. The ball club's leaders knew that the deal represented a risk for them, but they felt comfortable they had done everything within reason to justify the potential investment in "Poosh 'Em Up."

After Connery saw him, he told Barrow: "I don't care what he's got. Buy him. He's the greatest thing I've ever seen."[9] After Krichell told Barrow the same thing, the Yankees bought him for $50,000 in cash and five players to be delivered later.

In his autobiography, Barrow said this about Lazzeri and his physical condition:

> There was never a time thereafter that I didn't watch Lazzeri with the greatest apprehension, fearful always that he would have a seizure on the ball field. He never did. He had one attack on the train coming north that first spring; and he had another that I know about personally in the clubhouse before a game in St. Louis. I heard of a couple of others at secondhand. But he was never affected on the ball field, and I don't believe the public ever knew that about him. Certainly we took every precaution we could to see that the public never did, and in this the sportswriters traveling with the club were likewise as considerate of Tony's feelings and welfare.
>
> Lazzeri not only was a fine mechanical ballplayer and a powerful hitter, getting his great driving force from wrists and forearms developed as a boilermaker in his father's foundry, but he had a talent on the ball field that was part brains and part instinct.[10]

John Derks, who had been monitoring the interest in Lazzeri by major league baseball, wrote an article in the *Tribune* that was headlined: "They're After 'Our Tone'"[11] In his story he wrote that there was "a campaign in which the New York Americans [the Yankees] planned to spend $250,000 to develop their team from selected minor league players. Among them was Lazarre, Salt Lake's hard-hitting shortstop."[12]

By the time August rolled around, Derks said that the deal had been consummated with the Yankees and that "the cash was estimated all the way from $1,000 to $200,000. No doubt when the New York lads get their figures all compiled, it will be at least $250,000. Regardless, it is a fairly substantial sum."[13]

The purchase was in fact completed and announced publicly on August 1. In reporting on the signing, *The New York Times* described Lazzeri as:

> Considered the best infielder in the coast league today and perhaps the most outstanding prospect to be sent up to the majors from this league ... he has justified the confidence reposed in him by the officials of the Salt Lake Club by ripening into the most brilliant fielder that the coast league has seen in years.
>
> Lazerre has one of the best throwing arms in baseball today, easily being outstanding in that department in the coast league. He fields the ball well on either side of him, is fast in fielding and experiences no difficulty in

getting the ball away from him. Added to this he has a hitting power which ranks him fifth among the batters of the coast league.

Blessed with a large pair of hands Lazerre doubtless will be an unusual ball player. He stands out in practically every department.[14]

"Poosh 'Em up" promptly celebrated the successful conclusion of the deal by hitting his 34th and 35th home runs the following day. He also raised his batting average to .382.

Lefty O'Doul, yet another San Franciscan, also played for the Bees at the time. It was his first year as an outfielder after having begun his career as a pitcher. He led the league in hitting with a .421 batting average, but then he cooled off a bit and ultimately finished the year hitting a hefty .375. O'Doul was a big help to Lazzeri in that he hit in front of "Poosh 'Em Up" to take some of the pressure off the youngster.

Lazzeri hit his 40th home run of the year on September 2 in the Bees' 152nd game of the season. There were now 45 games left in the season. Tony then went on a home run binge, slamming 19 round trippers in the next 44 games. However, by concentrating on his home run output, he stopped stealing bases. He stole no more bases for the rest of the season after the middle of September.

On September 24, Lazzeri hit his 53rd home run of the season in a game that the Bees lost to San Francisco, 10–9. This was the first time that any mention was made in the press about his potential to surpass Babe Ruth's home run record of 59, set in 1921. However, that was the last home run he would get in Salt Lake City for the season, as the club departed on a season-ending two-week road trip.

Since "Poosh 'Em Up" had not been as successful on the road as he was at home, many doubted his ability to challenge the Ruth record. However, he hit three in Portland and two in Seattle to bring his total up to 58. In Salt Lake City, Derks' headline screamed: "Our Tone, She Poosh Um Oop Two Time, Maka da Feefty-Eight."[15]

Some controversy was attached to this particular home run. The Seattle center fielder, Bill Lane, reputedly the best in the league, let Lazzeri's line drive get past him and roll to the wall. While the official scorer generously gave Tony credit for hitting a home run, he just as well could have charged Lane with a two-base error.

In the final week of the season, the Bees were in Sacramento, where they had fared none too well throughout the year. Lazzeri was kept under wraps until October 17 when he hit Number 59 to tie the Ruth record. In Salt Lake City, John Derks' headline read: "The Bambino, He's Got Nothin' on Our Tone Now."[16] The subhead proclaimed: "Lazerre knocks out 59th homer; ties world record."[17]

A doubleheader to close out the season was set for the next day, Sunday, October 18. In order to give Lazzeri more times at bat, Manager Oscar Vitt moved him up to the leadoff position for both games. In the opener, Tony hit a double but nothing to resemble a home run. In the second game, he made outs on both of his first two times up.

However, in the seventh inning, he caught hold of one and drilled it into left center field. Normally this ball would have gone for a double had the outfielders not been so spread out. By the time Merlin Kopp chased it down, Lazzeri had rounded the bases to set a new record for home runs in organized baseball with 60.

The next day's *Salt Lake City Tribune* roared: "Gooda da Tone, She Poosh Um Up for Beat Bambino."[18] Veteran ball player Johnny Kerr, who played in the game, thought that Sacramento conceded the home run to Lazzeri. "They left a lot of room in the outfield that day," he said. "The left fielder and right fielder played him right on the line. No reason for that."[19]

Despite "Poosh 'Em Up's" late season heroics, the Salt Lake City Bees failed to win the Pacific Coast League pennant in 1925. The San Francisco Seals, perennial winners, took the flag once again. In addition to the 60 balls he hit for home runs, Tony produced 252 hits that included 52 doubles and 14 triples. He also drove in 222 runs and scored 202. All of this was accomplished in a long 197-game schedule in which he played in every single game, coming to bat no less than 710 times.

Whether or not his celebrity had anything to do with it, the Lazerre name was now spelled with another "z" and one less "r." Also the "e" was dropped off in favor of an "i" so that his last name forevermore would be Lazzeri.

Next stop for the new home run king of organized baseball was St. Petersburg, Florida, where the Yankees would begin training for the 1926 season.

3

A Breakout Rookie Season (1926)

When the New York Yankees arrived in St. Petersburg in the spring of 1926, the ball club was coming off one of the most catastrophic seasons in its history. The team had been in the World Series in three of the previous five seasons that included its first-ever world championship over the crosstown Giants in 1923. The club ended up second to the Senators in 1924 with an 89–63 record, and then toppled to a disastrous 69–85 record in 1925, finishing in next-to-last place in the American League standings.

One of the major reasons for this dramatic decline was that Babe Ruth started off the 1925 season by eating his way into the hospital. No sooner had the spring training camp been concluded than the Bambino, who was constantly either chewing, smoking, eating or drinking to excess, consumed a dozen hot dogs and some half-dozen bottles of pop, resulting in his hospitalization. W.O. McGeehan of the *New York Herald-Tribune* labeled it "the world's most important stomach ache."[1]

Reporters on the train carrying the team north put out bulletins on Ruth's condition at every stop. Some headlines proclaimed that he was gravely ill. There was even a rumor that he had died shortly after being admitted to the hospital.

Manager Miller Huggins, with whom Ruth had carried on a love-hate relationship, once fined him $5,000 for "breaking training rules." Ruth went into orbit over the fine. "I haven't been drinking or carousing," he claimed. "I came in a half-hour late Saturday morning. I know of guys who kill people and bootleggers who don't get that tough a fine. It just ain't right."[2]

Not leaving well enough alone, Ruth complained that Huggins was incompetent and threatened to take his case to Commissioner Kenesaw

Mountain Landis and to the owner of the club, Jacob Ruppert. However, Ruppert backed his manager in the dispute, as did American League President Ban Johnson.

The Babe not only repented but also apologized publicly to Huggins, which helped the manager gain added standing in the baseball community. Even New York City Mayor Jimmy Walker, from the podium of a preseason Elks Club dinner in Manhattan, told Ruth to grow up. Walker told him that he had to live up to the expectations of the youth of America who idolized him. The Babe tearfully accepted the challenge and promised to mend his ways from there on out.

The Yankees began the 1925 season without Ruth in the lineup. Thereupon the club started slowly and never really recovered their old spark. The Bambino played in only 98 games that year, batting what for him was a paltry .290. In hitting only 25 home runs, he was also far below his normal output. Thus the game's top slugger was virtually no help to his team that season. So while the Yankees had been competitive in 1924, finishing three games behind the ultimate World Champion Senators, the 1925 results were totally unacceptable to Colonel Jacob Ruppert, General Manager Ed Barrow and Field Manger Miller Huggins.

Although unheralded at the time, one of the changes that occurred during that forgettable Yankee season was the installation on June 2 of a rookie from Columbia University named Lou Gehrig at first base. A day earlier, Gehrig made his major league debut when he was sent up to pinch-hit for Pee Wee Wanninger.

The next day the team's regular first sacker, Wally Pipp, who had been ailing after being hit with a pitch earlier that year, asked out of the lineup. He never returned as Gehrig began his record 14-year, 2,130 consecutive game playing streak that would last until broken by Cal Ripken, Jr. of the Baltimore Orioles in 2001.

A drastic overhaul of the Yankee ball club was called for in 1926 and it would start up the middle at shortstop and second base. The services of the previous season's occupants, Wanninger, a rookie shortstop, and nine-year veteran Aaron Ward, the second baseman, were no longer required. Wanninger, who had hit an anemic .236, was given his pink slip immediately after the 1925 season. In fact, he was out of the major leagues entirely after the 1927 campaign at the age of only 25.

Ward, who batted but .246 in 1925, was to play in only 22 games the following year behind the club's new second sacker, the former Pacific Coast League shortstop phenom Tony Lazzeri. Ward would subsequently be traded to the White Sox in the off-season.

"Poosh 'Em Up's" double play partner on the Yankees was to be Mark

Koenig, also a native San Franciscan, who had been brought up from St. Paul late in the 1925 season. While Koenig had but 28 games of major league experience behind him, Tony's first game as a big leaguer would be the first one he had ever seen.

Even second-year first baseman Lou Gehrig had not yet been transformed into a gazelle at the position. Only the veteran "Jumping Joe" Dugan at third base, arguably the best at the hot corner in the American League, was considered reliable by Huggins.

The club had no concerns in the outfield with the likes of Bob Meusel, Earle Combs and the repentant Babe Ruth patrolling the outer reaches. Meusel had picked up Ruth's slack in 1925 by slamming 33 home runs for the Yankees to lead the American League while the Babe sat out over 50 games. Meusel thus became the only right-handed batter in Yankee history to win a home run title until Joe DiMaggio was to do it in 1937.

The catchers, Pat Collins and Benny Bengough, were more than adequate. And led by a rotation that included Herb Pennock, Waite Hoyt, Urban Shocker and "Sad Sam" Jones, with newcomers Myles Thomas and Garland Braxton in reserve, the Yankee pitching staff was solid as well.

The only real question mark at the outset of the season remained in the infield. First baseman Gehrig on defense could be a little shaky at times. Shortstop Koenig, a high-strung, jittery kid, added to the ball club's potential problems. But the player who was destined to hold the group together was the first-year man Lazzeri. He had poise and a knowledge of the game well beyond his twenty-two years of age. As a hitter, the strength in his forearms — undoubtedly aided by his work as a riveter in his father's boiler shop — would lead him to deliver 18 homers in 1926, a new rookie major league record. Second basemen at the time were not counted on to be power hitters. Tony Lazzeri promptly changed all of that.

When the team broke camp in St. Petersburg, only Huggins was confident that the infield would do its job. "I believe we will win the pennant. We'll either do that or fall apart. And I don't think we'll fall apart."[3]

Despite his well-documented problems with Babe Ruth and a few others on the ball club, the 5'6", 135-pound Huggins had the complete support of Colonel Ruppert and Ed Barrow, who had hired him away from the Cardinals after the 1917 season. Hug, as he was called, had begun his managing career in St. Louis in 1912 and remained there for five years. The best finishes he had in the "Mound City" were third place both in 1914 and 1917. Other than that, his teams wound up in sixth, seventh and eighth places in the standings.

Following the dismissal of Wild Bill Donovan as manager of the Yankees after the 1917 season, Huggins had not been the first choice of co-owner, Cap Huston. Huston, who was serving in the army in France during World War I, wanted Wilbert "Uncle Robbie" Robinson, then manager of the Brooklyn ball club. After Robinson had a disastrous interview with Colonel Ruppert, Ban Johnson, the American League president, was consulted for his opinion. "Get Miller Huggins," he said.[4]

At first Huggins was reluctant to leave the Cardinals since he had invested heavily in the ball club and it was just then starting to pay him dividends. However, he agreed to take the job after meeting Ruppert. Both men liked and respected each other immediately.

Huston was furious when he learned about the hire but when he came back after the war, Huggins was firmly entrenched as the team's field manager. This fact did not deter Huston from gunning for Huggins. He used every opportunity to denigrate Huggins up until he sold his interest in the team to Ruppert after the 1922 season.

The Cincinnati-born Huggins was never a big fan favorite or even that popular with his own players. He was retiring in nature, not blessed with good health, and he tended not to mix well with the fans. He preferred to stay in the background with his team of stars. A superstitious sort, he often changed his seat to change the team's luck in a game.

His diminutive stature forced him to look up to his players, many of whom literally and figuratively looked down on him and were critical of his managing tendencies. But when all was said and done, Huggins was a decent, honest individual who genuinely liked his players and was quick to forgive their indiscretions. "Great players make great managers," the self-effacing Huggins would often say.[5]

There was no doubt about his ability to judge talent, though, and he used it wisely on the ball field. But, he never received the complete respect of his players, particularly Ruth, who led a group that constantly caroused all night, flouted curfews and ignored what there was of team discipline.[6]

This all changed amidst the terrible 1925 season. Huggins resolved to keep Ruth in line no matter what. Matters came to a head one night in St. Louis. The Yankees were nearly in the cellar and Ruth, who was hitting only .246 at the time, finally hit his first home run of the season on June 11.

The Bambino, despite drawing a huge $52,000 salary, was not pulling his weight. After Ruth missed batting practice and stumbled into the ballpark in an unkempt fashion three days in a row, Huggins called the entire team together and read them the riot act. At the same time, he told them he was fining Ruth $5,000, suspending him indefinitely and sending him back to New York.

Huggins told the team that the fine was being levied for general infractions of training and disciplinary rules. No team had ever fined a player more than $500 up until then. Ruth promptly let loose an obscene tirade of epithets and threats against the manager, but Huggins stood firm. He told the Babe in no uncertain terms to go see Colonel Ruppert if he didn't like it.

With the combined backing of Colonel Ruppert and Barrow, which was all he needed, Huggins won out. "Eventually," claimed Waite Hoyt, "a very deep affection grew up between Babe and Huggins. One of my fondest memories is a picture of Babe spouting threats at an umpire and marching toward his victim while little Hug stood between Babe and the umpire, shoving hard at Babe's chest, and giving ground with each of Babe's charges."[7]

Waite Hoyt was Huggins' strongest supporter among the Yankee players. A graduate of Brooklyn's Erasmus Hall High School, he had pitched batting practice at the Polo Grounds for John McGraw's Giants when he was only 15. He drew one of his nicknames—"Schoolboy"—from that experience. As a rookie for the Giants in 1918 under McGraw, he would later say that Huggins was the better manager of the two.

Huggins was much admired for being a teacher. "He was a complete baseball man, highly respected," said Ken Smith, a former Yankee beat writer for the *New York Daily Mirror* and the *New York Evening Graphic* who later worked in public relations for the Hall of Fame. Author Leo Trachtenberg spoke to Smith about Huggins in a telephone conversation on March 26, 1986: "The first thing that strikes on your mind was that everybody trusted him, and admired him. He was no phony," Smith told Trachtenberg.[8]

Later in his career, Tony Lazzeri told *Literary Digest*: "I don't think anybody could bring along a kid player like Huggins could."[9] No one knew that better than Lazzeri, whom the manager took under his wing. It is certain that no one appreciated "Poosh 'Em Up" more than Huggins. "Here's the man who really made the 1926 team," the Yankee manager said of Lazzeri. "He was the tower of strength to Gehrig and Koenig when they were unsure of themselves. Ball players like Lazzeri come along once in a generation."[10]

Mark Koenig was equally effusive in his praise of Huggins as a manager. In 1984, he told sportswriter Norman Macht:

> Hug was the best manager I ever played for. He was a little guy, very quiet, very nervous. He'd sit on the bench in a tight game and you could hear him muttering to himself. "This guy has two hits already, we'll pitch to him, he can't get another hit, he won't get another one."
>
> He never bawled out a player in front of anybody else. There was one

stretch where I was making a lot of errors and the writers got on me. Huggins called me into his office and said, "I'm managing this ball club. As long as I say you're gonna play, you're my shortstop. Never mind what anybody else says." He gave me confidence.

He had the respect of all his players, even Ruth. Once he had a spat with the Babe, and Ruth and Meusel threatened to throw him off the end of a pier. But when he fined Ruth $5,000, it stuck.[11]

Koenig said that Huggins was not a disciplinarian. "There was no curfew. Guys would come into the hotel at two or three in the morning after a night on the town. The elevator boy'd say, 'Geez, I just took another bunch of you guys up.'

"Huggins didn't care as long as you delivered on the field. If you didn't get the job done, then he'd say something to you."[12]

In that same interview, Koenig told Macht: "We weren't expected to go anywhere in 1926. I came up from St. Paul late in 1925 when we finished seventh. We had power and good pitching, but a young infield. Gehrig was starting his first full season. Tony Lazzeri and I were 21-year-old rookies. We were an unknown quantity. Dugan at third was the only veteran.

"The first two games in spring training, the Braves beat us, 16–3 and 13 to something. The writers wrote us off. Then we went north with the Dodgers and beat them 13 straight. The writers changed their tune. They said Lazzeri and I were the glue that put the team together."[13]

Koenig always marveled at Lazzeri's ability to cope with his handicap. "Tony played 14 years in the big leagues, in seven World Series, with a lifetime average of around .290, and he was epileptic. I roomed with him on the road. He had these fits in the mornings but never in a game. He'd come out of it and never even remember it."[14]

On the trip north that season, the Yankees were to face Brooklyn ace Dazzy Vance in an exhibition game in Atlanta. As good a pitcher as Vance was, for some reason the Yankees usually hit him well in the spring. A young cousin of Vance's came in to see the game and the pitcher met him in the hotel lobby. Ever the egoist, Dazzy introduced his cousin to some of the Yankees and proceeded to tell him how he was going to handle them.

"This is Lazzeri," he said. "I'll strike him out.... This is Combs. He'll pop up.... Meet the Babe. He'll break his back swinging at my fast one...."[15] While the Yankee players smiled, Vance's cousin was dumbstruck by what Dazzy was going to do to them. Vance got his cousin a seat next to the Brooklyn dugout and told him to wait there for him so they could go back to the hotel together. Combs did pop out to lead off the game as Dazzy had predicted. The cousin thought it must be wonderful to be able to pitch like that and make $25,000 a year doing it. Vance at the time was the highest paid pitcher in the game.

Suddenly all hell broke loose as Koenig followed Combs' at-bat with a ringing double. Gehrig then tripled Koenig home and Ruth blasted one over the right-field wall for 3–0 Yankee lead. Meusel then came up and delivered a long triple and Lazzeri followed with a shot that hit a tree behind the left-field wall that shook loose three little youngsters from its branches. Yankees 4, Brooklyn 0.

Manager Wilbert Robinson came out to the mound to relieve the furious Vance. Ignoring his pre-game instructions to his cousin, Dazzy rushed out of the park and took a cab back to the hotel by himself. When Vance asked his cousin how he liked it, his rejoinder to the great Dazzy was: "Cousin Dazzy, that's the easiest way to make $25,000 I ever saw."[16]

It was evident from the very beginning of his big league career that Tony Lazzeri was not going to escape the fact that he would be looked down on because of his Italian heritage. For an exhibition game played in Atlanta on April 2, 1926, against the Brooklyn Robins, writer Harry Cross of *The New York Times* began his story: "Signor Tony Lazzeri, the famed spaghetti farmer, showed his fine Italian hand again today when the Yanks made it five straight against the Robins."[17] Although Tony had three hits in the game, readers could only find this statistic buried in the very last section of a twelve-paragraph article.

Even the immortal Ty Cobb, who was well known for his prejudices, couldn't help but admire Lazzeri's power. He once sneered in a supposedly joking manner that Tony's ability to hit 400-foot line drives was attributable to "eating spaghetti and drinking wop wine."[18]

If this kind of stereotyping bothered Tony, it was not apparent in his on-field performances. In an early season game against the Philadelphia Athletics at Yankee Stadium on April 28, 1926, a column titled "Pickups and Putouts" in the following day's *New York Times* declared: "Lazzeri took a hit away from [Mickey] Cochrane by speeding toward first base and making a one-hand stop. They have to hit them faster than that."[19] Grudging respect was beginning to enter descriptions of the rookie second baseman's work on the field.

Ed Barrow perhaps said it best in his autography: "Lazzeri, though only a rookie himself, took over the leadership of the infield, guided Gehrig on his left and Koenig on his right, and remained a leader thereafter. He will always be one of the greatest in my book."[20]

Tony was an enormously popular player with all Yankee fans, especially Italian-Americans, scores of whom came to their first baseball game just to see him play. Harry Jupiter, writing for the *San Francisco Chroni-*

cle in 1989, put Lazzeri "right up there with Caruso" as a hero to Italian-Americans of the 1920s and 1930s.[21]

As the 1926 season progressed, it did not take long for Lazzeri to become a hero not only in New York but in other American League cities as well. He was nearly as popular as Babe Ruth since the rest of the Yankees were low key, content to do their jobs and do them well.

Wherever "Poosh 'Em Up" and the Yankees were, be it Boston, Detroit or New York itself, large groups of Italian fans attended the games. Content with boxing and *bocce* up until then, they began streaming into the ballparks whenever Tony was in town with the Yankees. He was encouraged to "poosh 'em up," which now meant in their broken English that they wanted him to drive runners around the bases or, better yet, hit a home run, just as he had been implored to do while playing for Salt Lake City in the Pacific Coast League.

Tony renewed the warm memories of the old country within immigrant Italians and they adopted him as their own. They reveled in his calm assurance at second base and his surprising power for a young man who only weighed 165 pounds. Be that as it may, he hit the ball as hard as anyone on the Yankee team.

Tony Lazzeri probably attended more banquets than any other Yankee and he was always laden with gifts. Though he spoke very little Italian himself, the immigrants in every city where the Yankees played adored him. He radiated calmness both on and off the field that resonated with his growing army of loyal followers.

When he went to Detroit for the first time, he was honored at a dinner at the Book Cadillac Hotel. On the dais were the mayor of the city, the Italian consul and members of the faculty of the Jesuit-operated Detroit University. That day he had won the game in the top of the tenth inning with a home run over the left field fence with two men on. Everyone in attendance roared whenever his name was mentioned by any of the speakers.

When Tony was asked to say a few words, he simply said: "Reverend Fathers, Mr. Mayor, ladies and gentlemen, I can't make a speech. I'm only a ball player. But I promise you that out at that ballpark I'll give you the best I got every day."[22]

His brief presentation was greeted with thunderous applause. A reporter later said to him: "Tony, that was remarkable tribute to you, that dinner." And Tony said: "You're____ ____ right."[23]

All season long Miller Huggins was making changes that seemed confusing and strange, particularly to the writers covering the team. They were drawing a completely distorted view of the moves the manager was making to recover from the dark days of 1925. The writers considered the Yankee chances in 1926 to be all but hopeless.

Meanwhile, the players knew what was going on and they knew that Huggins was compelled to take some long chances. The difference between the players and the writers was that the players now were beginning to believe in their manager and were determined to see it through with him.

The Yankees stayed out in front of the American League from the month of April on. The hitting of Ruth, Gehrig, Meusel and Lazzeri was overwhelming. The latter was simply superb at second base and the team, which had always looked to Ruth for inspiration, was also now in awe of this amazing rookie. Players around the league were talking about him and so were the umpires, of all people.

"I shouldn't be saying this, being an umpire," Tommy Connolly, dean of the American League staff, said one night in Cleveland, "but I can't help it. That Italian is a great ball player. And he's got a surprising head on his shoulders. I never saw a young fellow like him."[24]

But that kind of evaluation was quite common not only then but even when Joe DiMaggio would reach the big leagues a decade later. In 1926, Arthur Daley of *The New York Times* called Tony Lazzeri "a ball player's ball player and one of the most intelligent athletes ever to patrol the diamond."[25] And a rookie at that.

Lazzeri did not possess blinding speed but he was always perched in front of the ball no matter where it was hit. His strong arm and his aim were virtually always on target. Although never a consistently high average hitter—he batted .275 in that first year—he could hit the long ball better than most and as a clutch hitter he had few peers. He actually seemed to thrive under pressure. He was a true leader because when the team would hit a bump in the road now and then it was Tony Lazzeri who would pull them up by the proverbial bootstraps. By mid-season, "Poosh 'Em Up's" name was as prominent in New York and throughout the American League as any other Yankee player except Babe Ruth.

As the season progressed, the Yankees continued to improve. First they won six games in a row, lost a pair, won twelve consecutive games, lost two more and then ran off another five in a row. The even-tempered and difficult-to-rattle Herb Pennock was the best southpaw in the game at the time and the ace of the Yankee staff.

Blessed with pinpoint control, "The Squire of Kennett Square"—from the town in Pennsylvania where he was raised—looked easy to hit because he was never overpowering. However, all that most batters could manage were lazy fly balls to the outfield. For a pitcher who once never knew where his ball was going and considered quitting the game, he was now just about faultless.

Spitballer Urban Shocker, while chronologically past his prime at 35, also had great control and got by with the guile and experience that a dozen years in the big leagues had afforded him. He also continued to win consistently that year. "Pitching is this and that," is the way he described his craft.[26]

Waite Hoyt had a sore arm on occasion, and Bob Shawkey and Sad Sam Jones were not quite what they used to be. However, Huggins pressed youngsters Garland Braxton, a left-hander, and Myles Thomas, a right-hander, into service as spot starters and they responded by registering a total of 11 victories in 1926.

The ball club also obtained Walter "Dutch" Ruether from the Senators late in the year. Although he was not quite what he had been in 1919 when he led the Cincinnati Reds into the World Series, the left-hander did pick up a couple of important wins when they were needed. While he had drifted from one team to another in his previous seven years in the majors, Ruether was a great competitor who, when his assignments were properly spaced, could be a valuable asset.

The starting catcher, Benny Bengough, was having trouble with his throwing arm in 1926, which forced Huggins to use Pat Collins to do most of the work behind the plate. To provide further assistance in the catching department, the club acquired the veteran Hank Severeid from the Senators.

The Yankees did falter as the season wore on and many of the so-called experts in the press remained convinced that they were not that good a team anyway. However, they continued to win when they had to, as the Indians led by player-manager Tris Speaker made a spirited run at them.

The New Yorkers were forced to play six games in five days against the Tribe in Cleveland. When the series started the Yankees were in front by four games. After winning the opener, the Yankees proceeded to lose the next four and their lead had dwindled down to a single game, leaving them very little margin for error.

The newspapers in Cleveland took delight in proclaiming that the Yankees were dead and that the Indians would overtake them in short order. The younger players were upset to the point they had difficulty eating. Huggins himself was concerned about the sudden turn of events.

Finger pointing began to set in and tempers flared to such an extent that a utility player, Mike Gazella, accused his teammates of being quitters. The Lafayette College graduate's remarks took place at a dinner at the Hollenden Hotel where the club was staying in Cleveland. Not one player on the ball club challenged him.

The next day before an overflow crowd at Cleveland's League Park, Huggins sent Ruether out to start for the Yankees. Three days before, he had lost to the Indians 2–1. Although Reuther wasn't used to pitching that often, Huggins was frantic and reasoned that the southpaw represented the club's best chance to pick up a win. The manager also replaced Koenig at short with the upstart Gazella.

As it turned out, Huggins made just the right moves. Gazella had a terrific game in the field and Ruether pitched into the ninth before tiring. The Yankees banged the ball all over the lot and prevailed, 8–3. At day's end, their league lead was back up to two games.

From Cleveland, the Yankees moved on to St. Louis to end their season against the hapless Browns. While in the Mound City, the Cardinals clinched the National League pennant against the Giants in New York. The city went wild since it was the first time the Cardinals had ever won a pennant. The crowds that descended upon the Buckingham Hotel where the Yankees were staying promised to give the New Yorkers their comeuppance in due course.

The next day, the Yankees won both games of a doubleheader with the Browns to clinch the American League flag. The steady Herb Pennock notched the first game victory and Waite Hoyt the nightcap. The club finished up at 91–63, or 22 games better than the previous year and three games up on second-place Cleveland. The stage was set for the soon-to-be memorable 1926 World Series.

At times during the season it seemed the Yankees were not all that good. Hoyt's arm was lame some days and both Shawkey and Jones were nowhere near what they had once been. But Thomas and Braxton had picked up some of the slack in their spot starts. Still many of the writers following the club were unimpressed and said so in print — often.

The Bambino bounced back from his miserable 1925 campaign with one of his patented monster seasons: a .372 average, a league-leading 47 homers and 145 RBIs. Lazzeri and Koenig not only shored up the middle defensively but left no doubt about their ability to hit big league pitching.

The steadily improving Gehrig with 107 runs batted in showed that he was well on his way to becoming a star of the future. And Combs was fast-establishing himself as one of baseball's premier leadoff men while scoring 113 runs. Pennock with 23 wins, Shocker with another 19 and Hoyt with 16 had accounted for a third of the club's victories.

Despite their late season misfortunes and their critics, the Yankees were still favored to win the World Series. The Cardinals on the other hand were making their debut in the Fall Classic and were the sentimental favorites throughout much of the country.

Twenty-two-year-old Tony Lazzeri was coming off a sensational rookie year in which he hit .275, smacked 18 home runs—a new first-year major league record for second basemen—and drove in 114 runs. In so doing, he became the first Yankee rookie ever to have exceeded 100 RBI, a record that lasted until Joe DiMaggio tied it in 1936 and Alfonso Soriano duplicated it in 2003. "Poosh 'Em Up" was also the first Yankee rookie ever to appear in all of his team's games, a record since tied by Billy Johnson in 1943 and Soriano in 2003.

Lazzeri was now poised to make his debut on the biggest stage in professional sports. Little did he know that he was destined to meet up with one of the greatest pitchers in the history of the game, Grover Cleveland Alexander, in one of the most talked about confrontations ever.

"Alex," as the legendary right-hander was called, had been waived over to the Cardinals from Chicago on June 22 that season. "Marse Joe" McCarthy, in his maiden year in managing the Cubs, had grown weary of the 40-year-old's well chronicled carousing, using him in only seven games. He carried a mediocre 3–3 record with him when he joined the St. Louis ball club. He was thought to be in the twilight of a once-meteoric career.

Nevertheless Rogers Hornsby, the Cardinals' player-manager and one of the game's all-time great hitters, put Alexander into his rotation immediately. "Pete," as he was also known, posted a very respectable 9–7 half-season mark and contributed mightily to the Cardinals' winning of the National League pennant. Hornsby apparently couldn't have cared less about Alexander's off-the-field escapades as long as the pitcher was able to take the ball every fourth or fifth day.

The clubs stood even at three games apiece on the eve of the seventh and deciding game to be played at Yankee Stadium on Sunday, October 1. Herb Pennock had bested Bill "Wee Willie" Sherdel in the opener at New York, 2–1, as Lou Gehrig plated Babe Ruth with a single in the sixth inning to break a 1–1 tie. Alexander beat Urban Shocker 6–2 in Game Two, thanks to a three-run homer by Billy Southworth in the seventh inning that broke open a 2–2 tie. The game was played before the largest crowd ever to see a Series game up to that time—over 63,000. Alex struck out ten Yankees and retired the last 21 batters that he faced.

The Cardinals took a two-games-to-one Series lead in St. Louis on October 5 as Jesse Haines blanked the New Yorkers on five hits, 4–0. Haines helped his own cause by getting two hits himself, one of which was a two-run homer. The Yankees stormed back to take Game Four, 10–5, behind Waite Hoyt, as Ruth led the way with a record three World Series home runs, two of them in succession.

Game Five was a nail-biter that the Yankees also won, 3–2, in extra innings as Pennock out-dueled Sherdel. Tony Lazzeri's sacrifice fly in the top of the tenth scored Mark Koenig after Sherdel's wild pitch put the Yankee shortstop in scoring position. Both pitchers went the distance.

The Cardinals knotted the Series at three-all when Alexander pitched his second complete game as St. Louis blasted the home-standing New Yorkers 10–2. Bob Shawkey, who started for the Yankees, and Urban Shocker were roughed up in the seventh for five runs when the visitors took a commanding eight-run lead to ice it.

That evening, Alexander, who was certain that he would not be used again, celebrated late into the night with some of his teammates who put him to bed early Sunday morning. The weather was damp and gray. It had rained early that morning and as the afternoon approached, Yankee Stadium was swept by a chilly wind.

What normally would have attracted a capacity crowd finally got underway with less than half that number in attendance. Only some 38,000 paid spectators were on hand to see what would turn out to be one of the most competitive World Series games ever to be played.

As the Cardinals made their way out to the field, Alexander told Hornsby: "I'm going down to the bullpen. If you need me, I'll be ready."[27] This from a man who had pitched and won two of the three Cardinals' victories already, the last being just the day before. Alexander also purportedly added: "But I'll tell you, I'm not going to warm up down there. I've got just so many throws left in this arm. If you need me, I'll take my warm-up pitches on the mound."[28]

One of the many myths that have grown up around this game is that "Pete" curled up on the bullpen and fell sound asleep. It never happened. He watched very intently as the game unfolded to see how far his team's starter, Jesse Haines, could go. Haines, a 33-year-old right-hander, had been troubled from the start by bloody blisters on his pitching hand, caused by throwing his knuckleball.

When the Yankees came to bat in the bottom of the seventh, the Cardinals led 3–2. The Yankees had been ahead early, 1–0, when Babe Ruth slammed a bases-empty home run in the bottom of the third. It was his fourth of the Series.

The visitors got all of their runs in the top of the fourth inning as a result of some shoddy fielding. The New Yorkers uncharacteristically committed three errors behind their starter, Waite Hoyt, interspersed between a couple of fly balls that fell between the fielders. The Yankees added a second run in their half of the sixth to narrow the gap.

Haines, obviously struggling, walked Earle Combs to lead off the Yankee seventh. Koenig bunted Combs along to second and Ruth was intentionally passed. Meusel then grounded to third as Ruth was forced out at second. With runners at the corners, Haines got two quick strikes on Gehrig but the blisters finally took their toll as the Yankee first baseman was walked on four straight balls to load the bases. Coming to the plate was the rookie sensation Tony "Poosh 'Em Up" Lazzeri.

Hornsby trotted out to the mound to check on Haines' pitching hand. The blister on the second finger of his right hand made it almost impossible for him to maintain any semblance of control. The manager, as they say, was in the horns of a dilemma. Yes, he had other pitchers in his bullpen who were younger and stronger than Alexander and completely rested. But only Pete had his total confidence.

Hornsby called time and walked part of the way into left center field and gave Alexander the signal to enter the game. "I wanted to look at his eyes," he later told the reporters.[29] Convinced that the pitcher's eyes were clear, he made the call as Lazzeri walked up to home plate. Second year pitcher Bill Hallahan said: "I think I smiled and nodded my head when I saw it was 'Alex' who was coming in. We all felt reassured. We just knew he was going to haul us out of it."[30]

Alexander strolled in looking like a man without a care in the world. As usual his uniform was rumpled much like an old bathrobe. Whether or not he was experiencing a monumental hangover from toasting his victory of a day earlier remains questionable to this day.

Cardinals' third baseman Les Bell debunked the hangover theory: "All a lot of bunk. No man could have done what 'Alex' did if he was drunk or even a little soggy. Not the way his mind was working and not the way he pitched. And as far as Hornsby walking out to meet him, that's for the birds, too. 'Rog' met him at the mound, same as the rest of us."[31]

Bell, who as a 13-year-old fan had first seen Alexander in Philadelphia in 1915, added: "'Alex' didn't pitch that day, but I saw him warming up on the sidelines. Couldn't keep my eyes off him. Doggone, there wasn't another man in the world I would rather have seen out there at that moment than Grover Cleveland Alexander.

"I can see him yet, to this day, walking in from the left field bullpen through the gray mist. The Yankee fans recognized him right off, of course, but you didn't hear a sound from anywhere in that stadium. They just sat there and watched him walk in. And he took his time. He just came struggling along, a lean old Nebraskan, wearing a Cardinal sweater, his face wrinkled, that cap sitting on the top of his head and tilted to one side — that's the way he liked to wear it."[32]

Upon reaching the mound to begin his warm-up pitches, Alexander

3. A Breakout Rookie Season (1926)

gave Hornsby this scenario: "I'm gonna throw the first one inside to him. Fast."[33]

"No, no," said Hornsby. "You can't do that."[34]

Alexander responded: "Yes, I can. Because if I do, and he swings at it, he'll most likely hit it on the handle, or if he does hit it good, it'll go foul. Then I'm going to come outside with my breaking pitch."[35]

"Rog looked at him for a moment," Bell recalled, "then gave 'Alex' a slow smile and said, 'Who am I to tell *you* how to pitch?'"[36]

Lazzeri had not looked good against Alexander in Game Six. Pete had gotten him out four straight times mostly on curve balls called by his catcher, Bob O'Farrell. Now he made his way out to his pitcher to talk about the situation.

"Remember what this guy did yesterday," whispered O'Farrell. "You can do it again."[37]

In a piece titled *My Greatest Day in Baseball* written years later by John P. Carmichael, Pete gave this version of what happened that afternoon:

> Some people say I celebrated the night before and had a hangover when manager Rogers Hornsby called me from the bullpen to pitch to Lazzeri. That isn't the truth. In the clubhouse after that game, Hornsby came over to me and said, "Alex, if you want to celebrate tonight, I wouldn't blame you. But go easy for I may need you tomorrow."
>
> I said, "Okay, Rog. I'll tell you what I'll do. I'll ride back to the hotel with you and I'll meet you tomorrow morning and ride out to the park with you." Hell—I wanted to win that series and get the big end of the money as much as anyone.
>
> Early in the game Hornsby said to me, "Alex, go down to the bullpen...." Well, I was sitting around down there, not doing much throwing, when the phone rang and an excited voice said, "Send in Alexander."
>
> I didn't find out what had happened until the game was over. Turns out Haines was breezing along with a 3–2 lead when he developed a blister on the knuckle of the first finger of his right hand. The blister broke and the finger was so sore he couldn't hold the ball. Before Rog knew it, the Yanks had the bases filled.
>
> So when I came out from under the bleachers I saw the bases were filled and Lazzeri was standing in the box. Tony was up there all alone, with everyone in that Sunday crowd watching him. So I just said to myself, "Take your time. Lazzeri isn't feeling any too good up there. Let him stew."
>
> I got to the box and Bob O'Farrell, our catcher, came out to meet me. "Let's start where we left off yesterday," Bob said. The day before [Saturday] Lazzeri had been up four times against me without getting anything that so much as looked like a hit. He'd gotten one off me in the second game of the Series, but with one out of seven I wasn't much worried about him.
>
> I said okay to O'Farrell. We'll curve him. My first pitch was a curve and Tony missed it. ...O'Farrell came out to the box again. "Look, Alex," he

began. "This guy will be looking for that curve next time. We curved him all the time yesterday. Let's give him a fast one." I agreed and poured one in, right under his chin. There was a crack, and I knew the ball was hit hard. A pitcher can usually tell pretty well from the sound. I spun around to watch the ball, and all the Yankees on the bases were on their way. But the drive had a tail-end fade and landed foul by eight, ten feet in the left field bleachers.[38]

A half century later, Bell remembered Lazzeri's foul home run this way: "Tony hit the hell out of it.... Now for fifty years that ball has been traveling. It has been foul from anywhere from an inch to twenty feet, depending on whom you're listening to or what you're reading. But I was standing on third base and I'll tell you — it was foul all the way. All the way."[39]

"So I said to myself, 'No more of that for you, my lad,'" Alexander told Carmichael. "Bob gave me the sign for another curve and I gave him one. Lazzeri swung where that curve started but not where it finished. The ball got a hunk of the corner and then finished outside. Well, we were out of that jam, but there were still two innings to go."[40]

Sportswriter Paul Gallico observed the strikeout pitch in his own inimitable style: "Lazzeri swung where that curve started but not where it finished. The ball got a hunk of the corner and then finished outside."[41]

To this day many people are convinced when they are asked to recall the details of the famed Alexander-Lazzeri matchup in the 1926 World Series that Pete struck Lazzeri out in the bottom half of the *ninth* inning to win the game and the Series. Not so. As Alexander himself said: "But there were still two innings to go." Grover Cleveland Alexander did not accomplish what he accomplished in the game for being naive.

Let him tell what happened after that:

> I set the Yankees down in order in the eighth and got the first two in the ninth. And then Ruth came up. The Babe had scored the Yanks' first run of the game with a tremendous homer. He was dynamite to any pitcher. I didn't take any chances on him but worked the count to three and two, pitching for the corners all the time. The Babe walked and I wasn't very sorry either when I saw him perched on first. Of course, Bob Meusel was the next hitter. He'd hit over forty homers that season and would mean trouble.
>
> If Meusel got hold of one, it could mean two runs and the Series, so I forgot all about Ruth and got ready to work on Meusel. I'll never know why the guy did it, but on my first pitch to Meusel, the Babe broke for second. He [or Miller Huggins] probably figured that it would catch us by surprise. I caught the blur of Ruth starting for second as I pitched, and then came the whistle of the ball as O'Farrell rifled it to second. I wheeled around, and there was one of the grandest sights of my life. Hornsby, his

3. A Breakout Rookie Season (1926)   39

Mark Koenig (left) and Tony Lazzeri formed the keystone combination for the Yankees' "Murderers' Row" team in 1927. (National Baseball Hall of Fame Library, Cooperstown, N.Y.)

foot anchored on the bag and his gloved hand outstretched, was waiting for Ruth to come in. There was the Series and my second big thrill of the day. The third came when Judge Landis mailed out the winners' checks for $5,584.51.[42]

Surrounded by reporters after the game, Alexander gave an honest appraisal of his meeting with Lazzeri. "Just a few feet was the difference of my being a hero and a bum."[43]

Asked how he felt after he had fanned Lazzeri, Pete replied: "How do I feel? Go ask Lazzeri how he felt."[44]

The famed author Harry Golden took note of the momentous occasion to write: "Where the myth gained circulation that there are men who excel only when drunk, I don't know. People remember Alexander struck out Lazzeri in the seventh inning of the World Series while working off a 'bender' the night before. But they also forget that just before Lazzeri fanned, he put a foul only inches foul into the leftfield upper deck."[45]

Alexander said that years after the confrontation, he would run into people everywhere and hear a new version of what actually took place, some of them pretty farfetched. One time he met Lazzeri in San Francisco and said to him: "Tony, I'm getting tired of fanning you." And Tony replied: "Maybe you think I'm not."[46]

Of course, Lazzeri, always the strong, silent type, remained reticent about this event as well as all of the many other good and not-so-good happenings in his remarkable career. Consequently, no one could get a grasp on exactly how the young rookie felt about failing to deliver in the most important at-bat of his still-early profession.

Westbrook Pegler wrote for the *Chicago Tribune*: "In the twilight of this gloomy and dripping Sunday afternoon, 38,000 hard-boiled New Yorkers rumbled down out of the stands in the Yankee Stadium bawling the name of Grover Cleveland Alexander, the ball player who won't behave because he doesn't have to, because old Aleck had just done something that would have brought a lump as big as an egg into the neck of a police captain."[47]

It was not only Alexander's clutch relief performance but also the sustained hitting of the team's shortstop, Tommy Thevenow, that sealed the decisive victory. Thevenow, a .256 hitter during the season, broke a 1–1 tie in the game with a two-run single in the fourth inning.

Overall, the Hornsby protégé was 10-for-24 against the Yankees, making him the leading batter in the 1926 World Series with a .417 average. Thevenow, who hit only two homers in a 15-year career beset by injuries, also ran one out of the inside-the-park variety in Game Two.

The Yankees got good run-production out of Earle Combs and Lou Gehrig, both of whom were appearing in their first World Series, and Babe Ruth. Combs was the Yankees' leading hitter with a .357 mark while Gehrig batted .348 and drove in the winning run in Game One. Ruth, who was walked no less than 11 times during the Series, smashed four homers, including the three he hit in Game Four at Sportsman's Park.

Yankee management was bitterly disappointed in the outcome, particularly after the resiliency the club had exhibited all season long. Even the players were troubled by the end result. Joe Dugan even went so far as to say to Waite Hoyt: "After the exhibition we put up in the last game, I feel as though as I was picking somebody's pocket."[48]

Despite it all, the team had made money that season and each player received $3,417.75 as his share of the prize money. There was some consolation in the fact that the club had bounced back from seventh place in 1925 to coming within a whisker of winning it all in 1926. And after all, there was still next year — 1927 — to look forward to.

Twenty-six years after that historic seventh game, Warner Bros. released a motion picture starring future President Ronald Reagan in the role of Grover Cleveland Alexander. The movie, *The Winning Team*, generally adhered to the highlights and lowlights of Alexander's life, although it took poetic license with the portrayal of the quite unlovable Rogers Hornsby, who comes off as an unvarnished hero.

Years later when the movie was re-released, Reagan expressed disappointment in Warner Bros.' insistence that the word "epilepsy" never be used. Alexander and Lazzeri both suffered from the disease.

Also, the script was written to state as fact — but quite incorrectly — that the Lazzeri strikeout took place in the ninth inning of the deciding game of the World Series rather than in the seventh. Obviously done to heighten the dramatic effect of the motion picture and in keeping with Hollywood's tradition of rewriting history to satisfy its audiences, the famed confrontation just never happened that way.

4

Murderers' Row (1927)

The Roaring Twenties helped produce a boom period for the fortunes of major league baseball. The bad taste left by the shocking "Black Sox Scandal" of the 1919 World Series—in which certain members of the Chicago White Sox were accused of throwing the Series and were banned for life—was now a distant memory.

As the 1927 season approached, the former federal judge Kenesaw Mountain Landis presided over major league baseball and ruled it with an iron hand. As a result of his stern and moralistic actions, the integrity of the game was being restored. Then, too, the public was spellbound by the exploits of Babe Ruth and the offensive style now in vogue.

Runs were being scored at an average of five per team and earned run averages had climbed to over 4.00, which was now deemed acceptable. Livelier balls were now being changed more frequently than ever during the course of a game, which added impetus to the newfound offensive displays. Also pitchers were barred from using the spitball and doctored balls were being outlawed as well. The fans loved it and responded at the turnstiles.

With a thriving economy, a reduction of working hours and increasing salaries, fans were flocking to the ballparks in greater numbers than ever. Attendance had soared to an average of 9.6 million in the mid–1920s. The drama evoked by the exciting 1926 World Series brought even more renewed interest in the national pastime.

Be that as it may, the gloom that hung over the Yankee training camp in St. Petersburg in the spring of 1927 could be cut with a knife. The disappointing finish to the 1926 World Series had the club primed for the launching of a mission. Yet few could have imagined how phenomenal a season it was to be for those wearing the pinstripes.

The team was bent upon meeting the Cardinals once again come the

4. Murderers' Row (1927)

fall and demolishing them. Most of the prognosticators among the press felt that a second consecutive meeting for the protagonists might indeed take place.

Of course, no one could have had a clearer goal in mind than 23-year-old Tony Lazzeri, now preparing for his second season in New York. The goat of the Series in the minds of many, "Poosh 'Em Up" was more embittered than any one of his teammates.

When it was announced that the team would be meeting the Cardinals in a series of meaningless exhibition games, Lazzeri reportedly raised clenched fists in the air and shouted: "Vendetta! I shall have revenge!"[1]

Both the Yankees and the Cardinals trained in St. Petersburg and the players were close enough so that they could walk from each other's respective fields to play the games.

Tony Lazzeri's intense resentment towards Grover Cleveland Alexander knew no bounds. The other players on both teams and the managers and coaches treated the spring training games as nothing more than what they were meant to be — getting in shape, trying out new players and working in various combinations of regulars to prepare for the upcoming season. Not so with Lazzeri — his only thoughts were of redemption.

The writers following each of the clubs were always on the lookout for a story angle, particularly at this time of the year when there was so little of a dramatic fashion to write about. They tabbed the forthcoming games between the Yankees and the Cardinals as the "Little World Series." The night before the first game, Lazzeri couldn't wait to face Alexander and gain some semblance of revenge. However, the confrontation would have to wait. Tony had developed a boil on one of his knees and was forced to sit out the training season for a while.

The Yankee team was virtually the same one that finished the previous season, so there was little for Manager Miller Huggins to do in camp. The resolve of the Yankees early in the year was unquestioned. The players were eager to redeem themselves and a new spirit had taken hold of them. It was not necessary for Hug to demand their allegiance since he knew now that he had it without reservation.

Throughout the history of major league baseball, nicknames have been thrust upon the players and even some of its events. Tony Lazzeri brought his own nickname along from his Pacific Coast League playing days—"Poosh 'Em Up." Babe Ruth had been called by various nicknames throughout his career: "The Babe," "The Bambino" and "The Sultan of Swat," among others.

Lou Gehrig was identified as "Larrupin' Lou" and later when he was to be in the midst of his incredible consecutive game playing streak, "The

Iron Horse." Third baseman Joe Dugan carried the moniker of "Jumping Joe" ever since he arrived in the big leagues ten years before with the then-perennially last place Athletics. And Pebworth, Kentucky, native Earle Combs could answer to the names of either "The Kentucky Colonel" or "Mail Carrier."

But what the impending season would bring to the New York Yankees was a name that would forever distinguish them as a team from any other ball club in the history of the game: "Murderers' Row."

The Yankees were still a relatively young ball club when the season began. The 32-year-old Babe Ruth was the elder statesman among the starting eight position players. He was easily now one of the most recognized American sports hero of the era along with the likes of Jack Dempsey, Bill Tilden, Bobby Jones and Red Grange.

The Bambino had earned a reported $25,000 for 17 days' work over the winter while filming a new motion picture in Hollywood called "Babe Comes Home." It was an unheard of amount of money in those days, especially for an athlete who didn't know the first thing about acting. He didn't have to; his name was solid box office for the movie moguls.

Babe Ruth was now the ultimate baseball player of the day, as he not only hit for average but also with unbelievable power. His skilled fielding, throwing and running abilities also enhanced his game. Shortly before training camp opened, he had signed a three-year contract with the Yankees calling for a salary of $70,000 a year, another unprecedented amount of money.

The Babe's outfield mates included 30-year-old Bob Meusel, in left, who possessed a rifle arm, and the speedy 29-year-old Earle Combs in center. Meusel's arm was generally considered the best in the game at the time. Joe Dugan claimed that Meusel's throws were so hard and so accurate that "he could hit a dime at 100 yards and flatten it against a wall."[2] And Ruth's "soup bone" was just a shade behind the Yankee left fielder's. Both had to have good arms to make up for Combs' weaker throws.

Meusel was starting his eighth season in New York after being acquired from Vernon of the Pacific Coast League for the 1920 American League season. The younger brother of the Giants' Irish Meusel, the Yankee outfielder at 6'3" was the tallest player on the 1927 squad.

In seven of his first eight years in the big leagues, he hit .313 or better although he was often accused of having an indifferent or lackadaisical attitude. Meusel and Babe Herman hold the distinction of hitting for the cycle more times than any other hitters in history — three.

Meusel had always played the sun fields for the Yankees ever since Ruth lost a fly ball in 1918 and vowed never to play any sun fields again.

Consequently, he always played left field at Yankee Stadium and often traded places with the Bambino on the road. The Yankee hierarchy reasoned that it was absolutely necessary to keep the most valuable eyes in baseball out of the sun.

Combs was recognized as the best leadoff man in the American League, if not in all of baseball, in 1927. His speed alone enabled him to lead the league in triples three times during his career. He was to hit three of them in one game in 1927 and 154 overall for his lifetime.

The Eastern Kentucky State Teachers College graduate had played for Joe McCarthy in Louisville of the American Association. The Yankees purchased Combs for $50,000 and five players for delivery in 1924. His speed also allowed him to cover much ground in the outfield but he was forced to get rid of the ball quickly; his arm was always suspect.

Combs was a lifelong teetotaler and some of his teammates could never fathom how a Kentuckian did not drink. He claimed that one of them actually told him in 1925 that he had better learn to drink if he expected to stay with the ball club. Despite the "advice," he remained a non-drinker, a non-smoker and a devoted Bible reader throughout his stay in the majors and beyond. His natural quickness and lifetime .325 batting average more than made up for his so-called shortcomings in the area of social drinking.

When he was inducted into the Hall of Fame in 1970, the ever-modest Combs stayed totally in character in his acceptance speech: "I thought the Hall of Fame was for superstars, not just average players like me."[3] He could not have been more wrong.

Cedric Durst, a 30-year-old off-season acquisition from the St. Louis Browns, and Ben Paschal, age 31 and now in his third year with the Yankees as a backup, were the team's spare outfielders. Each was counted upon to rest the regulars on occasion. Durst had come to New York along with Pitcher Joe Giard. Paschal had been out of the majors for three years before the Yankees acquired him for the 1924 campaign. He was a very capable reserve fly chaser who rarely made an error and owned a career .319 batting average as a role player.

Lou Gehrig, who like Lazzeri was also only 23, had not yet begun to scratch the surface of his remarkable career. He batted fifth in 1926 and then Huggins switched Gehrig to the cleanup spot in 1927. It was the best thing that ever happened to Ruth's career, as no pitcher would deign to pitch around the Babe to get to Gehrig.

Using a 34-inch, 38-ounce Louisville Slugger bat, "Larrupin' Lou" had attended Columbia University originally on a football scholarship. He pitched as well and his school record for strikeouts—17 against

Williams College — still stands. In 1927, the third-year player was now set to combine his talents with those of Ruth and embark upon a devastating offensive display that would help earn him the league's Most Valuable Player award.

Mark Koenig, the light-hitting shortstop who was but 24 years of age, had led the AL in errors with 52 in 1926. Hitting just ahead of Ruth and Gehrig, he also had suffered through an awful World Series by striking out seven times, often on critical occasions. Koenig also hit into three double plays and committed three errors, one of which was crucial in the seventh and deciding game. He was also to endure a poor spring training camp in 1927, and his playing time was to be further limited during the season due to a severe leg injury.

"Jumping Joe" Dugan at third was the oldest player on the infield at 30 and was generally regarded as one of the game's best fielders. It was alleged that the former shortstop received his nickname for being occasionally absent without leave from his original team, the Philadelphia Athletics, when things did not go his way. The name was later attributed, perhaps apocryphally, to his flawless fielding of bunt attempts.

Dugan had next to no power with the bat, averaging only three home runs a year in his previous 11 seasons in the majors. However, he was quite adept at the hot corner and led the league in fielding twice while with the Yankees. In fact, he established a major league record for third basemen when he made four unassisted double plays in 1924. Fielding his position well was all the Yankees expected of him and that, he did, probably better than anybody playing the position at that time.

A former Holy Cross student, he had come to the Yankees on July 23, 1923 along with outfielder Elmer Smith from the A's in exchange for four players and $50,000 in cash. The controversial deal, which came late in July of 1922 during a heated pennant race, led to the creation of major league baseball's June 15 deadline for trades.

A superstitious sort, Jumping Joe would never throw a ball directly to his pitcher unless it was for a putout. During infield practice, his teammates would often turn their backs when warm-ups were over so that he wouldn't be able to throw the ball to the shortstop or any other infielder. Whenever that happened, Dugan would simply walk over to the pitcher and hand him the ball rather than throw it directly to him.

One of Babe Ruth's best friends on the team, Dugan always sat next to the Bambino on the bench. "Born? Hell, Babe Ruth wasn't born, he fell from a tree," Jumping Joe was fond of saying.[4]

Julie Wera, a 25-year-old utility infielder, had been acquired from St. Paul primarily to serve as an adequate backup for Dugan when needed.

He had good speed but, like Dugan, hardly any pop in his bat. At $2,400 he was a bargain as the lowest paid player on the team.

Pat Collins, who was to do most of the catching in 1927, was 30 years old like Dugan. After playing six seasons with the St. Louis Browns, he had also been obtained by the Yankees from St. Paul just prior to the 1926 season. A veteran of eight years in the big leagues, Collins had some power and was coming off a year in which he led all American League catchers in double plays with 14. Ruth, who always called everyone "Kid" because he could never remember names, made an exception in Collins' case and disparagingly nicknamed him "Horse Nose."

Collins' backups, Benny Bengough and Johnny Grabowski, were 28 and 27 years of age respectively. Bengough, a former Niagara University student who once studied for the Roman Catholic priesthood, had been the starting catcher until hobbled by a nagging arm injury throughout most of the 1926 season. Bengough was scheduled to be the team's starting catcher again in 1927 but the injury that had occurred in the previous season limited his availability considerably. Oddly enough, he played in his first game for the Yankees on the very day that Gehrig replaced Wally Pipp at first base — June 1, 1925.

Grabowski, who had been obtained just prior to the 1927 season from the White Sox as insurance due to the uncertainty of Bengough's injury, would go on to have his best season ever. A Schenectady, New York, native, he was the Yankees' "Opening Day" catcher. Grabowski had been acquired along with Ray Morehart in exchange for the second baseman that Lazzeri had replaced in 1926, Aaron Ward. The latter had started at second for the Yankees for five consecutive years before Lazzeri arrived on the scene.

The 27-year-old Morehart, a Texan out of Stephen C. Austin College, was a left-handed hitter who was brought in to back up the right-handed hitting Lazzeri. The three-year veteran would turn out to be a pleasant surprise — he also filled in capably for Koenig during one of the shortstop's prolonged injuries.

Mike Gazella was a 30-year-old utility infielder with next-to-no clout in his third year with the Yankees. He had joined the team in 1923 after playing for the Atlanta Crackers of the Southern Association. A .221 hitter for his abbreviated time in the big leagues, Gazella was to achieve career highs in batting average, doubles and triples in 1927.

The biggest question mark that the Yankees had for the approaching season was with their pitching staff. Waite Hoyt, a hot-tempered and headstrong 27-year-old right-hander, and Herb Pennock, a 33-year-old southpaw who was coming off a personal best 23-win season, headed the group. Pennock, one of the classiest players in the game, was another of those Red Sox castoffs who seemed to move on to New York endlessly from Boston.

All of these moves were directly attributable to General Manager Ed Barrow, himself an ex-member of Red Sox management. Barrow, who went on to become one of the greatest general managers of all time, was a major factor in the 14 pennants and 10 world series championships that the Yankees were to win during his 1921–1945 tenure. A strict disciplinarian with an explosive temper, he even challenged Ruth to a fight once. Barrow was elected to the Hall of Fame in 1953.

Former Washington Senator Dutch Ruether, another 33-year-old left-hander, George Pipgras, a 28-year-old right-hander, and Urban Shocker, a 36-year-old right-hander, rounded out the starting rotation. A husky, balding 29-year-old rookie right-hander, Wilcy Moore, was ticketed for the bullpen but was also capable of starting now and then.

A second-year man, 29-year-old right-hander Myles Thomas, a Penn State graduate, helped Moore to anchor the pen. Moore had become a hard-to-hit side-armed sinkerball pitcher after hurting his shoulder several years earlier in the Sally League.

Thirty-seven-year-old right-hander Bob Shawkey, a former 20-game winner who was in the last year of a fine 15-season big league career, now worked primarily out of the bullpen. Southpaw Joe Giard, another ex–St. Louis Brown, was also in the final season of an undistinguished three-year stint in the majors. But what a year it would be for Shawkey and Giard to complete their rather diverse stays in the big leagues.

Before the season began Huggins believed that Hoyt would be a better pitcher if he would only learn to curb his temper. "There is no reason why he should not win 20 games every year. He has the stuff and knows how to use it."[5]

In an interview twenty-five years later, Hoyt claimed that being on the Yankee bench with Huggins was akin to "a deportment as rigid and stiff as one directed by a New England schoolmaster. There was no goofing off. You watched the game and you kept track not only of the score and the number of outs, but of the count on the batter. At any moment Hug might ask you what the situation was."[6]

About the tough, agile and sure-handed Lazzeri, who was now playing under full strength following a winter of battling boils, Huggins opined: "I've seen a few better second basemen, but not many. He has a phenomenal pair of hands, a great throwing arm and he covers acres of ground."[7]

Training camp was nothing to write home about principally because there was little for Huggins to do. The ball club was basically the same one he had a year earlier. The players were eager to redeem themselves as a result of the Series letdown and a new spirit was emerging. Huggins was not planning to get in the way. He knew he had no need to demand their loyalty since he already had it.

Lazzeri, though, felt that he was on the spot with the press corps despite having had a marvelous rookie season overall. He knew full well that he would have to prove himself all over again because of the lingering doubts caused by that infamous strikeout in Game Seven against Grover Cleveland Alexander. The writers were determined to find out what effect, if any, the incident would have on Lazzeri's upcoming season. It was destined to haunt him forevermore.

One prominent sportswriter, Ford Frick of the *New York Evening Journal*, had Lazzeri under his personal microscope during spring training. Frick, who was later to become the president of the National League and eventually the commissioner of major league baseball as well, observed Lazzeri's performance in camp this way: "Tony Lazzeri is the key man of the Yankee infield—and a good one. No man in camp is hitting the ball harder than Tony—or holding up in the field with quite the same brilliance. A budding star last season, this year Lazzeri gives promise of full bloom to stardom."[8]

Just a handful of games into the season, the April 13 "Pickups and Putouts" column in *The New York Times* proclaimed: "Tony Lazzeri picked up yesterday where he left off at the Stadium last October. He swung at a third strike and missed."[9] It would be slow going indeed for the sensitive and quiet San Franciscan. He knew what he had to do to regain everyone's confidence and he was determined to do exactly that.

For 1927, the capacity at Yankee Stadium was increased from 58,000 to 62,000. The price of a ticket for the wooden bleachers, which could seat up to 22,000 fans, was actually lowered from 75 cents to 50 cents by Colonel Jacob Ruppert. Grandstand seats went for $1.10. Left field extended a mere 281 feet down the line, which made it a convenient target for Tony Lazzeri, while the right field line of only 295 feet was an inviting objective for powerful sluggers like Babe Ruth and Lou Gehrig.

The Babe, who was credited with being responsible for creating "The House That Ruth Built," claimed that he despised hitting there. "All the parks are good except the Stadium," he had said earlier. "There is no background there at all... I cried when they took me out of the Polo Grounds."[10]

Ruth never believed he could break his 1921 record of 59 home runs that he had set across the Harlem River at the Polo Grounds. The Bambino did not think he could establish a new record; he was convinced that he had to have an early start and historically he always came on later in the season.

It was also his contention that opposing pitchers would have to pitch to him and he thought they had not done so in the previous five seasons. Further, he also complained that he was only thrown bad balls to hit. Obviously, as it would turn out, "The Sultan of Swat" was not nearly as good at predictions as he was with a bat in his hands.

The dimensions in center field and in the power alleys in Yankee Stadium were a sight to behold. It was 490 feet to left center, 487 feet to dead center and 429 feet to right center. Speedy outfielders could have a field day for themselves by having the chance to run down fly balls hit in the gaps. Small wonder that the new ballpark's outfield would come to be known as "Death Valley" over time.

The dark green Yankee dugout was on the third base side in those days and the bats were lined up at the top of the dugout stairs. The bullpen looked out over left center field. The batteries for the day's games, which usually began at 3:30 in the afternoon, were announced over a megaphone. It was to be another couple of decades before lights would be installed in Yankee Stadium, one of the last in the majors to be so equipped. A manually operated scoreboard, which also displayed scores of other major league games, was installed above the bleachers in right center field.

On opening day in 1927, an unofficial overflow attendance of 73,206 welcomed the Yankees and their opponents, Connie Mack's Philadelphia Athletics, whom most writers had picked to win the pennant. The previous record at a major league game was the 63,000 fans who sat in on Game Two of the 1926 World Series at the Stadium.

The incomparable Graham McNamee did the play-by-play on radio, the colorful New York City Mayor Jimmy Walker threw out the first ball and even tea magnate and boating enthusiast Sir Thomas Lipton was on hand for the festivities. The stage was set for the start of the greatest season in New York Yankee history. For an unexplained reason, Mayor Walker presented Babe Ruth with a three-foot-high silver loving cup just before the game began.

Mr. Mack, as everyone called him, had obtained an aging Ty Cobb and equally ripening Zack Wheat during the winter to help buttress his outfield. He had also reacquired second baseman Eddie Collins of his famed "$100,000 infield" from the White Sox to back up the youthful Max Bishop.

While all three veterans were fast nearing the end of their illustrious individual careers, each was still a major drawing card. With eight future Hall of Famers on the club and arguably the best southpaw in the game, Lefty Grove, as his ace, A's owner-manager Mack felt he had the makings of a solid team in 1927 with which to challenge the defending league champions. Al Simmons, Jimmie Foxx, Mickey Cochrane and Mack himself would ultimately be enshrined in Cooperstown along with Cobb, Collins, Wheat and Grove. It was indeed a formidable array of big league stars.

Early in the opening day contest, Grove and his blazing fastball struck out Ruth, Gehrig, Combs and Lazzeri. However, the home club caught up with him in the fifth and put up a four-spot. The Yankees added another four runs in the sixth to chase the left-hander and tag him with the loss. Lazzeri's double to start the sixth led the way while "Brooklyn Schoolboy" Hoyt went the distance. The Yankees prevailed, 8–3.

From that day on and as the season progressed, there was little doubt that the Yankees would win the pennant and perhaps even another World Series. Ruth, Gehrig, Meusel and Lazzeri pounded opposing pitchers unmercifully. Although Meusel did not possess the power of the other three, he and all the others in the starting lineup were capable of breaking open a game by hitting one out of the ballpark.

Huggins said without equivocation in late May:

> I have a much better club than last year and if we don't run into misfortunes we ought to stay on top. It's possible for us to take a slump at any time, but just now I'm not worrying a great deal. You see my boys are hitting the ball consistently and my pitchers are working very smoothly. The Yankees, as a team, have improved in every way.
>
> Gehrig, Lazzeri and Koenig, the young infielders, are showing the result of last year's experience by playing with more confidence and steadiness. Koenig is destined to become one of the finest shortstops in the majors. He is handling balls that he couldn't reach a year ago and is throwing wonderfully. Gehrig is the hardest hitting first baseman I've seen and that is saying a whole lot. Lazzeri is the best second basemman in the American League today.
>
> Joe Dugan isn't hitting but his third base play is excellent. In case of accidents to my regular infielders, I'll be well fortified. [Cedric] Durst can play first base, while [Ray] Moirehart [sic], [Mike] Gazella and [Julie] Wera are ready to jump into the other positions.
>
> The pitchers? They've surprised me, particularly Hoyt and Ruether. Pennock hasn't lost a game yet [he lost his first on May 27] and Shocker is coming along nicely. Moore ... has done splendid relief work.[11]

Grantland Rice agreed wholeheartedly with the manager's assessment of the infielders when he wrote: "Gehrig, Lazzeri and Koenig are still only a trifle more than baseball kids. Two of them have less than two years' experience under the big top. So here is three-quarters of an infield with ten or twelve more years to go, and there is no other combination so valuable to baseball in spite of their brief experience."[12]

Lazzeri had one of his greatest days ever on June 8 at Yankee Stadium.

Using the best "purple prose" he could muster to describe Tony's afternoon, James R. Harrison of *The New York Times* wrote:

> In a story book finish that made Dick Merriwell look like a pallid piker the Yankees scored five runs in the ninth inning yesterday, tied up a game that looked hopelessly lost and then beat the White Sox in the eleventh, 12–11.
>
> The fine Italian hand of Signor Tony Lazzeri was plainly to be seen in the gala proceedings. In fact, it would not be stretching the truth to say that Tony wrecked the White Sox single-handedly, for the handsome Signor broke out into a rash of home runs — one in the second inning, another in the eighth and a third in the ninth.
>
> It was in the ninth that Tony brought 20,000 customers to their feet, screeching and screaming like so many maniacs. The Yanks needed five runs to tie and six to win. They had scored three of the five and Durst was on first and one man was out.
>
> Signor Lazzeri strode to the plate with determination and a heavy tan on his face. He looked like Dick Merriwell in the flesh....
>
> Tony adjusted his sights, aimed toward the right field bleachers and swung. And while 20,000 fans let out a roar that shattered the eardrums, the ball sailed out along the foul line, poised in the air for a second and then fell a foot inside the white line and two feet inside the wire fence.
>
> It was a close shave, but a miss is as good as a mile and a homer is much better than long foul. The Signor had done it, and when he jogged from the plate to the bench he met the greatest ovation that a Yankee athlete has faced since Miller Huggins was knee high to a bat bag.[13]

The game ended dramatically in the eleventh when Cedric Durst led off with a triple, Lazzeri was intentionally walked to bring up seldom-used Ray Morehart, who singled to win it.

On June 21, the Yankees were in Fenway Park to play a doubleheader with the last-place Red Sox. Between games, a delegation of proud Italians from Boston's North End presented Lazzeri with a jeweled ring. To demonstrate his appreciation, Lazzeri responded with a 2-for-3 performance after having gone 2-for-4 in the first game. He also filled in at shortstop for the injured Mark Koenig that afternoon while Ray Morehart took over for him at second base.

Later that month, Ruth and Gehrig were tied for the league lead in home runs with 24 apiece. Writing in his column in *The World*, the Babe wrote: "If I am to break my 1921 record, I believe I will do it this year. Unless I can break my record this year, I believe there are only two men in baseball who have a chance to do it. One of them is Lou Gehrig and the other is Tony Lazzeri."[14]

Paul Gallico, one of the several distinguished sportswriters of the day, was in awe of what the Yankees were producing offensively in 1927: "There never has been anything like it. Even as lines are batted out on the office typewriter, youths dash out of the AP and UP ticker rooms every two or three minutes shouting, 'Ruth hit one! Gehrig just hit another one!'"15

Two months into the season, only two games separated the Yankees from the second place White Sox. However, the Yankees won 21 of 27 games in June and led both the White Sox and Senators by 10½ games. It was never a pennant race again once July began.

In a Fourth of July doubleheader at Yankee Stadium before a record crowd of 74,000, the Yankees blew away the Senators, 12–1 and 21–1. The visitors were on a roll, having won 10 straight and were now seven and a half games behind the front running Yankees. A double dip over the New Yorkers would have put them back in the race, or so they thought.

Following the holiday devastation, Washington first baseman Joe Judge had this to say: "Those fellows not only beat you, but they tear your heart out. I wish the season was over."16 The rout was officially on.

The next day the Senators came back to score five runs in the first inning but the Yankees crept back until Gehrig tripled and a long sacrifice fly by Meusel tied the score at 6–6 in the bottom half of the seventh. What happened in the ninth inning was probably a foregone conclusion as Lazzeri, who had looked at a couple of bad pitches, missed the next one and then delivered a blast over the wall to win it all.

As one account described it, "He was mobbed at the plate by Joe Dugan, Pat Collins and a dozen cash customers and acclaimed in the headlines as a diamond Mussolini, a sawdust Caesar some considered worthy of emulation, who even then was calling on Fascists to obey his book of faith and accept the commands of history."17

During a visit to Boston that same month, Babe Ruth was invited to speak at a testimonial dinner there in Tony Lazzeri's honor. The Bambino spoke glowingly of Tony's accomplishments as well as his own ability to break his home run record set in 1921. He and Gehrig were tied with 29 homers apiece at the time.

Ruth admitted that he wanted to set a new record "but if anyone is going to beat me out I hope it will be Lou Gehrig," he said to loud applause.18 Gehrig, who was also in attendance, just took a bow. Lazzeri was presented with a diamond ring and $1,000 in cash by his many admirers from the city's Italian-American community in the North End.

Tony heard himself compared to Columbus and Mussolini by other speakers that evening. "He didn't discover America," the *Times* noted in their report the following day, "but Columbus never went behind third for an overthrow to cut off the tying run in the ninth inning."19

"Poosh 'Em Up's" popularity was clearly now second only to that of

Ruth's. It was evident that his presence on the team was responsible for attracting many new fans bringing wicker baskets of fruit, bottles of wine and Italian flags to Yankee Stadium and to other parks on the circuit. *Time* magazine called him "the craftiest, quickest-thinking player in the major leagues and a settling influence on the jittery Koenig on one side of him and the yet uncertain Gehrig on the other."[20]

The Yankees were constantly in demand to play games on open dates during the season in such minor league cities as St. Paul, Dayton, Buffalo and Indianapolis. Even some National League teams like the Pittsburgh Pirates and Cincinnati Reds brought them in to play exhibition games.

Some of the players resented these games on their "off" days, but no one loved these bookings more than Babe Ruth. Wherever he went, traffic jams ensued just to catch a glimpse of him. And the Bambino did not disappoint. He would go so far as to leave his dinner or one of his beloved card games to go out on a railroad platform to welcome his admirers and shake their hands. It is said that he would even get out of bed occasionally to meet and greet his fans.

One time in Indianapolis, the Yankees were playing on a field located near the railroad tracks. The first three times Ruth came to bat he hardly managed to get the ball out of the infield. The fans had a great time giving the "Bronx Bomber" the "Bronx Cheer." However, on his last time up, he got hold of one and drove it well over the right field fence where it landed among the boxcars in the freight yard. The crowd loved it and so did the Babe. He couldn't have been happier if it was hit to win a World Series game.

Another time the club went to Sing Sing to play the prison team. In batting practice, the Bambino hit one over the right field wall and then over the center field wall, which was an even longer shot. The prisoners roared with delight.

The Babe was in his glory. When a convict umpire called one of the prisoners safe on a close play at home, the Babe yelled: "Robber!"[21] While clowning with the prisoners, the Yankees allowed one of them to steal a base. The Babe asked if there weren't any cops in the joint. Turning in the direction of the first base bleachers, he asked them what time it was and when a group of them told him, he countered: "What difference does it make to you guys? You ain't going any place."[22] Only Ruth could have gotten away with that remark to such a gathering.

Tony Lazzeri's epilepsy was never a problem when he was on the field, according to Mark Koenig, who roomed with him for a while. The shortstop claimed that a hairbrush flew out of Tony's hand as he stood at a mirror once and narrowly missed him. "The comb went whipping out of his hand," said

4. Murderers' Row (1927) 55

Ever the jokester, Lazzeri, who never caught a game in his life, donned the so-called "tools of ignorance" for this photograph during the record-breaking 1927 season. (*The Sporting News*)

Koenig to Stan Grossfeld of *The Boston Globe* in a December 1989 interview, "and he went down and started having convulsions. I was strip [*sic*] naked and I ran out into the hallway looking for [Waite] Hoyt." Why Hoyt? "'Cause he was an undertaker in the off-season. Hoyt took care of him."[23]

Hoyt was even called "The Merry Mortician" because of the undertaking business he had begun to supplement his income in the off-season. "I'm knocking 'em dead on Seventh Avenue while my partner is laying 'em out up in Westchester," Hoyt was quoted as saying once.[24] A man of many talents, he also was an artist, a writer and a vaudevillian who actually played the famous Palace Theater in New York City during the 1920s.

Whether or not his epilepsy contributed to his reluctance to talk, Lazzeri was known as the "silent man of the Yankees." Sportswriters following the club recalled that Lazzeri would join them in the railroad club car with a "hello" as he sat down and they would get nothing more than a "goodbye" when he departed.[25]

His infield sidekick Koenig declared: "Tony was a nice kid. He didn't say much, but he was a Sicilian and he got a temper. You couldn't say anything against him. Once I was in infield practice and I called him a Sicilian. Boy, he got madder'n hell. He was gonna kill me."[26]

Koenig dressed next to Ruth and had the train berth across from the Yankee slugger on road trips. He admitted in an interview long after he retired that he got into a fight with the Bambino once over a play that involved Lazzeri. "It was a silly thing. He was playing first base and he musta had a date or something. Lazzeri threw a ball 10 feet over my head. He [Ruth] thought I shoulda caught the ball and started bawling me out. I waited till he got through and, oh boy, what I didn't call him."[27]

When the team reached the dugout, Koenig said Ruth "was picking up a bat from the batting rack, and he grabbed me from the back and shoved me down the stairs. There were no punches thrown; it was a wrestling match. I used to have the berth across from him on the train, and Huggins moved me. Then after we clinched [the pennant], we shook hands and forgot about it. We got along good after that....

"Y'know, I don't think Ruth even knew my last name. He'd say, 'Hiya, kid,' to everybody."[28]

The Yankee juggernaut continued to roll through the months of July and August. Heading into the final month of the season, the club chalked up another 40 victories against only 17 losses. The Bronx Bombers had opened up an insurmountable 17-game deficit between them and the second place A's.

At one point during the year, third baseman Joe Dugan remarked: "It's always the same. Combs walks. Koenig singles. Ruth hits one out of the park. Gehrig doubles. Lazzeri triples. Then Dugan goes in the dirt on his can."[29]

The Yankees scored runs with such regularity in the late innings that the erudite Earle Combs labeled this delayed attack "Five O'clock Lightning." The phrase caught on and spread throughout the league and into the heads of opposing pitchers. Along about the seventh or eighth innings, hurlers on the other teams came to dread the approach of five o'clock as the sign that something ominous was about to befall them.[30]

Lazzeri was on his way to another stupendous season both at bat and defensively. Fans and writers alike marveled at his finesse. In a game played against the White Sox at Comiskey Park in Chicago, "Poosh 'Em Up" made one of his patented fielding gems.

The "Pickups and Putouts" column in the next day's edition of *The New York Times* reported it this way: "Tony Lazzeri made another one of those 'impossible' plays for which he is famous when he skidded over behind second base, picked up [Bibb] Falk's hot hopper with his bare hand and flipped the ball to Koenig to start a double play. It would have been brilliant enough if he had just stopped the ball."[31]

For the final game in August, the Yankees hosted the Boston Red Sox and beat them 10–3 behind George Pipgras. Lazzeri socked two homers with strict impartiality as to location: the first went into the left-field bleachers, the second among the right-field customers. Ruth walloped home run number 43 in the same game to put him two up on Gehrig.

The cry of "Break Up the Yankees" was given its first soundings as September arrived. "Runaway Race Starts Talk of Yankee Trades to Other Teams" was the *Times* headline. Rumors abounded that Gehrig was going to Detroit because having Ruth and Gehrig on the same ball club was deemed too powerful a combination to be the exclusive property of one team. Meusel was supposedly ticketed for White Sox for third baseman Willie Kamm, and Lazzeri was also thought to have been mentioned in trade talks.[32]

Of course, none of this ever materialized, proving to be nothing more than newspaper talk. "When the Yankees were last, did anybody give me players?" asked the owner, Colonel Jacob Ruppert. "Maybe they did give me a couple of lemons, and now I should give away Gehrig or Ruth or Lazzeri?"[33]

On September 2, the A's, buoyed by winning 12 of 14 games on a trip out west, came home hopeful of whittling down the huge Yankee lead. The Bronx Bombers crushed them 12–1 on two home runs by Gehrig—numbers 42 and 43—and one by Ruth—number 44—while Combs went 4-for-6 and "Poosh 'Em Up" added a double and two triples to the club's total of 20 hits. So much for hopefulness.

On September 5, the Yankees visited the last place Red Sox. Some

36,000 fans jammed Fenway Park and spilled onto the playing field to the point where the police had to be called in to preserve order. Another 15,000 packed the nearby streets hammering at the locked gates. The locked-out fans missed a great one, which lasted 18 innings and featured a home run by Gehrig — his forty-fourth — that actually put him in a flat-footed tie with Ruth. The Babe only had a double in seven trips to the plate as the Beantowners pushed over a run in the bottom half of the 18th to win the marathon, 12–11.

Gehrig actually passed Ruth on September 6 in the first game of a doubleheader at Fenway when he connected for home run number 45. Ruth, his competitive juices apparently flowing, followed with a blast over the center-field wall in the same game. The ball traveled some 488 feet, over the center-field wall with plenty to spare. It was by far the longest homer ever hit there.

Also in the opener, the Bambino connected for number 46 into the right-field bleachers and then belted number 47 into the right-field stands during the nightcap. The following day, Ruth hit numbers 48 and 49 during a 12–10 slugfest win over the Red Sox at Fenway to pull four ahead of Gehrig.

When the Yankees returned to New York on September 8 it was "Tony Lazzeri Day" both at the Stadium and at a testimonial dinner that evening in the grand ballroom of the Hotel Commodore. The Lazzeri Day Committee was headed by a prominent businessman and fellow Italian-American, Humbert J. Fugazy, who presented Tony with a horseshoe floral wreath prior to the game.

Guests of the Lazzeri Committee at both the ball game and the dinner included acting Mayor Joseph V. McKee, Judge Francis X. Mancuso, Judge Salvatore A. Cotillo, Judge Albert H. Vitale, Judge Joseph Raimo, Judge Daniel E. Direnzo, Frank K. Bowers, Michael Lauria and many other distinguished members of the sporting, business and financial world of New York City. Another well-known Italian-American, Edward Corsi, presided over the banquet as master of ceremonies. Corsi, the editor of *La Follia*, was also the president of the Italian Republican League.

Over 1,000 attended the dinner, including congressman and future New York City mayor Fiorello H. La Guardia, boxing commissioner James J. Farley and Yankees general manager Ed Barrow. Speeches by Babe Ruth, Lou Gehrig, Miller Huggins and Colonel Jacob Ruppert lauded the brilliant work of the popular Lazzeri on the playing field and his exemplary conduct both on and off the field.

Other members of the Yankees were also on hand, as were, members of the visiting St. Louis Browns and delegations from Italian societies in

4. Murderers' Row (1927)

Boston, Providence and Jersey City. Tony was presented with a $1,000 silver service from honorary committee chairman Fugazy, which he accepted graciously and prepared to "poosh up" a few runs the next day. The presentation was met with a deafening roar from those in attendance.

In his talk, Ruth reminded the audience, as he always did, that he wasn't being pitched to enough to break his 1921 home run record of 59. It was then that he added, perhaps even needlessly but maybe even kindly, that the only player that had a chance to top it was Lou Gehrig.

There could be little doubt now that Lazzeri had become the idol of Italian fans everywhere and the first true Italian-American superstar in professional sports in the United States. Though the press referred to him in such seemingly unflattering terms as "Tony the Wop," "The Walloping Wop" and "The Foremost Spaghetti Farmer," the descriptions had little effect on Lazzeri himself. When asked how he got nickname "Poosh 'Em Up," Tony would reply: "When I was in San Francisco, there were these old wops who used to sit together in the bleachers and they didn't speak English very well and...."[34]

The nation was a great deal more relaxed and a lot less politically correct than it is today. Remarkably, as we shall see later in this book, the situation would not change that much a decade later when Joe DiMaggio entered the big leagues.

With winning the pennant a foregone conclusion, interest began to center more and more around the Ruth-Gehrig home run duel. Whether Ruth's big days in Boston on September 5 and 6 put additional pressure on Gehrig cannot be measured. Suffice it to say, Gehrig was never to get closer than four behind again. It took him until September 27 to get his forty-sixth home run. Meanwhile, the Bambino had collected ten more to pull well ahead of his teammate.

Gehrig was only able to hit one more out on the last day of the season, October 1, when the Yankees beat the Senators, 4–3, to put the capper on an unbelievable record 110–44 season. The Bronx Bombers finished a distant 19 games ahead of the Athletics, the pre-season pick of most writers. Meanwhile, the Babe had cracked out three more dingers by September 30 to assure him of the record-breaking 60 home runs he so eagerly sought.

Gehrig's season was spectacular—47 home runs—which actually exceeded the totals of four teams, and a major league record 175 runs batted in, 218 hits and a .373 batting average. "Larrupin' Lou" led the American League in doubles with 52, and in total bases with 447 and 18 triples, which gave him 117 extra-base hits, the highest total in major league history. As if this were not enough, Gehrig also scored 149 runs and drew 109 walks.

To go along with his record-breaking 60 home runs—more than any entire team in the league—Ruth had 192 hits, 164 runs batted in and a .356 batting average. He also led the AL in slugging percentage with .772, a .486 on-base percentage and 158 walks.

The outfield alone—Ruth, Bob Meusel and Earle Combs—combined for 158 home runs, 597 hits and a .350 average. Combs set the pace in the American League that year with 231 hits, 23 triples and 137 runs scored.

Lazzeri was no innocent bystander himself that year, finishing with a .309 batting average, 176 hits, 102 runs batted in, 18 home runs and 22 stolen bases. It was the second year in a row that he had hit 18 homers, tying his own record for major league second basemen that he had set as a rookie a year earlier. He equaled that total in two later years but never surpassed it.

Lazzeri's home run and stolen base totals were good for third place in the league, making him the only player in the AL to finish in the top five in both categories. His third place finish in stolen bases left him just two behind the league runner up, Bob Meusel.

Yet despite this unbelievable display of offensive power, it was the pitching staff that Miller Huggins gave the most credit. "The backbone of any ball club is the pitching staff," he said. "The New York Yankees are sometimes spoken of as an exception. I have heard it said their tremendous batting punch carries them through. Now, I appreciate that batting punch as much as anyone, but no team would lead its league as we did in 1927 unless they possessed some real pitching strength."[35]

The statistics certainly backed the little manager up. The rotation included the winingest pitcher in the league, Waite Hoyt with 22, and the leader in earned run average, Wilcy Moore at 2.28. Hoyt was second in ERA at 2.64 while Urban Shocker was third at 2.84 and Herb Pennock was fourth with an even 3.00. As a whole, the American League's ERA was 4.13 while the Yankees alone recorded a 3.20 mark.

Murderers' Row had now completed its mission of getting to a second consecutive World Series but, unfortunately, the Cardinals were not destined to be their opponents. Revenge for the previous year's defeat would have to be kept on hold for the time being.

The winners of the National League pennant in 1927 were the Pittsburgh Pirates under Donie Bush, who had prevailed in a year in which the Senior Circuit had a number of strong teams in contention. Included among them were the 1926 champion Cardinals, who fell short of repeating by a scant one and a half games. The Giants had played one more game than the Cardinals and lost it, consequently finishing in third place only two games off the pace.

Fellow San Franciscans Lefty O'Doul (right) and Lazzeri prepare for an off-season golf game following the disappointing 1930 season. (*Baseball Magazine*)

The Corsairs were led by an outfield comprised of the future Hall of Fame Waner brothers—"Big Poison" Paul, the right-fielder, who led the league with a .380 average, and "Little Poison" Lloyd, the center-fielder, who batted .355. Clyde Barnhart in left for most of the season had a .319 average. Lloyd Waner had a better arm than Earle Combs and although Barnhart may not have had an arm like that of Bob Meusel, he fielded his position well while Meusel could sometimes appear rather lackadaisical. The big problem with the Pittsburgh outfielders offensively was that there wasn't a long ball hitter in the bunch. Paul Waner led all Pirate batsmen that season with a mere nine home runs.

The infield was solid, led by the veteran Pie Traynor, another future Hall of Famer, who hit .342 that year. In fact only the shortstop, Glenn Wright at .281, batted under .300. Light hitting Johnny Gooch and Earl Smith shared the catching duties.

Right-hander Carmen Hill had 22 victories to lead the mound staff, followed by a pair of 19-game winners, Ray Kremer and Lee Meadows, also right-handers. Still another righty, 15-gamer winner Vic Aldridge, rounded out the rotation. Not a single southpaw starter graced the crew to negate the hard-hitting Yankee lefty sluggers like Ruth and Gehrig.

Nevertheless, former Cardinals manager and now Giants second baseman Rogers Hornsby boldly predicted that Pittsburgh would win the Series based on what he considered the ability of their pitchers to hold the powerful Yankee bats in check. However, some observers felt that the Pirates were in awe of their opponents. The story goes that their players lost all hope as they watched the Yankee sluggers hit during batting practice.[36] According to Mark Koenig, the Pirates became intimidated as they "watched us take batting practice before the first game. Ruth, Gehrig and Meusel kept hitting the ball out of the park. The Pirates were beaten before they started."[37]

After Gehrig belted ten out of the park, Ruth stepped in and hit ten more. Pirate players watching the display were in awe of the Bambino, who had hit six more home runs during the regular season than their entire team combined.

To add insult to injury, Ruth admonished the Pirate players who were gawking at the awesome display thus: "Okay, sunnies. If any of you want my autograph, go out there and get those balls and I'll sign them for you."[38]

"We really put on a show," was how Ruth summed it all up.[39] A Pirate player later declared: "If the two teams had played a hundred games, I honestly think the Yankees would have won all. That's how intimidated we were."[40]

Waite Hoyt opposed Ray Kremer in Game One at Forbes Field, won by the Yankees, 5–4, despite the fact that the Pirates actually out-hit them nine to six. The Pirates were obviously jittery. They committed two errors in the top of the third inning to let in three unearned runs. The Yankees carried a 5–2 lead into the top of the fifth; the Pirates battled back to score single runs in both the fifth and eighth but couldn't close it out.

Ruth had three of the Yankees' six hits while Paul Waner also banged out three safeties. Hoyt developed a blister on his throwing hand during the fourth inning but lasted until the eighth, when Wilcy Moore relieved him and preserved the victory.

The Bambino credits Tony Lazzeri with the most important play in Game One. In his book, *Babe Ruth's Own Book of Baseball*, Ruth wrote:

> George Grantham, a sweet ball player and a mighty fast man on the bases, was first up to open the inning. He worked Hoyt for a base on balls and the stage was set for a sharp Pirate attack.
>
> Joe Harris, one of the best of the Pirate hitters, followed Grantham at

the plate and he signaled Grantham for the hit and run. Just as Hoyt drew back to pitch, Grantham leaped for second and Joe Harris smacked the ball squarely on the nose. Lazzeri had leaned toward second with the pitch and was starting as if to cover, but caught himself in time. With perfect timing, he scooped up the ball and tagged Grantham out as he tore for second. Then with the same motion he shot the ball to Gehrig and Harris was doubled at first base.

So far as actual play was concerned the play was good and snappy, but not spectacular. But it was a deathblow to the Pirates just the same. For when that play was pulled it showed them that we had an infield that could click under pressure, and a second baseman who knew what to do in the face of a hit and run attack. Right off the bat it made the Pirates doubtful about their best attacking method, and when a bit later, Tony pulled the same play they were thoroughly convinced. The point is that second base is the pivot of all infield play."[41]

The 6–2 victory in Game Two came much more easily for the visitors as George Pipgras, aided by his thunderous fastball, went the distance. Vic Aldridge, who pitched into the seventh for Pittsburgh, was tagged with the loss. The Yankees, led by Mark Koenig's three hits, put all of their runs together in two innings with three-run rallies in the third and again in the eighth.

The Yankees did not produce a single home run but their 11 hits were more than enough to take a two-games-to-none lead on their way home to the friendly confines of Yankee Stadium.

Before the second game, some critics speculated that Miller Huggins might have bitten off more than he could chew by starting the inexperienced Pipgras. After Lloyd Waner led off with a triple in and scored the first Pirate run via a sacrifice fly by Clyde Barnhart, the right-hander settled down to pitch a complete game. Only five assists were needed. The manager's faith in the youngster had been justified, as Pipgras scattered seven hits over the first seven innings.

The Yankees were determined not to have to return to Pittsburgh. A newspaperman riding in a cab to the railroad station with Tony Lazzeri and three other Yankees told them: "If you fellows don't wind this series up in the next two days, I'll shoot you." Lazzeri responded: "If we don't beat these bums four in a row, you can shoot me first."[42] The other players simply nodded since it was the way everybody on the ball club felt.

Babe Ruth's two home runs, the first of the Series by either team, gave the Yankees another easy triumph, 8–1, in Game Three at Yankee Stadium. The so-called "smart money" had it that no left-hander could beat the Pirates. Once again Huggins flew in the face of logic by starting his 33-year-old veteran ace, Herb Pennock. The southpaw promptly went the route for the home team, allowing only three hits. In fact, Pennock, who entered the game with a perfect 4–0 World Series record, retired the first 22 Pittsburgh batters he faced while taking a perfect game into the eighth. Pie Traynor spoiled the no-hit bid by touching up the left-hander for a single.

After Lou Gehrig scored Earle Combs and Mark Koenig on a triple in the bottom of the first inning, the Yankees themselves were stalled until the home half of the seventh by Pirates starter Lee Meadows. However, the New Yorkers drove the Pittsburgh right-hander out of the box when they rallied for six runs featuring a three-run blast by Ruth, his first home run of the Series; yet another example of "Five O'clock Lightning." The Yankee rally was aided by another Pirate error, their fifth of the Series. Lazzeri, who had been hit by a pitch in Game Two, played the entire game with his left wrist in a bandage but fielded flawlessly nevertheless.

The long wait in the dugout may have cooled off Pennock, who surrendered his first hit in the top half of the eighth. The Pirates' cleanup man, Glenn "Buckshot" Wright, led off the inning by grounding out to Koenig. Traynor, however, got a loud groan out of the Yankee Stadium crowd when he singled to left for the visiting team's first hit since the first inning. Barnhart followed with a run-scoring double to spoil the Yankee left-hander's shutout bid.

With one out in the ninth, Pennock allowed a third hit — a single by rookie Lloyd Waner, who had delivered 223 hits during the regular season. Hal Rhyne then flied out and Paul Waner grounded out to end the game, leaving the home club just one game away from becoming the first American League team to sweep a World Series.

With their commanding three games-to-none lead in hand, Huggins started his 30-year-old rookie sensation Wilcy Moore in Game Four. Moore had only made 12 starts that year in 50 appearances.

Donie Bush countered with his ace, Carmen Hill, a 22-game winner who had never recorded more than three victories in six previous seasons. The Pirates made a game of it before falling in the bottom of the ninth, 4–3, in a bizarre turn of events.

Hill had permitted a run-scoring single by Ruth in the first inning and was touched up once again by the Bambino in the fifth when he smacked a two-run homer, his second of the Series, giving the Yankees a 3–1 lead. Bush pinch-hit for Hill in the top of the seventh; an inning in which the Pirates scored two runs off Moore to tie the game at 3–3. It remained tied into the bottom of the ninth.

Johnny Miljus, who had relieved Hill in the seventh, walked Combs to begin the inning. Koenig's pop fly sacrifice then bounced off the ankle of the usually sure-handed Traynor. With Ruth at bat, Miljus wild pitched

Combs and Koenig to second and third base respectively. After walking Ruth to load the bases, Miljus reached back in his arsenal to strike out both Gehrig and Meusel.

Up came "Poosh 'Em Up" Tony Lazzeri, who could possibly have been swept up in a wave of *déjà vu* since he had batted in a similar scenario a year ago almost to the day. While the players urged Huggins to put the squeeze on, the manager declined, claiming that Miljus was "bearing down too hard. If Tony doesn't hit one, he'll wild pitch."[43]

Tony sent Miljus' first pitch screaming into foul territory in the left-field stands. On the next pitch, Miljus let loose a "sailer" that kept rising out of the reach of the catcher, Johnny Gooch. In raced Combs with the winning run as Huggins had clearly prophesied and the first-ever World Series sweep was complete.

Writer Paul Gallico described the finish of the Series in his own inimitable style thus:

> How that [Johnny] Miljus is pitching! The bases full and none out and he fans Gehrig and Meusel in full view of 57,000. Who is this? Ah, Tonee Poosh-em-opp — Tony Lazzeri. Sure enough, fate has stored up this moment for The Wonderful Wop. We shall be decorated by Mussolini.
>
> He shall have free haircuts and shaves wherever he goes. He shall have as much spaghet as he can eat. O, Tonee! Tonee, poosh 'em, poosh 'em up! Wow! Wow! Wow! The ringing sound of bat and ball. No, no. Foul. Foul! Into the left field stands, but foul. It shows that our Tony has his eye on the ball. Miljus is winding up again. Come on, Tonee! Poosh—!!"Does Tony connect solidly with the ball to send tens of thousands into ecstasy? No, my friends, he does nothing of the kind, because Mr. Miljus lets go a wild pitch that hits the top of Gooch's glove and caroms to the stand, and Earle Combs gallops over with the winning run, the championship, the shekels, and the integrity of baseball. He does a little war dance, and everybody goes home.
>
> The slapstick is mightier than the bludgeon and for that reason the New York Yankees are champions of the world, and if ever a dramatic ball game came to a sillier ending, I would like to be informed.[44]

Miller Huggins was the epitome of class when he received the reporters in his office following the game. "Say something nice about the Pirates," he said. "Don't be hard on them. It was tragic to lose a ball game that way, and they were a much better ball club than they showed in the Series."[45]

Grantland Rice had another view of the Pirates' performance in the Fall Classic. "Pittsburgh was badly outclassed," he wrote. "The weary-looking Pirates were out batted, out fielded and out pitched. They were badly out fought. For three days that Yankee juggernaut had rolled in Ruth and ruthless fashion."[46]

Huggins called in Lazzeri immediately after the Series ended to ask him what he intended to do with his winning share. "I haven't given it a thought," replied Tony. "Turn the check over to me," Huggins told Lazzeri. "I'll make this Series worth a lot more money to you. If there was any doubt about it, I wouldn't suggest it, but I know."[47]

Three weeks later, Huggins asked Lazzeri if he still held the stock that the manager had recommended. "It's in the middle eighties now. It will go beyond a hundred. That World Series will keep on making money for you for a long time."[48]

During the regular season, Huggins was noted for how he handled each of his players on an individual basis. While sitting in the dugout chewing tobacco and spitting, he would sometimes indulge himself in conversation along the lines of: "That Lazzeri. He's no good. Can't do nothing."[49]

Lazzeri, within earshot of the manager's criticism, would bear down and perhaps hit a home run, steal a base or make a spectacular fielding play. Then he would walk up to Huggins and say: "Well, how do you like that?"

"Routine," Hug would respond.

When Huggins passed away two years later, a tearful Lazzeri did not think of the money that his manager had helped make for him after the 1927 World Series. "He made me. That's all."[50]

As far as the 1927 season was concerned for the New York Yankees, sportswriter Arthur Robinson put it completely in perspective when he wrote: "This is just not a ball club. This is Murderers' Row."[51]

5

Back-to-Back Champions (1928)

If Yankee management had the slightest idea that signing the players without contracts from 1927's Murderers' Row for following season was going to be easy, it was sadly mistaken. The players truly believed much of what they had read about themselves throughout the winter — that they were the greatest major league baseball team that had ever been assembled. And they wanted to be compensated accordingly.

Every contract that was sent out by General Manager Ed Barrow in early February was returned unsigned. The exceptions were Babe Ruth and Herb Pennock, who had been inked to three-year deals a year earlier, and Lou Gehrig, who had also been signed for three years just weeks before training camp opened.

Ruth was signed for the unparalleled sum of $80,000 a year, by far the highest in the history of the game. The Bambino's new salary gave rise to the often-quoted remark he made regarding the fact that he was now making more money than the president of the United States. The Babe told reporters that he was entitled to it because he had had a better year than the president.

Ruth's teammates and even players from opposing teams were not envious. After all, in the long run, the Babe's new salary set a standard from which their own future paydays would be measured. Besides, many of them liked "The Sultan of Swat" and felt as he did — that he had earned it.

The non-signers were a diverse group and even included players like utility infielder Gene Robertson. He was in the minor leagues in 1927 and, therefore, not even with the team. After balking at the club's first offer, Robertson ultimately capitulated and sent his signed contract back to Barrow with a note saying: "I give up. I just can't stand the thought of walking around New York next summer and having people point at me and say: 'There goes the guy who broke up the Yankees.'"[1]

After several weeks of haggling, most of the Yankee players did sign. By the end of February only pitchers Waite Hoyt and Urban Shocker and "Poosh 'Em Up" Tony Lazzeri had failed to provide Yankee management with their "John Hancocks." Hoyt was enjoying the baths at Hot Springs, Arkansas, while Shocker had announced he would change the direction of his life from baseball to aviation. It was also believed that the ball club wanted Lazzeri to sign a two-year deal, which the second baseman supposedly rejected, believing he could make more money by signing a new contract every year.

While Hoyt wanted a two-year deal, it was said that Barrow felt he hadn't earned it. "Show a better earned run average and we will give you a long-term contract," Barrow supposedly told Hoyt.[2] Meanwhile, Mark Koenig, Wilcy Moore and Earle Combs each did sign two-year deals.

"I'm not worried about any of them," said Manager Miller Huggins, referring to the three holdouts. "Maybe they've signed and I haven't been informed yet. They'll all be in there at the gong."[3] Less than a week later, the manager was already making plans to install either Mike Gazella or Robertson at the keystone sack should Lazzeri fail to show in training camp.

Huggins also was preparing to have a cocky first-year shortstop named Leo Durocher on the roster as a backup. The Yankees had looked Durocher over a couple of years prior to the 1928 season but had judged him not quite ready. A year in Hartford and another in St. Paul convinced the ball club that the brash infielder would be the first rookie to make the team.

The manager also indicated that he was planning to retain right-handers Hank Johnson and Al Shealy on his roster, particularly if Shocker failed to report. Hug told the press in no uncertain terms that if the veteran wasn't going to show: "Let him stay away." Should that, in fact, be the case, Huggins said that he would employ both Johnson, a third-year man, and Shealy, a rookie, on his staff.[4]

It was now evident to all concerned that the manager was playing hardball with the holdouts on his team. Huggins also seemed quite taken with the abilities of a couple of outfielders, Allen "Dusty" Cooke and Sammy Byrd, who were trying to catch on with the World Champions. Neither one, though, was able to make the club in 1928. While Byrd would come on board a year later in 1929, Cooke was still two years away from a spot on the Yankee roster.

Referred to as the "California delegation" by James R. Harrison of *The*

New York Times, Bob Meusel, Mark Koenig and Tony Lazzeri were all characterized by the writer in the March 4 edition of the newspaper as having "never been known to arrive on time, and it will be a great big surprise if any one of them shows his face tomorrow."[5]

With the 38-year-old Shocker seemingly retired, Hoyt and Lazzeri, two key cogs from the 1927 world championship squad, could now be officially classified as holdouts. Barrow sent a telegram to Huggins allowing the field manager to negotiate personally with both players. Hoyt and Lazzeri quickly made their way to St. Petersburg to begin their quest for more Yankee dollars.

If Hoyt and Lazzeri thought that Huggins would be a softer touch than Barrow, both discovered early on that this was not the case. "Hoyt and Lazzeri have been handsomely treated by the Yankees," Huggins told James R. Harrison of *The New York Times*.

> In fact, I can say with truth that in all my experience with the Yankees as a manager, I do not recall one player not being treated well by the New York club.
>
> We are not trying to inveigle them into a bad contract. We are not trying to pay them less than they have earned. But we are offering them exactly what we think they are worth, and I see no prospect of the New York club going one step beyond that figure.
>
> I will be glad to talk to both Hoyt and Lazzeri, but I don't intend to retreat. If I can persuade them that their demands are unreasonable, well and good. If not — well, then the Yankees will have to stand pat and see what happens.[6]

The same reporter asked if during salary negotiations the Yankees posited that the team might be in the World Series again and that the players would obtain extra money in any event. "Never," the manager said emphatically. "We pay ball players what we think they are worth, regardless of the World Series money. The Yankees have never underpaid a player... That would be manifestly unjust. A player should be entitled to a fair wage for his season's work, and the World Series money should be regarded as a just reward for victory."[7]

To conclude his article, Harrison apparently could not resist the chance to use the situation for a bit of editorializing: "Lazzeri, of the warm Italian blood, is also what is known in baseball as a tough customer," he wrote. "Tony doesn't say much but when he makes up his mind all the king's horses and all the king's men cannot budge him.

"Mr. Huggins may find that all his oratorical skill, developed in the Cincinnati bar years ago, will be needed in the present argument. At any rate, it looks like a keen and merry battle."[8]

The very next day, March 6, 1928, "Poosh 'Em Up" Tony Lazzeri arrived in camp along with his double-play mate and fellow San Franciscan Mark Koenig, and, after a meeting with Huggins, promptly signed a new contract. The manager was ecstatic. "Yep, Lazzeri is signed to a two-year contract and everything is jake," the manager exclaimed. "And will you just look at that [Ben] Chapman digging them up out there at third? And I want to say for the benefit of all concerned that Leo Durocher is as fine a young shortstop as I've ever seen in a southern training camp."[9]

Lazzeri, who was now earning the same amount of money as Lou Gehrig—$8,000 annually—dressed quickly and took his turn in the afternoon workout at second base. Harrison reported in the same article that announced Lazzeri's signing: "Charley O'Leary slapped a slow one down to Leo Durocher who sallied in at top speed, collared the pill and blazed a perfect throw into the [Lou] Gehrig mitt. Not to be outdone by a pair of mere rookies, Mr. Lazzeri accomplished the same feat with singular ease and dexterity."[10]

Hoyt and Shocker eventually came around just before training camp ended but the Yankees did make a few changes. Julie Wera, the youngster who backed up Joe Dugan at third base in 1927, was sent to Hollywood of the Pacific Coast League. The contracts of Lyn Lary and Jimmy Reese, an exciting young shortstop/second base combination, were purchased from Oakland of the PCL for $100,000 with the proviso that they not report until the spring of 1929.

All during spring training in St. Petersburg, Huggins approached the players in a unique manner. He knew that he needed to provide them with an incentive that was not just centered on their salaries and the prospect of hauling in another World Series check.

Consequently, he talked to them about the value of the money they received in return for their talents. Huggins reminded them it was not just important for what it could buy but rather for what it could do for them and their families in the long term. He talked to them constantly about buying better homes for their families and providing better schooling and other returns for their children.

The manager emphasized investments and not just in the stock market. In fact, he told them to get out of the market. Therefore, when the market crashed in the following year very few of his players were hurt financially. And those that were got off relatively lightly. In the final analysis, the plan worked marvelously well for those Yankee players who heeded Huggins' advice.

A lanky catcher named Bill Dickey whom Huggins really liked was brought in from Little Rock but was sent out to Buffalo for more season-

5. Back-to-Back Champions (1928)

ing at the beginning of the year. The manager told the young receiver not to emulate sluggers like Ruth, Gehrig, Lazzeri and Meusel with free-swinging, "go-for-the-downs" cuts.

"Stop unbuttoning your shirt on every pitch," Huggins warned the youngster. "We pay one player here for hitting home runs and that's Babe Ruth. So choke the bat and drill the ball."[11] The manager wanted his catcher-of-the-future to stop trying to pull everything and just meet the ball. Dickey wised up quickly and proceeded to follow Huggins' directions to the letter not only in Buffalo but also later on in New York for many years to come.

Durocher, who had the proverbial cup of coffee with the Yankees in 1925, made the club as a utility infielder as everyone believed he would. Now Huggins had the team he wanted on the field to start the 1928 campaign and defend its championship.

One day during spring training, an interviewer asked Ruth if he had ever had an idol. Lazzeri, who was within earshot of the question, barked out: "Sure he has, 'Babe Ruth.'" "Go to hell," Ruth said, and to the reporter, "Excuse me, it's my turn to hit."[12]

The Yankees began the season on a fast track but then stumbled briefly in April while losing their lead to the Red Sox. That was it for the Beantowners, who were to wind up in last place for the second year in a row by a distant 43½ games. As usual the Athletics were considered to be the Yankees' chief contenders.

Lazzeri had a back injury early in the season, so much so that he winced in pain with every throw he made. It then became necessary for the inexperienced 22-year-old Durocher to jump in and spell "Poosh 'Em Up" at second base. While the youngster's fielding was superb, his hitting was spotty. Durocher would hit well for a week or so and then seemed to have trouble getting the ball out of the infield.

A reporter asked Huggins why the rookie could only hit well part of the time. The manager replied: "If you can tell me, I'll give you $50,000 because a fellow like that would be worth that much more to this club if he could hit consistently. I've watched him, studied him and talked to him. And between us we can't figure him out."[13]

Picking up where they left off in 1927, Ruth, Gehrig, Meusel and Lazzeri — when he returned to the lineup — pounded opposing pitchers with regularity. Their own mound staff led by the ever-reliable Herb Pennock, George Pipgras and Waite Hoyt was virtually unhittable.

Hoyt, despite his attempted holdout, said: "It's great to be young and a Yankee."[14] He also held that the secret to success as a pitcher in the major leagues "lies in getting a job with the Yankees."[15]

The group was bolstered by the addition of Bradenton, Florida's Hank Johnson. The right-hander, who had been with the Yankees briefly in 1925 and 1926, had been in the minors in 1927. He would go on to become a 14-game winner for the Yankees in 1928 and, incredibly, would best the A's ace, Lefty Grove, on five separate occasions.

It was evident early on that Shocker would be of no value to the ball club. He had dropped from his normal playing weight of 190 pounds to an alarming 115 pounds in the off-season. He worked hard to regain the weight he had mysteriously lost and began the season with the team. However, while pitching batting practice in Comiskey Park in Chicago in April, he collapsed. He was only able to give the Yankees a total of two innings of work for the first half of the season and eventually would be released in July.

The first game of a doubleheader played at Philadelphia's Shibe Park on May 27, 1928, had no special significance at the time, but no less than 17 future Hall of Famers were involved in the contest. Connie Mack, Ty Cobb, Tris Speaker, Mickey Cochrane, Al Simmons, Eddie Collins, Jimmie Foxx and Lefty Grove represented the Athletics. The Yankees' cast of characters included Babe Ruth, Lou Gehrig, Tony Lazzeri, Earle Combs, Waite Hoyt, Leo Durocher and Miller Huggins. Umpires Tommy Connolly and Bill McGowan rounded out the sparkling list of some of the greatest names in the history of the sport.

Although Shibe Park's capacity in those days was estimated at anywhere between 27,500 and 33,600, the *Philadelphia Public Ledger* reported paid attendance that day at nearly 42,000, and unpaid attendance inside the park—pass holders, wall scalers, etc.—at another 2,000. It was also reported that still another 15,000 to 20,000 disappointed patrons (many holding scalped tickets) were denied entrance to the park that day.

Writing in the *Philadelphia Public Ledger,* Bill Brandt said the multitude outside the park "retreated from the barricaded portals or lingered outside the concrete horseshoe to listen to the noises of the long and rapid-turning battletide."[16] It was the largest crowd up to that time in Philadelphia baseball history.

Inside the ballpark fans scuffled for every possible venue from which to view the action. They filled the aisles, climbed to the top of the scoreboard and even atop its steel girders. As many as 3,000 of them scaled the walls to reach the sloping left-field roof. *The Philadelphia Inquirer* provided this account of the game:

> Over the low (12-foot) wall in right field, rabid rooters scaled the barbed wire walls like doughboys in France when the word was given "over the

5. Back-to-Back Champions (1928)

top." Despite the efforts of the police, several ladders were smuggled into the vast throng of ten thousand, which banked itself on Twentieth Street. As if by prearranged signal, four of them were placed against the walls and the fans surged over them like Greeks over the Trojan battlements. Many, once they reached the top, were caught on the barbed wire, and their antics in extricating themselves kept the fans in riotous good humor.

One rooter in jumping to the ground had his coat sleeve caught on a barb. As he slipped to earth the coat remained in the wire, much to the delight of the vast throng who followed the progress of the invasion with as much interest as they did the batting practice of the Yanks.

Another less fortunate wall climber caught his trouser leg in a steel prong and dangled in the air as thousands roared. His belt, however, did not give way and companions pulled him back to safety.

Even the white pole along the right field foul line served as a practice ground for embryonic steeplejacks, and several of them, instead of dropping to earth [from] atop the wall, "shinnied" up to the top pavilion. Each successive climb was met with a vast cheer from the crowd until so many accomplished the goal that it became monotonous.

The new scoreboards did double work, serving as a parking place for a hundred more fans as well as flashing the progress of the game. The porch and top roofs of the houses on Twentieth Street held five thousand more baseball bugs [fans] despite feeble efforts by the police to keep them off. On roofs two blocks away, fifty or more [fans] were sighted viewing the battle through field glasses. They must have had a good view of the tilt for in the sixth inning of the first game when a doubtful strike was called on Cobb, one threw his hat on the roof, stamped on it, shook his fist at [umpire] Van Graflan and then disappeared from sight over the sidewalk."[17]

The A's were riding the crest of a five-game winning streak when the Yankees came to town. The team was almost but not quite the ball club that Connie Mack had wanted. He had an outfield consisting of 41-year-old Ty Cobb in right, 40-year-old Tris Speaker in center and 26-year-old Al Simmons in left. Another 41-year-old, Eddie Collins, attempted to shore up the infield at second base while the 25-year-old Mickey Cochrane had no peer behind the plate in the American League at the time.

With their ace, Lefty Grove, on the hill, the A's failed in their quest for a sixth consecutive victory as the New Yorkers, led by Tony Lazzeri's three hits and six runs batted in, prevailed, 9–7. Grove had long since left the game when "Poosh 'Em Up" blasted a triple with the bases loaded in the ninth inning to break the game open.

The home club made a game of it in the bottom of the ninth as they rallied and had the tying runs in scoring position on second and third with two down. Cobb smacked a line drive in the direction of left center field when Hoyt, whom Huggins had brought in to relieve, knocked the ball down and beat Cobb with a throw to first base to end the contest. Rookie

Al Shealy, the starter, was credited with the win, en route to a 6–0 won-lost record that season.

The A's gained a split on the day by winning the second game, 5–2. Mr. Mack started a rookie lefthander, Ossie Orwoll, and he completely stifled the Yankees as he tossed a six hitter against them.

As the season progressed, Huggins had to do some fine-tuning of his pitching staff due to the illness of Urban Shocker for most of the year. Shocker, who only appeared in that one game in April for the Yankees in 1928, retired to his home in Denver following his release to try and regain his health. Sadly, it never happened; the popular veteran succumbed there on September 9.

Wilcy Moore had also suffered through a season of assorted arm problems. No amount of doctors, bonesetters and muscle manipulators could help him and he retired for the year on September 27, returning to his home in Hollis, Oklahoma.

In an attempt to patch up his ailing staff, Huggins brought up Fred "Lefty" Heimach from St. Paul in late July. Also, the veteran southpaw Tom Zachary was purchased from the Senators in August to further help strengthen the manager's banged up group of hurlers.

"Poosh 'Em Up" also continued to endure some lingering injuries in 1928. After having played in nearly every game in the previous two years, Lazzeri had been forced to miss some games early in the year due to his recurring shoulder problems. The Yankees were indeed fortunate to have Leo Duorcher fill in for him and do a creditable job.

The youngster, who would later be known as "Leo the Lip" for obvious reasons, was probably the most irrepressible rookie to come along in years. He had no compunction about riding opposing players, particularly such veteran superstars as Ty Cobb. In the last year of his extraordinary career, "The Georgia Peach" was urged to "give yourself up" by the brash Durocher. The more Cobb hurled threats at him, the more Leo would try to enrage him.

"Go home, Grandpa," Durocher would yell to Cobb. "Get wise to yourself. If you keep on playing with us young fellows, you might get hurt."[18]

In one game with Cobb on first and two out, the next batter singled to right center. Cobb took off immediately after the ball was hit and as he rounded second, Durocher, standing near the bag, gave him the hip. Cobb stumbled but regained his composure and kept running toward third. However, he was thrown out by at least three feet. Durocher laughed and while heading for the dugout, Cobb snarled at him: "The next time you try that, I'll cut your legs off."[19]

5. Back-to-Back Champions (1928)

"You'll cut nobody's legs off," Durocher shot back. "You've been bulldozing young ball players in this league for years, but you can't frighten me. I'll give you the hip every time you come around that bag, if I can. And if you try to cut me, I'll stick the ball down your throat."[20]

Durocher also went out of his way to antagonize a former umpire, George Moriarity, who was managing the Tigers in 1928. Although Moriarity had neither done nor said anything to Durocher, the young rookie taunted him every chance he could. Moriarity had a reputation as a fighter and Leo took special delight in tormenting him. Moriarity was twice as big as Durocher and probably could have taken care of him easily, but knew he would get into big trouble if he did. Durocher knew this also and kept up his acerbic remarks until finally called off by Huggins.

According to Durocher, Miller Huggins felt that Lazzeri had to be motivated once in a while. In his book, *Nice Guys Finish Last*, Durocher wrote:

> Huggins would wait until Lazzeri was picking up his bat, and then he'd give me the wink and say, "Get your glove and warm up. You're going in at second base."
>
> Hooooo, it was like setting off a bomb under Lazzeri. "*He's* going to play second! HE's going to play in my place! That humpty-dumpty? The All-American Out!" "That's right," Huggins would snap, "I've seen all I want to see of you for the day. I don't want to have to look at you any more."
>
> And just about that time, Lazzeri would go up and rip one. Hit it about 30 miles. And come back to the bench swaggering, look right at Huggins as if he were going to spit in his eye and say, "How do you *like* it?"[21]

It was no secret that the Yankee players were enjoying life off the field as well as on it. Huggins took note and, while concerned, decided to let things stand as long as the team enjoyed a comfortable lead. One day in Chicago, he did opt to hold a meeting. The players were shocked, as he had not held one in years.

After shutting the clubhouse door, he paced up and down and looked at them somberly. The players were puzzled as they looked at each other wondering why the little manager had called the meeting in the first place. Finally, Huggins broke the ice and said: "Chicago is a bad town for you fellows. Be careful."[22] Then he just walked out. After presumably the shortest team meeting history, the players followed Hug out to the field and promptly destroyed the White Sox.

Another time in the Windy City, Huggins thought it might be best for him to confront Ruth. At first he decided to talk to the big fellow before the game, then decided against it. That afternoon the Bambino belted two home runs, one off Red Faber and the other off Ted Lyons.

That evening while Huggins was sitting in the lobby after dinner with the team's traveling secretary, Mark Roth, Ruth got off the elevator. Roth encouraged Huggins to approach the Babe. "Shut up," Huggins told Roth. "Go on, talk to him," Roth said. Huggins got up and again told Roth to shut up. "Come on. Let's go the movies," the manager said.[23]

In late August, it was discovered that Tony Lazzeri had torn a muscle in his right shoulder and Huggins was forced to bench him. "I don't expect Lazzeri to play regularly the rest of the season," the manager told the press. "He is practically through for this year. I gave him two weeks' rest with medical treatment; then he played a week, and now the old trouble has returned. I consider that conclusive proof that he cannot play regularly.

"Besides [affecting] his throwing, Tony's sore shoulder has interfered with his hitting and fielding. Knowing that his arm is weak, he is trying to throw the ball before he has it, resulting in fumbles. A long rest will cure him; abuse of the shoulder might result in permanent injury."[24]

It was decided to limit Lazzeri's participation to an occasional pinch-hitting chore through the end of the season. All in all, Tony wound up missing 38 games in 1928 due to the recurring pain in his shoulder. Although Durocher would wind up with a decent .270 batting average, the young man simply could not deliver the long ball the way "Poosh 'Em Up" could.

Lazzeri's bat was definitely missed in the lineup. The Yankee lead, which had been as high as seventeen games at one point, dwindled to where the Athletics were breathing down their necks in early September. Besides Lazzeri's injury, Ruth was nursing a bad leg, Meusel was taped from head to foot and Pennock's arm was bothering him. It was not a pleasant situation and it cost the Yankees dearly. By September 8, it was the A's and not the Yankees who were in first place in the American League. New York's big lead had frittered away and many doubted that they would ever recover.

It all came to a head with a big doubleheader against the A's at Yankee Stadium on September 9. It was estimated that there were over 80,000 fans in the ballpark that afternoon. The Yankees realized that this could represent a do-or-die day for their pennant hopes. They were more than equal to the task and won both games, coming off a shutout pitched by George Pipgras in the opener, and another victory behind Waite Hoyt in the nightcap. The second game featured a grand slam by Bob Meusel to provide the icing on the cake.

The Yankees felt they had left Mr. Mack's club by the wayside that day but there was no cause for joy in the clubhouse. They were informed

5. Back-to-Back Champions (1928)

by their road secretary, Mark Roth, that Urban Shocker had passed away early that morning at his home in Denver. The news had been kept from the team for obvious reasons. The popular Shocker was only 35 years old.

The very next day, Hank Johnson recorded his fifth straight win over Lefty Grove and the Athletics. Philadelphia was hanging by a string. The Yankee machine rolled on for the next three weeks with the clincher coming in Detroit on September 28. The New Yorkers had withstood the furious rush that the A's had fashioned to finish two and one-half games up on them and capture their third straight American League pennant.

Although the club had piled up some impressive offensive numbers, this team was not nearly the equal of the 1927 Murderers' Row. Babe Ruth had smashed 54 home runs — twice as many as any other player in the American League — batted .323 and tied Lou Gehrig with 142 runs batted in. "Larrupin' Lou" led the club with a .374 batting average even though his home run production had dipped to 27 from the career-high 47 he had drilled the year before.

Earle Combs and Bob Meusel had decent years but not quite as good as the ones they had both enjoyed in 1927. And "Jumping Joe" Dugan, who had been nursing an old knee injury for most of the year, wound up being waived to the Braves at the end of the season.

Despite being hobbled by injuries for most of the year, "Poosh 'Em Up" still managed to get into 116 games, batting .332, his best average yet. However, his limited duty decreased his home run contribution to ten and his runs batted in total to 82. In his previous two years, he had established the all-time mark for home runs by a second baseman with 18 each year and had driven in 114 runs as a rookie and 102 in his second season.

Catching had been a problem all year long for the Yankees. Johnny Grabowski, Pat Collins and Benny Bengough divided the receiving chores, but none of them had any real power or could even hit for a decent average. Ultimately it was decided to bring up the left-handed hitting Bill Dickey to take over the position in 1929.

The hard-throwing George Pipgras had come along extremely well and turned in a magnificent 24–7 season. Wait Hoyt was 23–7 and was even credited with saving eight games to lead the American League in that department. Although Herb Pennock posted a 17–6 mark and a 2.56 earned run average, he suffered an injury to his arm and would never again be the pitcher he once was. He was to be sidelined for the entire 1928 World Series. Garland Braxton was the one who led the AL in ERA that year with a 2.52 mark.

The New York club was far from its best physically coming into the World Series against the National League's best team, the St. Louis Cardinals. Lazzeri's right shoulder was extremely tender and he was in pain not only every time he had to throw a ball but also when he had to swing a bat. However, it was impossible to keep him out of the lineup.

Ultimately it was decided that Lazzeri should play through the injury and have it taken care of in the off-season. Tony didn't care because all he wanted to do was to play. He reasoned that he would have plenty of time after the World Series to attend to the injury.

With two of three Yankee catchers also hurting, Benny Bengough, who had only played in 58 games that year, was forced to do all of the work behind the plate. Apart from the fact that Herb Pennock's sore arm had shut him down completely, Ruth had a charley horse that made him limp every time he just thought about it.

The busiest member of the club in 1928 was the trainer, Doc Woods, who did a great job by getting every regular ready for the first game except Earle Combs. The center fielder would have to sit this one out but for a single pinch-hitting appearance. Cedric Durst and Benny Paschal were to spell the "Kentucky Schoolmaster" in the Series.

The stage was set for sweet revenge for the Bronx Bombers, who were still smarting from their loss to the Cardinals in 1926. Even Grover Cleveland Alexander, now a seemingly ancient 41 years of age, was still with the NL club and penciled in to start Game Two in Yankee Stadium. "Old Pete" was still good enough to win 16 games for the Redbirds and help them beat out the runner-up Giants by three games in 1928.

Bill Sherdel, a 21-game winner, was to open the Series in New York and also pitch Game Four in St. Louis. Twenty-game winner Jesse Haines was set to start Game Three in Sportsman's Park.

The Yankees, even without Herb Pennock and with injuries to assorted players, were poised to repeat their 1927 Series triumph while counting upon Waite Hoyt and George Pipgras for Games One and Two at Yankee Stadium. A surprise starter was to be the journeyman left-hander Tom Zachary, whom the Yankees had obtained on waivers from Washington on August 23. He was scheduled to start Game Three. The veteran had posted a combined 9–12 mark for both clubs.

Bill McKechnie was now the pilot of the Cardinals, having replaced player-manager Bob O'Farrell. O'Farrell had left St. Louis after the 1927 season when his club was edged out by the Pirates by two games. McKechnie had been the skipper of the Pirates from 1922 to 1926.

The Cardinals were a fearsome team with future Hall of Famers Rabbit Maranville and Frank Frisch as their double-play combination, and another Hall of Famer to be, Jim Bottomley, anchoring the infield at first base. Bottomley led the NL in homers with 31 and runs batted in with 136.

5. Back-to-Back Champions (1928)

Andy High, a .285 hitter that season, his first with the ball club, rounded out the infield at third base.

The outfield featured Chick Hafey, another of that long line of San Francisco–native ballplayers in left, Taylor Douthit in center and George Washington Harper in right. Hafey slammed 27 home runs that year while Harper chipped in with another 17. Hafey, also in the midst of a Hall of Fame career, led the team in batting with a .337 average.

Jimmie Wilson was now the St. Louis catcher, as former player-manager O'Farrell had been traded to the Giants on May 1 in exchange for Harper.

"Poosh 'Em Up" had to be considered a liability in the field when the Series began because of his inability to throw accurately. The scenario was for Leo Durocher to come in as a late-inning defensive replacement for Lazzeri, much the same as Huggins had done during the regular season.

In Game One the Cardinals were only able to muster three hits against Hoyt, who went the distance in an easy 4–1 victory for the Yankees. Bottomley accounted for the lone St. Louis run via a seventh-inning home run, the only one the visitors were destined to hit throughout the entire Series.

Bob Meusel led the way offensively for the Yankees with a two-run homer into the right field bleachers. Ruth, injured ankle and all, contributed a single and two doubles and scored two runs while Gehrig was 2-for-4 with two RBI. Hoyt was superb throughout — Bottomley was the only Cardinal to get past second base.

Game Two in New York was an even easier victory for the Yankees, who prevailed 9–3 behind George Pipgras' complete game four-hitter. None other than their old nemesis, Grover Cleveland Alexander, was on the hill for the Cardinals. The Yankees pummeled him from the start, driving him from the mound in the third inning as they roared to an 8–0 lead. Gehrig got the team off and winging in the first inning with a three-run blast into the bleachers with Cedric Durst and Ruth aboard. The Babe, who was on fire, got two more hits — a single and a double and scored another pair of runs.

Pipgras, known as "The Danish Viking" because of his roots and 6'1½" frame, was a little shaky at the outset. Some of the Yankee players felt that Huggins should have lifted him when the Cardinals tied the game in their half of the second inning. However, the manager had complete faith in the World War I veteran and the right-hander did not let him down. By going all the way, the rookie gave the Yankees a two-games-to-none lead as the teams headed to St. Louis.

The situation didn't improve at all for the Cardinals in Game Three despite being on their own turf in Sportsman's Park. Zachary surprised many when he gave the Yankees their third consecutive complete game outing. The defending world champions, behind two home runs by Gehrig, won it easily, 7–3.

The aging left-hander Jesse Haines lasted six innings and gave up six of the Yankees' seven runs. After the Cardinals had jumped out to a quick 2–0 lead in the first inning, Gehrig's first homer, a bases empty blast into the right field pavilion in the second inning, halved the margin.

The Yankees took the lead in the fourth by virtue of a run-scoring single by Ruth and Gehrig's second home run of the game, a two-run shot, which was of the inside-the-park variety. "Larrupin' Lou" drove the ball over Douthit's head in straightaway center and promptly circled the bases for his third four-bagger of the Series.

The Cardinals came back to tie the game in their half of the fifth but the Yankees erupted for another three runs in the sixth. One of the runs resulted when Ruth, although obviously out at the plate, barreled into the catcher, Jimmie Wilson, and dislodged the ball from his grasp. The Yankees added their seventh and final run of the game in the top half of the seventh.

Lazzeri's injury woes continued to daunt him in this game as he suffered still another painful injury. The middle finger of his right hand was puffed and bruised as a result of his attempt to snare a hard-hit ball off the bat of Taylor Douthit in the second inning. Nevertheless, always the gamer, "Poosh 'Em Up" remained in the game until the eighth inning when Durocher was sent in to replace him.

The Yankees completed the sweep in Game Four, once again behind Hoyt, by the same score of the previous game, 7–3. Hoyt struggled somewhat here and there, giving up a total of 11 hits. He even trailed 2–1 as late as the top half of the seventh inning. Sherdel had given up a number of hits too but pitched himself out of several jams while surrendering a solo homer to the Babe.

A controversial call in the Yankees' half of the seventh opened the floodgates for the New Yorkers. Ruth's second home run came after Sherdel had thrown a third-strike quick pitch to the Yankee slugger. "You can't do that!" Ruth screamed.[25]

Huggins and many of the Yankees ran out of their dugout and surrounded Charlie Pfirman, a National League umpire, who was working behind the plate. Pfirman had his hands full as Wilson, Sherdel, Maranville and Frisch of the Cardinals soon joined the argument.

After conferring with the other umpires—Cy Rigler, Brick Owens and Bill McGowan—Pfirman declared: "Ruth isn't out. Sherdel will have to pitch over to him." "But it is legal," McKechnie and his players shouted at Pfirman. "It is legal in the National League and this is a National League game."[26]

Before the Series had begun, this type of quick-delivery pitch was indeed legal in the National League but not in the American. The umpires had conferred with Commissioner Kenesaw Mountain Landis to get a ruling before Game One. It was agreed that it would be prohibited but, for some reason, they forgot to tell the managers or the pitchers about it. Therein lay the rub, which resulted in a delay of over ten minutes before play was resumed.

Thereupon, Ruth was permitted to reenter the batter's box and, given another swing, he deposited his controversial home run into the right field stands. Obviously shaken by this wild turn of events, Sherdel was tagged for yet another home run, this time by Gehrig. This one turned out to be an even longer blast than the Bambino's. The homer was Gehrig's fourth of the Series and put the Yankees in front for good.

The New Yorkers added a pair of runs in the seventh and two more in the eighth, one via a solo home run by Cedric Durst, and another bases empty blast by Ruth. It marked the second time in three years that Ruth had hit three home runs in a World Series game. Ironically, each performance had come at Sportsman's Park.

Knowing that their heroes were out of the game at this point, Cardinal fans rose as one to cheer the grinning Bambino as he circled the bases. Later he would end the game and a sensational individual Series performance by making a spectacular one-hand running catch of a foul fly at the end of the left-field stands. Without breaking stride, the Babe, ever the showman, would run directly to the clubhouse while still holding the ball.

The offensive displays turned in by Ruth and Gehrig in particular were marvelous to behold. The Babe hit a thunderous .625, the highest in Series history, to go along with his three home runs. Meanwhile, Gehrig was no slouch himself with a .545 mark to accompany his four homers and nine runs batted in. It was the greatest two-man offensive display in Series history.

Together Ruth and Gehrig had ripped Cardinal pitchers for 16 hits in 27 at-bats, a combined .593 average. It seemed like the rest of the Yankee hitters were merely observers as they hit a collective anemic .196.

Cedric Durst ably filled in for Combs by batting .375 and was the only other Yankee to hit over .300. And the four complete games by the Yankee starters marked the first and only time that the feat had ever been accomplished up until then or since in a World Series.

Lazzeri had to be satisfied with a mere three hits in twelve trips to the plate for a .250 average. Of those three hits, only one was an extra-base hit—a double. But who gave up the double? Ironically, none other than his old nemesis, Grover Cleveland Alexander, who had been brought in as a reliever to face Lazzeri just as he had two years earlier. Tony also scored a couple of runs in the 1928 Series but was unable to drive in any.

Only one Cardinal regular—shortstop Rabbit Maranville—hit over .300 and just one other Redbird—Jim Bottomley—had more than one run batted in. Maranville hit .308 while Bottomley drove in three runs. Bottomley's home run was the only one St. Louis registered throughout the entire Series.

"Old Pete" Alexander, who mystified the Yankees in the 1926 World Series when he turned in a 1.33 earned run average in 20⅓ innings, fell off to a 19.80 ERA in the five innings he worked in 1928. Tommy Thevenow, the Cardinals' leading hitter in the 1926 Series, was now playing behind Maranville and made just one brief appearance in the 1928 set.

The train ride back to New York was a raucous one led by Babe Ruth, who ripped the shirts off all the players, club officials and newspapermen on board. He even had the temerity to strip Colonel Ruppert to the waist. Bewildered, the Colonel asked: "Is this usual, Ruth?"[27]

Wherever the train would stop on its way back to New York, people flocked to the platforms just to try and get a peek at the marvels of the baseball world. For the Yankees, the 1928 World Series made amends for their late-season decline during the regular season and gave proof positive that they were the greatest ball club in the major leagues once again.

Determined to leave his physical ailments behind him before the next season began, 25-year-old Tony Lazzeri checked into St. Vincent's Hospital in New York City shortly after the Series ended. Despite playing in all the games in intense pain, he never considered asking to be left out of the starting lineup. And Huggins never once thought about replacing him either.

As determined as he was prior to the start of the 1928 World Series, "Poosh 'Em Up" had his right shoulder operated on right after its conclusion. Preliminary reports from the doctors indicated that they were well satisfied with the results. However, Tony was not given permission to leave for his home on the West Coast until he made a succession of daily visits to the hospital for about a week's time.

6

Also-Rans (1929–1931)

Following the 1928 season many major league teams—particularly those in rival cities—believed that the Yankees had built themselves a fearsome dynasty. After winning three pennants in a row and sweeping two consecutive World Championships, a cry began to resound throughout the big leagues calling for the team's breakup.

Obviously, it fell on deaf ears in New York where the club's owner, Colonel Jacob Ruppert, insisted that he, General Manager Ed Barrow and Field Manager Miller Huggins would exert every effort to strengthen rather than to weaken their ball club. Barrow and Huggins, when asked to comment on the "Break Up the Yankees" theme cropping up among opposing teams, simply echoed their owner's statement.

The loudest complaint to be heard around the American League was that Babe Ruth and Lou Gehrig had to be split up. Since it was generally assumed that Colonel Ruppert would never sell the Bambino, the suggestion was made that he could easily garner at least $150,000—a "king's ransom" at the time—for Gehrig. Naturally Ruppert, Barrow and Huggins would hear nothing of it.

Ruppert, a former colonel in the National Guard's 7th Regiment, was an interesting portrait in his own right. He grew up a Giants fan and, after working in the family's brewery as a teenager, went on to serve in the United States Congress for four consecutive terms.

The Colonel had actually wanted to buy the Giants but his friend, John McGraw, told him that they were not for sale. "But I think the Yankees might be," McGraw told Ruppert.[1] So Ruppert and his partner at the time, Cap Huston, purchased the Yankees for $450,00 in 1915. Up until then, the franchise had been a loser for all twelve years of its existence and was only drawing an average of 345,000 fans a year to its games.

While he permitted Barrow and Huggins to handle the day-to-day operations of the team, Ruppert was the ultimate decision-maker. An innovator, he was the one who put the Yankee players into their famous pin-striped home uniforms, primarily in the hope that it would make the portly Babe Ruth look thinner.

"I found out a long time ago there is no charity in baseball," Ruppert was fond of saying. "Every club owner must make his own fight for existence. I went into baseball purely for the fun of it. I had no idea I would spend so much money ... the only return I even sought was to make ends meet."[2]

Changes were coming to be sure for 1929 and they started by dispatching the veteran Dugan and his cranky knee to the Boston Braves in a waiver deal following the previous season. Dugan had spent the better part of seven years as the club's regular third baseman and was considered among the best in the game at third base. However, the Babe's best friend was now 32 years old and he had only played in 24 games at the hot corner for the Yankees in 1928.

"Jumping Joe" had been relegated primarily to utility infielder and pinch-hitting chores for the better part of the past year. In short, he had been reduced to the status of a role player. And within two years he would be gone from the major leagues for good. However, Dugan's departure did weaken the left side of the infield and management knew that it had to take steps to solidify the position for the 1929 season.

Mike Gazella was farmed out to the Newark Bears, also never to return to the big leagues. Shortstop Lyn Lary, whom the Yankees had purchased a year earlier from the Oakland Oaks of the Pacific Coast League for delivery in 1929 along with Jimmy Reese, was to be brought into training camp. However, Reese, a second baseman, was ordered to remain with the Oaks for another year. Team management was convinced that Tony Lazzeri had recovered fully from his assorted injuries so there was no need to add Reese to the roster, at least for the time being.

Although it pained him to do it, Huggins had decided to replace Koenig at shortstop with Lary in 1929. The manager realized full well that he was breaking up the double play combination that had brought the team so much success from 1926 to 1928.

"For better or worse, I must do it," lamented Huggins. "They Lazzeri and Koenig were born in the same town in the same year only six months apart and they have been living happily together around second base for three years, but as much as it hurts me they must be separated for the good of the forces."[3]

Outfielder Sammy Byrd was recalled from Albany and southpaw Ed Wells, who had been in the big leagues earlier with the Tigers, was picked up from the Birmingham Barons of the Southern Association.

6. Also-Rans (1929–1931)

The biggest addition to the starting lineup was the rangy 22-year-old Arkansan Bill Dickey. He was the catcher that the Yankees had used sparingly late in 1928 but who they now were certain was fully prepared to be their number one receiver. They saw him as their prime backstop not only for the 1929 season but also for many years to come. And how right they were. For the next 13 years, Dickey would go on to establish a new American League record by catching in over 100 games every year, and actually making it look easy.

Also that year the Yankee uniforms got numbers on the back that corresponded for the most part to players' positions in the batting order. Consequently, Earle Combs wore number 1, Mark Koenig, number 2, Babe Ruth, number 3, Lou Gehrig, number 4, Bob Meusel, number 5, Tony Lazzeri, number 6, Leo Durocher, number 7, Johnny Grabowski, number 8, Benny Bengough, number 9 and Bill Dickey, number 10.

The club believed that the fans in the stands would have an easier time of recognizing the players if they could use the numbers for reference. Five years earlier, Branch Rickey had ordered small numbers to be placed on the sleeves of the Cardinals but hardly anyone paid any attention to them because they were almost impossible to see. Consequently, no other clubs followed suit. However, when the World Champion Yankees did it, it wasn't long before baseball fans universally accepted the practice and other teams began adopting it as well.

In the American League in 1929, Connie Mack, whose Athletics had not won a championship since 1914, had slowly built another contending team over the past several years. With the powerful Jimmie Foxx at first base, Max Bishop at second, Joe Boley at shortstop and Jimmy Dykes on third, Mr. Mack had put together a formidable infield with which to challenge the Yankees.

His outfield was not too shabby either with Al Simmons, Mule Haas and Bing Miller roaming the outer reaches. Mickey Cochrane, the future Hall of Famer who was perched behind the plate, had a trio of talented, proven starters throwing to him. They included the unrivaled Lefty Grove, the much-heralded second year right-hander, George Earnshaw, and a consistent annual double-digit winner, southpaw Rube Walberg. Overall Mr. Mack had assembled a young and aggressive ball club determined to overtake the Yankees at long last.

At the start of training camp in St. Petersburg on February 28, 1929, and for the first three days of workouts, Huggins and the rest of the Yankees were all smiles. Why? First of all, because Lazzeri's arm was again as accurate and as strong as it had always been. "Poosh 'Em Up" was firing bullets all over the infield. The throwing arm that was the talk of the base-

When spring training opened for the Yankees in 1929, Tony Lazzeri's arm, which had been injured through most of the previous season, regained its former strength. (National Baseball Hall of Fame Library, Cooperstown, N.Y.)

ball world when it cracked the previous August and probably should have been shut down in the World Series was back to its original prominence. All seemed to be right with the Yankee world.

Then all of a sudden, Tony was nowhere to be found. Leo Durocher had taken over Lazzeri's spot at second base working with Gehrig, Koenig and Gene Robertson, now apparently the team's new third baseman, during the morning and afternoon workouts.

Although Lazzeri wasn't talking as usual, the word was that he was now suffering from soreness near his elbow. Consequently, trainer Doc Woods felt it was best for him to confine his training activities to some calisthenics in the morning and afternoon hours while Durocher worked out with the regulars.

Woods and the Yankee brain trust were convinced that this new problem was far less serious than the previous year's muscle tear. They believed that it was likely to disappear entirely with a few days of rest and treatment.

Evidently the diagnosis was proper; five days later in an inter-squad game, Tony was up to his old tricks and seemingly devoid of any physical problems. While playing for the "Regulars," Tony speared a line drive off the bat of Ruth — who was playing first base for the "Yannigans"— in the third inning and threw out the Bambino with plenty to spare.

In the same game, Lazzeri also veered far off his position at second base to snare an infield fly that Ruth had lofted in the sixth. There appeared to be little doubt that Tony was in mid-season form much to the delight of Huggins and the rest of the ball club.

Lazzeri's value to the club could never be underestimated. William E. Brandt, writing in the March 1, 1929, edition of *The New York Times*, summed it up this way: "The Yanks need Lazzeri's big bat at home plate in line with Ruth's and Gehrig's and Meusel's in the middle of their great firing line. If Lazzeri's sore arm is a temporary condition, all is still well. If it is going to be an ever-recurring weakness, it will mean that one of Ruppert's deadliest rifles must be hung on the rack every so often and the run-making barrages periodically impeded."[4]

However, much of the 1929 regular season though turned out to be a roller coaster ride for the New York Yankees. The club started well, faltered for a time and then came on strong again for a while. What they could not do was shake the resolve of the A's. The team dropped back into third place at one point and moved up again into the second spot, but just could not overtake the Philadelphia ball club. The Yankees probably would have fallen further behind had it not been for Babe Ruth.

Ruth and Gehrig, although not as potent as they were in 1927 and 1928, were once again on their way to their usual big seasons. And Lazzeri was en route to what would turn out to be his best offensive year ever in the major leagues. Unfortunately, though, Meusel had begun to slow down both offensively and defensively. The club had not bargained on the 33-year-old leftfielder's wavering as quickly as he did and was sadly disappointed.

The left side of the infield was an even bigger problem due to its inconsistency. Robertson was not doing the job at third so Huggins was forced to shift Koenig into the position. Lary was installed at shortstop but he, too, was unable to deliver. Huggins eventually pulled Lary and replaced him with Durocher, who was all right with the glove but a pronounced liability with the bat.

Finally, the manager was forced to return Koenig to his original shortstop position and try Lary at third. That experiment didn't produce the desired results either. The move had fellow San Franciscans Koenig and Lazzeri, the longtime Yankee keystone combination, reunited for the remainder of the season in an attempt to win a fourth straight American League pennant.

Pitching-wise, the Yankees of 1929 had their troubles as well. Herb Pennock was still having arm problems. Waite Hoyt was afflicted with an assortment of illnesses, which would contribute to a so-so year. And George Pipgras was a far cry from the pitcher he had been in 1927. The only member of the staff pitching with any degree of consistency was the veteran Tom Zachary. Overall, though, the staff was sub-par all year long.

A major bright spot on the club was the expected development of catcher Bill Dickey. The kid from Little Rock was absolutely terrific throughout the year. He was a blessing since Benny Bengough and his constant nagging arm injuries made it almost impossible for him to reach second base anymore. In fact, he wasn't even able to catch a game at all until late June.

The Yankees suddenly sprang to life in July, winning seven games in a row at one point. Ruth hit his historic five-hundredth home run on the eleventh of the month against Willis Hudlin of the Indians. It appeared that the Yankees might be on their way once again to claim what they believed to be rightfully theirs—the American League flag and another World Series appearance. The euphoria was short-lived, however, as the surprising Browns, of all teams, proceeded to shut them out in St. Louis in three consecutive games on August 23, 24 and 25.

When they returned to the Bronx, Huggins held a closed-door meeting with his club and read them the riot act. The players seemed to tune out their manager's words and he knew it simply by looking at each of their faces.

Ruppert and Barrow were anxious to find out what was troubling their team.

"What's the matter with the boys, Hug?" the Colonel asked.

"They're through, Colonel," Hug said.

"But we still have a month—"

"Forget about it," Hug said. "Start getting ready for next year. These fellows are through."

"But how do you know?" Ruppert wanted to know.

"I just finished talking to them," Hug said. "I talked to them for twenty minutes. I talked to them calmly. I pleaded with them. Then I abused them. No matter what I said, or how I said it, it didn't make the slightest difference. I couldn't make them mad. I couldn't even make them laugh. When I realized that I might just as well have been talking to that wall over there, I quit."

"But why?" Ruppert asked, "Why should they be through?"

"I guess they're just tired, Colonel," Hug said. He got up and walked to the door.

"I'm tired myself," he said. "I'm tired out — and I can't sleep."[5]

Huggins was not only tired but also seriously ill. He had suffered from neuritis for years and now the plight of his team only added to his physical miseries. His condition worsened as the team's fortunes waned. It got so bad at times that his right leg would shake in nervous spasms. He had trouble sleeping and he started to lose his appetite, both of which lowered his resistance considerably.

On September 20, Coach Art Fletcher noticed that Huggins had developed a sore under one of his eyes. Fletcher suggested that the skipper seek treatment for it. "Go to the doctor because I have a red spot on my face?" Hug declared. "Me, who took the spikes of Frank Chase and Fred Clarke."[6]

He did turn the club over to Fletcher that day, admitting that he was not feeling well and that he would depart for home. That was the last time his players and coaches would ever see him alive. Five days later, 50-year-old Miller Huggins succumbed from what was diagnosed as a form of blood poisoning. The news stunned the ball club. Although the players had known for a long time that their manager was not well, they had no idea how seriously ill he had really been.

As crusty as many of them were on that team, they still wept openly in the clubhouse when told that their little manager had passed away. That group included some like Babe Ruth who had battled openly with Huggins over the years. The manager's body was taken to Woodlawn Cemetery in Cincinnati where Ruth, Lou Gehrig, Tony Lazzeri, Earle Combs and Herb Pennock acted as pallbearers along with Hug's three coaches, Art Fletcher, Bob Shawkey and Charley O'Leary.

Lazzeri was devastated by Huggins' death to the point where he did not play another game in 1929, going directly from Cincinnati to his home in San Francisco. The rest of the Yankees had no heart for what was left of the season either. The year had not gone that well anyway and under the circumstances the team felt there was no point to it.

The Athletics ultimately won the pennant by 18 games. George Earnshaw won 24 games and Lefty Grove contributed his usual 20. Al Simmons belted 34 homers and led the AL in RBI with 157. Jimmie Foxx was only one behind Simmons at 33 dingers and the first sacker drove in 117 runs as well. The A's defeated the Cubs easily in the World Series in five games, finally winning their first world championship after a 15-year drought.

Suffice it to say, the Yankees had fallen well off their pace of 1928, when they had been victorious with a 101–53 record. In 1929, they won only 88 games despite the fact that some players like Tony Lazzeri had sensational years.

"Poosh 'Em Up" had 193 hits and batted .354 in 147 games. He also hammered out 18 homers and drove in 101 runs. It was simply a great year for Tony Lazzeri after suffering through an injury-prone 1928 season.

Babe Ruth was still the league's home run king with 46 along with a solid .345 batting average. Lou Gehrig, though mired in a series of slumps, still managed to hit .300 and deliver 35 homers. Bob Meusel, on the other hand, fell off to a career-low .261 mark. On the other side of the coin, Bill Dickey hit a resounding .324 in his first full year of action in the big leagues along with 10 home runs.

George Pipgras won 18 but lost 12 and posted an elevated 4.23 ERA. The closest to Pipgras in wins was newcomer Ed Wells, who delivered 13 victories. Meanwhile Waite Hoyt struggled through a 10–9 season and a lofty 4.24 ERA. Hank Johnson, who turned in a fine 14–9 mark in 1928, was wracked with back pain all season long, and fell off to a mediocre 3–3 record while appearing in only 12 games.

It was evident that the Yankees would have to undergo some serious overhauling for the 1930 campaign, beginning with the appointment of a new manager. The quest to find a new pilot would turn out to be a lot more difficult than management had originally believed. The club's first choice was Donie Bush, who had managed the Pirates in the World Series against Murderers' Row in 1927. Bush's club had dropped to fourth in 1928 but bounced back to a second place finish in the 1929 National League pennant race. Both Colonel Ruppert and Ed Barrow liked Bush and coveted him openly.

Bush had disagreed with his owner, Barney Dreyfuss, once too often and was released immediately following the 1929 season. The White Sox snapped him up days later and he was signed on the very same day that Barrow called to offer him the Yankee job.

Disappointed, Barrow then went after Eddie Collins, who had man-

Joe Sewell (right) who replaced "Jumping Joe" Dugan at third base for the Yankees in 1931, joined the team's infield regulars (left to right) Lou Gehrig, Tony Lazzeri and Mark Koenig. (National Baseball Hall of Fame Library, Cooperstown, N.Y.)

aged the White Sox in 1925 and 1926. Collins piloted Chicago to two straight fifth-place finishes before rejoining Connie Mack in Philadelphia as a player in 1927. After talking it over with Mr. Mack, Collins turned down the Yankee job. He shared Mack's opinion that he wasn't ready to accept the challenges and attendant pressures of managing in New York.

Next Barrow turned to long-time Yankee third base coach Art Fletcher, who had been Miller Huggins' most trusted lieutenant and a great favorite of the players. Fletcher had some previous managing experience in the National League when he led the Phillies from 1923 through 1926. With little or no material to work with in Philadelphia, he finished seventh twice and last in the other two years before joining the Yankees for the 1927 Murderers' Row season.

Fletcher told Barrow that his time in Philadelphia had soured him on ever managing again. Although he greatly appreciated the offer, his preference was to stay on as a coach for the Yankees and that is precisely what he did in 1930 and for many more years thereafter.

Colonel Ruppert was now beside himself with worry, but that fear was soon dissipated when Barrow hired former Yankee pitcher Bob

Shawkey. Now 37 years of age, Shawkey had spent over 14 years with the Yankees as a player. A World War I Navy veteran sometimes called "Sailor Bob" and "Bob the Gob," the Brookville, Pennsylvania, native spent most of 1918 as a yeoman petty officer on the battleship *Atlantic*.

Shawkey had come to the Yankees on waivers from the Athletics in 1916 and had been with them continuously ever since, excepting his time out for military service. He was a fine pitcher for them over the years but by 1929 he had begun to slow down considerably.

Yankee management was convinced that the unassuming Shawkey knew the players as well as or better than anyone else. Although considered somewhat colorless, he was extremely likable and a keen student of the game. Yet following a legend like Miller Huggins would have been a difficult task for anyone, let alone an untested presence like Shawkey.

The new manager's other major potential problem was that he had been a teammate of nearly all of the players that he was now to command. Barrow and Ruppert had no doubt that Shawkey had what it took to overcome both obstacles.

Just before bringing Shawkey on board as manager, the club sold Bob Meusel to the Reds. Although Meusel respected for his on-field accomplishments, the writers, fans and even many of his teammates had never really warmed up to him during his 10 seasons with the ball club. Forming the most feared quartet of batters in baseball along with Ruth, Gehrig and Lazzeri, he never came close to receiving the acclaim that the other three received regularly from the media and the fans.

Despite having, arguably, the strongest throwing arm in the major leagues and being as good a base runner as there was in the game, Meusel gave the appearance of being cold and indifferent. He was viewed by many as a player who did not care much whether he was cheered or booed. Writers following the team found him to be withdrawn and sometimes even antagonistic.

Meusel was even accused of being lazy on occasion. His teammates found him to be indifferent as well. The only players that he spent any time with was his roommate, Herb Pennock, as well as Joe Dugan and Waite Hoyt.

Huggins, whom Meusel grew to like after a while, had always defended his left fielder to the media, claiming that they never gave him the credit he deserved for his contributions to the success of the Yankees. The record would bear out those contributions. He batted over .300 seven times and in the two years that he missed that mark, he still managed to hit an above average .297 and .292. But at 31 years of age, the Yankees felt he simply was no longer the player that he had been.

6. Also-Rans (1929–1931)

Huggins always had praised Meusel's character, although he admitted that he lacked the warmth the writers would have preferred him to have. Consequently, the press and the fans by and large did not mourn his departure.

Another loss was in the person of the slick fielding but light hitting Leo Durocher. Convinced that he would never hit big league pitching well enough to suit them, the Yankees also peddled him to Cincinnati for the waiver price just before spring training began.

When training camp opened in St. Petersburg on March 1 that season, Tony Lazzeri was still on his way in. "Poosh 'Em Up" was the last to report after a five-day train trip across the country. He quickly donned his uniform and began to work out with his long-time double-play mate, Mark Koenig. Jimmy Reese, finally with the Yankees following his purchase from Oakland two years earlier, spelled Lazzeri while Lyn Lary took over for Koenig at short during the workouts.

One of the brightest spots in the Yankee training camp in 1930 was a rookie left-hander whom the club had purchased from the San Francisco Seals named Vernon "Lefty" Gomez. Constantly smiling and with a twinkle in his eye, he became an instant favorite of the players and writers alike. The Rodeo, California, native had a smoking fastball punctuated by a high leg kick.

The Yankees could not get over the speed with which Gomez delivered the baseball, since he only weighed in at 146 pounds when he reported. However, after a couple of years on major league meal money and the natural maturation of his body, he tipped the scales at 178 pounds for most of his major league career. Gomez needed more seasoning in 1930 and he got it by spending most of the year with the St. Paul farm club. With only two years of professional baseball behind him, he may have been short on experience but not on talent.

Right after the season began, it became evident that Shawkey's control over the team was eroding dramatically. The older players with whom he had played for so many years laughed at him while the younger ones did just about whatever they pleased. The lack of discipline on the ball club was far removed from the years that Miller Huggins had been in charge of the Yankees.

Shawkey made a deal on May 6 that would benefit the Yankees for years to come–a trade with the cash-poor Red Sox (them again?) in which Cedric Durst was swapped for pitcher Charlie "Red" Ruffing. Despite a league-leading 28 losses in 1928 and 22 more in 1929, the right-hander had a blazing fastball but a minor flaw in his delivery. Shawkey was convinced that Ruffing's problem could be fixed. The situation was addressed in camp and Ruffing would go from a 39–96 record in six years with Boston to a fine 15–5 record in his first year with the Yankees.

The next trade for which Shawkey was responsible had more to do with the questioning of his authority than his skill in picking talent. Following a dispute with Waite Hoyt on how to pitch to certain hitters, Shawkey had the veteran hurler traded to the Tigers along with Mark Koenig on May 30.

Two weeks earlier, Al Simmons had hit a long home run off Hoyt in Philadelphia. When Shawkey asked Hoyt about the pitch he had thrown to Simmons, the pitcher told him it was a fastball. Shawkey told Hoyt to never do it again and that he should make hitters like Simmons try to hit his curve ball. Hoyt exploded and told his manager that he would pitch to hitters the way he wanted. When Shawkey told Hoyt that he would have to pitch the way he was told, the "Brooklyn Schoolboy" knew he was gone.

The trade turned into a self-fulfilling prophesy for Hoyt, who had once said that Yankee pitchers should never hold out or quarrel with their manager, else they would have to come back and face their lethal lineup. Truer words were never spoken. The first time Hoyt pitched against the Yankees, he was driven from the mound in the second inning.

After his career ended, Hoyt became one of the first ex-players to go into broadcasting. Starting in 1939, he did both pre- and post-game commentary for the Dodgers in Brooklyn for a couple of years before moving on to Cincinnati. The former pitcher then became the play-by-play broadcaster for the Reds for 25 years before retiring. No less a legend than Hall of Fame broadcaster Red Barber said that Waite Hoyt was the best of all the former athletes who went behind the microphone, because of his intelligence, industriousness and storytelling ability.

In return for Hoyt, who made it to the Hall of Fame as a player in 1969, the Yankees obtained a pitcher, Owen Carroll, an outfielder, Harry Rice, and an infielder, Harry Wuestling. All were used sparingly during the season and contributed little to solving any of the club's pressing problems.

Not that he needed any encouragement to "paint the town," but Babe Ruth after one particular evening out in New York asked the trainer if he had anything for his bloodshot eyes. The trainer gave him some eyewash that the Bambino proceeded to apply to his eyes. Then he went out and got himself three hits.

For the next six days, Ruth used the eyewash whether he needed it or not and got at least one hit every day. Tony Lazzeri, who had been watching the scenario unfold, bought a bottle of eye wash, emptied it, rinsed it and filled it with water. Then in front of Ruth, he drank the contents.

6. Also-Rans (1929–1931)

Ruth thought Lazzeri had lost it. "Look at the dumb guy," he announced to the entire locker room. "He drinks the eye wash."[7] In that afternoon's game, Lazzeri delivered three base hits. Ruth was dumbfounded.

The very next day the Babe got a bottle of eye wash from the trainer and drank every drop, remarking to Lazzeri, "Sure tastes terrible, doesn't it, Tony?" Ruth's hitting streak continued and he repeated the procedure every day until it ended.[8]

Ruth had always been fond of Lazzeri whom he affectionately called "Dago" and "Wop." To demonstrate their liking for each other, the pair took delight in destroying each other's equipment, which cost both of them a great deal of money. The Yankees' clubhouse man, Fred Logan, sold the players their inner hose, kangaroo-leather baseball shoes and undershirts, all at prices well beyond their original cost.

Ruth would take trainer Doc Painter's scissors and cut the feet out of Lazzeri's inner hose, and the next day the Babe would find his shoes nailed to the floor and the arms cut out of his sweatshirt.

Though the season did not go as well for the Yankees as they would have liked, "Poosh 'Em Up" never lost his dry sense of humor. Late in the year in a game against the Indians, his second base counterpart, Johnny Hodapp, slid into second after hitting one of his patented doubles. Hodapp led the American League that year with 51 two-base hits.

"I remember Tony Lazzeri looking at me after I slid into second base," Hodapp later remembered, "'I hope to God you rot here!' he said. 'I'm tired of seeing you down here.'"[9]

Both Ruth and Gehrig had excellent offensive years in 1930. In fact, the team as whole averaged .309, the highest batting average in its history. The Babe batted .359, smacked 49 homers to lead the American League, and drove in 151 runs. Gehrig hit a career-high .379 while slamming 41 homers and driving in a league-leading 174 runs. Lazzeri had his usual steady season with a .303 batting average, nine home runs, and 121 RBI. As usual, he was rock-solid at second base.

However, pitching was the real Achilles heel for the Yankees throughout the year. It was not at all consistent and no amount of hitting could make up the difference. Waite Hoyt was no longer there, Herb Pennock was vanishing rapidly and George Pipgras was no better than a .500 pitcher at 15–15. Only Red Ruffing at 15–8 pitched with any authority for the Yankees in 1930.

Also, the left side of the infield continued to be as shaky as it had been in 1929 and the issue was never completely resolved. Wuestling was not an adequate replacement for the departed Koenig and using rookie Ben

Chapman, an outfielder by trade, at third base proved to be disastrous as well. All in all, Shawkey, with his assortment of woes, did well to have his club finish in third place behind the Senators.

The Athletics, to the surprise of no one, repeated as American League pennant winners and Jimmie Foxx edged out his teammate, Al Simmons, for the home run crown — 36 to 35 — while driving in 156 runs. Simmons led the league in batting with a .381 mark along with a runs-batted-in total of 165. Mr. Mack's club became World Champions for the second year in a row as they dispatched the Cardinals in six games.

Both Ruppert and Barrow knew that Shawkey, whom they had only signed for one year, was not the man they needed for the job. After years of stability and success under Miller Huggins, the Yankees found themselves looking for a new manager for the second consecutive year.

It was not a pleasant departure for "Sailor Bob." The day after the season ended, he went up to the club's offices to discuss some business. When he saw Joe McCarthy walking out the door as he entered, Shawkey was convinced that the end was near.

The man whom the Yankees had wanted for some time was the recently released McCarthy, a man who had never played a day in the major leagues. "Marse Joe," as he was called for his authoritarian method of operating, had led the Cubs to five consecutive first division finishes beginning in 1926 that included winning the 1927 National League flag.

Rogers Hornsby replaced the 44-year-old McCarthy, who had been dismissed by the Cubs with just four games to play in the 1930 season. Chicago had been involved in a season-long dogfight with the Cardinals, who ultimately won the pennant by a mere two games. However, St. Louis went on to lose the world championship to Connie Mack's A's in six games.

Joe blamed Hornsby and former baseball writer and then-president of the Cubs William C. Veeck for his firing. He was extremely bitter over the episode and didn't let go of it for quite a while. It turned out to be the best thing that ever happened to him.

McCarthy had been instrumental in the early development of Yankee centerfielder Earle Combs, whom he had managed years earlier at Louisville. Barrow knew that. He had also observed McCarthy as a player when Barrow was president of the International League when Joe played for Buffalo. In fact, the Yankee general manager had even tried without success to land him as a player for New York at one time.

Barrow watched Joe's managerial career progress with interest and liked what he saw. He was convinced that McCarthy was ready to accept "the best job in baseball," as Art Fletcher had described it.[10] Barrow called Ruppert and got his approval to hire McCarthy during the 1930 World Series.

"I never played in the big leagues. Not one game," Joe McCarthy once said. "Wasn't good enough, I guess. But I think I spent more time trying to get up there than anybody I know of. I was twenty years in the minor leagues as a player and manager before I made it."[11]

McCarthy became the standard against which all future Yankee managers would be judged over time. He was indeed shrewd and serious but far from humorless. He confounded his players with his vast knowledge of the game, his remarkable memory and his attention to detail. "He never made notes," one of his players said years later. "He didn't have to. He never forgot anything."[12]

"Marse Joe" never roamed the dugout. "I was in there in the middle, the command post," he would say later.[13] Arguing with the umpires was also something he abhorred. "I wanted to be around to manage," he declared. "I'm no good to the team if I'm not there."[14]

Needing a third baseman desperately after the failed Ben Chapman experiment of the previous season, the Yankees acquired veteran infielder Joe Sewell from the Indians. Cleveland had converted Sewell, originally the team's shortstop for eight years, into a third baseman in 1929. Known for his durability and a good bat, he fit in well with his new ball club. Now only Tony Lazzeri, Babe Ruth, Lou Gehrig, Earle Combs, George Pipgras and Herb Pennock remained from 1927's fabled Murderers' Row team.

Originally McCarthy had installed Tony Lazzeri at third base early into the training season. "Marse Joe," new to the American League, did not know that much about some of his players' abilities and had to be shown their individual strengths. He had both Jimmy Reese and Ben Chapman around as backups to Lazzeri but when Sewell was given the chance to show his wares, the future Hall of Famer responded. Consequently, the job at the hot corner was his for the 1931 season and Lazzeri was returned to his normal spot at second base.

The manager wanted to have both Lazzeri and Sewell in his everyday lineup. "I want Tony in the game," McCarthy said. "A man who can drive in as many runs as the records show he drove home last year is too powerful an asset to keep out of the lineup."[15]

The no-nonsense McCarthy was not that popular with many of his players, mostly because they believed they could never satisfy him. He was also surrounded by a group who liked to have fun on a regular basis. This was a bunch of tough, rollicking players, some of whom were fully capable of breaking training rules at any given moment.

One of McCarthy's first acts that did not exactly endear him to the team was to order the clubhouse man, Fred Logan, to take an ax to the team's card table. "This is a clubhouse, not a clubroom," McCarthy

"Poosh 'Em Up" crosses home plate and is greeted by Bill Dickey after hitting his second home run of the fourth game of the 1932 sweep of the Cubs. (*Baseball Magazine*)

thundered. "Do your card playing in your homes. When you come in here, I want you to have your minds on baseball."[16]

He also insisted that his players wear jackets and ties whenever they were on the road. There were no hot dogs, peanuts or snacks of any kind permitted to be consumed on the Yankee bench. To McCarthy — and he hoped to convey his philosophy to the team — the Yankee tradition of pride and winning was something that should be passed on from player to player and team to team.

McCarthy the manager allowed himself no other diversion besides what he was paid to do. He had no hobbies or other distractions that would get in the way of the task at hand. His only focus was on the game of baseball and how his team would play it.

Lazzeri was one of those players who was not enamored of the new manager and his seemingly unending rules and regulations. "Poosh 'Em Up" especially did not appreciate it when he saw McCarthy verbally rip a teammate to shreds one afternoon just before a game. However, when Lazzeri saw that "Marse Joe" was tearing into the player because he was cheating both himself and the team by not putting out, he won Tony over.

The incident took place when the Yankees were in Washington.

McCarthy was alone in the clubhouse while the team was taking batting practice. The player in question whom the manager had never confronted before arrived in his street clothes an hour late.

"Who do you think you are?" McCarthy screamed. "And what do you think I am? A dope? What do you mean by coming in here at this time, when you should be dressed and on the field?"[17] "Marse Joe" kept on berating the player when Lazzeri walked in to get a new bat that he had put in his locker. The manager had never attacked one of his players verbally up to then.

Lazzeri, who admired McCarthy as a manager, wasn't sure whether he liked him as a person. He was certain that he despised him now. He was determined to tell off his manager after the player left the locker room. "That was a fine thing to do," Tony said coldly. "You ought to be —"

"I'm glad you were here, Tony." McCarthy said. "I'm glad you heard what I had to say to him. Now I want you to understand why I said it. I know that boy doesn't like me. I'm not interested in whether he does or not. But I am interested in him as a ball player. He could be one of the best ball players in this league, but he isn't because of his attitude. He thinks he's been getting away with something around here, just to spite me. But he hasn't. I took this opportunity to tell him so because I hope that by scaring him — as I think I did — I can wake him up. I didn't like to do it that way. But I had made up my mind it was the only way. I wasn't in here by accident when he came in an hour late. I was waiting for him. Do you understand now what it was all about?"

Tony nodded. "I do, Joe," he said. "I've known all along how he felt about you — and how some of the others feel. I didn't know just how I felt about you myself. But I do now. I want you to know that from now on, I'm on your side."[18]

It wasn't long before other players followed Tony's lead and accepted McCarthy with open arms. From the time Lazzeri joined the Yankees six years earlier, he was always well respected by his teammates for his judgment. Once they knew that he backed the manager, most of them, especially the ones who were indifferent in their enthusiasm for "Marse Joe," followed suit.

The lone exception was Babe Ruth, who was out to get McCarthy's job from the day he was hired. Ruth truly believed that he had earned it and should have been given the job over anyone else. He also resented the fact that McCarthy was a National Leaguer and, worse still, had never played a day in the major leagues. Ruth was truly obsessed with the notion that he should have been made the manager of the Yankees over anyone that the Yankees might have been considering.

McCarthy was fully aware of the situation and let it ride as long as the Babe produced, and that he did. Ruth was also smart enough to know that he should never try to rattle the cages of Yankee management or question the manager's authority. And regardless of how he felt personally, he continued to give it his all on the field.

McCarthy was no fool either. He gave in to the two sets of rules that he had inherited — one set for Ruth and the other set for everyone else. He let the Babe have his lifestyle just as long as it did not interfere with his performance between the white lines.

Ruppert and Barrow were behind their new manager all the way and they gave him their complete support to run the club the way he wanted. They believed that Ruth could no more manage the Yankees than he could his own life.

Just after training camp broke in 1931, the Yankees were involved in a historic exhibition game played in Chattanooga, Tennessee, on April 2. The club was booked to play against the Lookouts of the Southern Association, whose owner, Joe Engel, had gained nationwide attention a week earlier by announcing the signing of a 17-year-old girl named Jackie Mitchell to pitch for his team. Mitchell, a lefty, was the first woman ever to be signed to a professional baseball contract.

On the day of the game, more than 3,000 fans were in the stands. Although Clyde Barfoot, who had pitched for the Cardinals briefly at one time, started the game, Mitchell warmed up on the sidelines.

Earle Combs led off for the Yankees and doubled. Lyn Lary promptly singled Combs home. It was then that a signal was given to have Mitchell enter the game to pitch to none other than Babe Ruth.

Here's how Jack Orr described the scene in his article, "The Girl Who Struck Out Babe Ruth," in the June 1954 issue of *Sport* magazine:

> The Babe diplomatically tipped his cap. Jackie, disdaining his awesome figure, wound up as if she were cranking the handle of a coffee-grinder and pitched. Lary could have stolen several bases and Ruth could have knocked the ball into the outlying yards. But Lary stayed where he was and the Babe, taking careful aim, swung and missed by a foot. The next two pitches were wide and Ruth pretended her speed was making the ball take off. He made the umpire throw in a new ball. He swung again and missed. On the next pitch he let the ball go by and shook his head as he walked back to the bench.
> Gehrig came next and took three mighty swings and sat down. Lazzeri swung at one, fouled another and eventually walked. At this point, with Ben Chapman up, Jackie was taken out. There was some serious editorial comment the next day. *The New York Times* asked, "Whither baseball?" But from other quarters there were hints of skepticism. "Maybe her curves were too much for them," said one paper.

6. Also-Rans (1929–1931)

Jackie, of course, never did pitch for Chattanooga or for any other pro club. In fact, she wasn't heard from again. Rud Rennie, reporting in the *New York Herald-Tribune* probably had the right answer. He wrote: "After striking out Ruth and Gehrig and issuing a pass to Lazzeri, Virnie Beatrice (Jackie) Mitchell, organized baseball's only woman player, was taken out and sent back to the kitchen for further seasoning."[19]

The season itself wasn't as successful as all involved would have wanted it to be. The still-powerful Athletics finished a distant thirteen and a half games ahead of the second place Yankees to chalk up their third straight American League pennant. Al Simmons led the league in hitting once again with a resounding .390 mark while belting out 22 homers and driving in 128 runs. His partner, Jimmie Foxx, hit 30 homers and drove in 130 runs.

"Double-X" as he was most often called, Foxx debuted in the majors in 1925 at the age of 17, going 6-for-9 as a pinch-hitter and a catcher. A protégé of Frank "Home Run" Baker for whom he played in the minor leagues, his powerful physique and far away home run blasts also earned him the additional nickname of "Beast."

Lefty Grove posted an astounding 31–4 record for the A's that season while both George Earnshaw and Rube Walberg won 21 and 20 games respectively. However, the Cardinals, now managed by Gabby Street, got revenge for their 1930 World Series loss to the A's by defeating them in an exciting seven-game set.

Lou Gehrig had a career year with the Yankees in runs batted in with 184 to set an American League record. Gehrig also tied Ruth for the league lead in home runs with 46. It was the only time in their careers as teammates that Gehrig was able to match Ruth's home run total.

The Babe was no slouch either as he batted .373 and drove in 163 runs himself. Gehrig hit .341 but Lazzeri had an off year, finishing with only eight homers, 83 RBI and a .267 batting average. Meanwhile, second-year man Ben Chapman drove in 127 runs and Lyn Lary added another 107.

Despite having what for him was an off year, Lazzeri was always doing things from time to time to illustrate how good a player he could be. Once when Lefty Gomez was wrapped up in a tie game with the Tigers, Lazzeri stole second and then home in the twelfth inning to earn the southpaw a complete game 2–1 victory.

Gomez, who had come into his own in his second year in the majors, had an excellent year by posting a 21–9 record along with a 2.63 earned run average. McCarthy contributed to Gomez's success by converting the southpaw from a sidearm thrower to an overhand pitcher.

However, the rest of the staff had mediocre seasons. Red Ruffing was up and down and finished up with a 16–14 record and a rather lofty 4.41 ERA. And the veterans Herb Pennock and George Pipgras fell off to what for them were unproductive marks of 11–6 and 7–6 respectively.

Nonetheless, Barrow and Ruppert were satisfied and so were the fans. The Yankees improved by winning seven more games than they had the year before. They also moved up a notch in the standings. The lone dissenter was Joe McCarthy, who had wanted to win a pennant in his first year in New York. To him the season was a complete failure and he vowed not to let it happen again in 1932.

7

Back on Top Again (1932)

When the Yankees opened their training camp in St. Petersburg on March 1, 1932, Tony Lazzeri had not yet signed a new contract. The 28-year-old was now a six-year veteran but was coming off a so-so year. However, he was in his prime and felt that he was entitled to a substantial raise. Whether he got one remains to this day a deep, dark secret.

Suffice it to say, Manager Joe McCarthy reported that Lazzeri was indeed signed on the first day of training camp. William E. Brandt of *The New York Times* simply reported that "details of Tony's truce with the club on the question of his contract were not disclosed, but it is understood that both sides made concessions before an agreement was finally reached."[1]

Brandt described "Poosh 'Em Up" as the "star second baseman of the 1927 and 1928 world's champion Yankees and last of the thirty-two players in this year's spring training squad to report for duty … joined his teammates for his first practice (on March 3) at Huggins Field.

"Lazzeri brought with him a thick veneer of sunburn which enabled his face to harmonize with the color scheme of his brothers-at-arms," Brandt went on to write. "He did considerable preliminary baseball training at his home in San Francisco. He was excused from the infield workout, which was the finishing touch to today's practice session.

"While the first squad was at bat Lazzeri and Crosetti teamed as a second-base combination in fielding grounders. Both live in San Francisco."[2]

McCarthy apparently had no set lineup in mind at the opening of training camp. Since he felt that Lazerri had shown signs of wear and tear toward the end of the previous season, he decided to give Jack Saltzgaver a shot at second base. Saltzgaver was a 27-year-old rookie up from the Yankees' Newark farm club, who had spent a number of years in the minors before finally being called up to the big leagues.

McCarthy also inserted 26-year-old Lyn Lary at shortstop while another rookie, 21-year-old Frank Crosetti, was installed at third base in place of the veteran Joe Sewell. The 33-year-old Sewell was beginning his thirteenth year in the big leagues, all but one of those seasons as a starting third baseman. A future Hall of Famer, he had always been known for his consistency with the bat and his durability. Only in 1931 had he failed to hit under .299.

Crosetti had been purchased from the Pacific Coast League's Seals following the 1931 campaign. Once the season got underway, it was evident that Saltzgaver was not going to be able to hit big league pitching so he quickly gave way to Crosetti, a natural shortstop. "Crow," as Crosetti was called, coincidentally, was not performing all that well at third base either. Thereupon, Sewell was returned to his natural position at third, and Lazzeri went back to second. With the streaking Lou Gehrig solid at first base, the infield was once again intact.

Sewell was truly remarkable with the bat. He almost never struck out. He was to make 503 appearances at bat in 1932 and, remarkably, struck out only three times. In fact, in 7,132 times at bat during his 14-year major league career, he fanned only 114 times. Years later when an interviewer asked him what his secret was, Sewell responded simply: "You have to keep your eye on the ball."[3]

Entering his fourth full season in the big leagues, 24-year-old Bill Dickey, a catcher who had few peers, was again the man behind the plate while Babe Ruth, Earle Combs and Ben Chapman comprised an impressive outfield. The decision to move the 23-year-old Chapman from the infield to the outfield permanently the year before was dictated by his "scatter" arm. Whenever he played the infield, on plays that required shorter throws, his naturally strong arm often contributed to a failure in accuracy. McCarthy believed the longer throws from the outfield would be much more suited for Chapman. In addition, he thought Chapman's blinding speed would allow him to run balls down that many other outfielders just could not reach. The manager was proven right on both counts.

The Nashville, Tennesseean's base stealing prowess was another plus for the sometimes-volatile Chapman. Although some referred to him as a second Ty Cobb in this regard, he never really was. He was undoubtedly swift but on occasion he would run when there was no reason to do so, which angered McCarthy to no end.

But Chapman was immensely popular with Yankee fans that had never seen much base stealing before. The club's home run power was what they had lived by since Ruth, Gehrig and Lazzeri arrived, so there was never the necessity to steal bases. Nevertheless, followers of the team reveled in Chapman's success with it.

7. Back on Top Again (1932)

The irrepressible Lefty Gomez, the hard-throwing Red Ruffing, the veteran George Pipgras and a newcomer up from Jersey City, 26-year-old Johnny Allen, anchored the pitching staff. McCarthy would juggle the rotation at times during the 1932 season and it seemed to work more often than not.

Ruffing, who was always in tip-top condition because of his insistence on running and running some more in spring training, was one of the best fielding and hitting pitchers ever. As a batter he hit over .300 eight times in his 22-year Hall of Fame career, which included 521 hits, 98 doubles, 13 triples and 36 home runs. In 1932, he was to bat .291 and smack five home runs.

McCarthy often used Ruffing as a pinch-hitter. In his career, he was called off the bench over 200 times to pinch-hit. He was inducted into the Hall of Fame in 1967. Bill Dickey said of Ruffing: "If I were asked to choose the best pitcher I've ever caught, I would have to say Ruffing."[4] As a pitcher, although he would never boast of it, he gave up Ted Williams' first major league base hit—a double.

Other contributors included a late season acquisition from who else but the Red Sox, 25-year-old right-hander Danny MacFayden, southpaw Herb Pennock, who was now 36 years of age, and 35-year-old right-hander, Wilcy Moore, who had been reacquired from Boston.

The 23-year-old Gomez, who was known for his fun-loving antics, could be counted on for a wild comment or two on occasion. Once when Dickey came out to the mound to advise him about how he should pitch to Jimmie Foxx, "Goofy," as Gomez was aptly called from time to time, confessed: "I'd rather not throw the ball at all."[5] He also once boasted that he had a new invention. "It's a revolving bowl for tired goldfish," Gomez deadpanned.[6]

As good a hitter as the 27-year-old Ruffing was, Gomez was plainly atrocious. The right-hander had lost four toes off his left foot in a mine accident as a youngster. The mishap cut down on his speed and the pain never left him.

Although Ruffing could be cold on the field, he was just a regular guy and a good teammate off of it. Together he and Gomez would prove to be the mainstays of the Yankee pitching staff throughout the 1930s, with each of them winning 20 or more games in four different seasons.

Despite the coolness that existed between McCarthy and Ruth, the Babe never let it affect his play on the field. Ruth continued to be convinced that he should have been named manager and a few of the players on the team agreed with him. Where he could though, McCarthy disposed of those players quietly and efficiently, especially if they were not helping his ball club. He knew which players he could drive and those he couldn't, particularly the ones who regularly sided with the Bambino. No one could accuse the manager of making a personnel move that would hurt his team.

McCarthy chose to give the appearance of ignoring the situation between him and Ruth. The Babe was now 37 years old and the manager sincerely believed that the matter would resolve itself in due course. He was to be proven right.

Following a sputtering start to the 1932 season, the Yankees were in a position to make a move and that they did. As the season progressed, there was little doubt about the eventual outcome. The Yankees were thrashing the opposition with a regularity that had not been seen in the American League since the 1926 through 1928 seasons. They were never out of first place after the middle of May.

On May 16, Yankee starters posted their fourth consecutive shutout to tie a league record set by Cleveland in 1903 and Boston again in 1906. The successive shutouts were hurled by the rotation of Johnny Allen, George Pipgras, Red Ruffing and Lefty Gomez. All told that season, Yankee pitchers tossed 11 shutouts, recorded 96 complete games and posted a league-leading 3.99 earned average and 780 strikeouts.

On May 30, the Yankees honored the memory of their beloved late manager, Miller Huggins, by unveiling a plaque dedicated to him that enumerated his many accomplishments. The plaque was installed in deep center field at Yankee Stadium. Other monuments were also installed there as the years went on to honor former Yankee "greats." It is the basis of today's historic "Monument Park."

The defending champion Athletics were still a potent ball club in 1932 but not nearly as dangerous as they had been in the previous three seasons. Also, the Washington Senators, now managed by the immortal pitcher Walter Johnson, were challenging the A's for the runner up position in the American League. Lefty Gomez did his part to do in the Athletics by vanquishing Mr. Mack's ball club no less than seven times without a loss in 1932.

On June 3 of that year, several things happened to make that day one of the most memorable in baseball history. First off, Gehrig, now being hailed as "The Iron Horse" because of his ever-growing string of consecutive games played, belted four home runs in Philadelphia. In a slugfest won by the Yankees, 20–13, the 29-year-old Gehrig hit three of them off George Earnshaw and another off Leroy Mahaffey. In fact, he barely missed a fifth home run when he drove a ball to the deepest part of center field in the ninth inning only to have it run down and caught.

"Larrupin' Lou" thus became the first man to perform such a feat in

7. Back on Top Again (1932)

the twentieth century. Only twice before in the game's history had it been accomplished — once by Bobby Lowe of Boston on May 30, 1894, and again by Ed Delehanty of the Phillies on July 13, 1896.

In the same game that Gehrig made his record-tying accomplishment, Tony Lazzeri hit for the cycle, including a grand slam home run, and as the team established a new single game major league mark of 41 extra bases. Unfortunately for Gehrig, Lazzeri and the Yankees, none of these achievements drew the banner headlines that they normally would have. John McGraw chose the same day to announce his retirement as manager of the Giants.

After 30 consecutive seasons at the helm of the Giants and 40 games into the season — with only a 17–23 record at the time — McGraw was replaced by first baseman and future Hall of Famer "Memphis Bill" Terry. The emphasis by the members of the fourth estate that day was placed on the legendary McGraw.

It seemed inevitable that the modest Gehrig, who appeared to be overshadowed throughout his career first by Ruth and later by Joe DiMaggio, was once again to be eclipsed, this time by the venerable McGraw. As usual he took it all in stride. His motto and what he would live by was summed up in this quote: "The ballplayer who loses his head, who can't keep his cool is worse than no ballplayer at all."[7]

When the Yankees were in Boston to play the Red Sox after the events of June 3, Gehrig was asked to pose for a picture with Bobby Lowe. One of the Yankee beat writers who saw the picture in a late edition of a local newspaper asked Gehrig why he didn't tell him that Lowe was in the ballpark, because he would have wanted to write a story about him. "The Iron Horse," who just posed for the photograph not knowing it was Lowe, was flabbergasted. He said he wished he had known who it was himself. All he knew was that he was asked to take a picture with some older gentleman and he did.

All sorts of stories persist about the love-hate relationship that supposedly existed between Gehrig and Ruth. Early in Gehrig's career, the two had been close friends until the Babe reportedly made a pass at a female friend of Lou's. Ruth also was supposed to have made a disparaging remark about Gehrig's mother. A coolness did exist between the pair thereafter, but they maintained a cordial professional relationship during their many years together with the Yankees.

Lazzeri was also involved in an unusual turn of events in a game played against Detroit on August 1 at Tiger Stadium. Since the departure of Bob Meusel, Lazzeri had been inserted into the starting lineup to bat fifth in the order after Ruth and Gehrig. Chapman was now hitting sixth, where Lazzeri customarily had hit since joining the team in 1926.

However, on that August afternoon Lazzeri and Chapman were listed in reverse order on the lineup card that had been submitted to home plate umpire Dicky Nallin. At the start of the second inning, Lazzeri questioned the lineup placements to McCarthy, who promptly brought it to the attention of Nallin, asking that the mistake be corrected forthwith.

Nallin agreed to have the Yankees change the order and reverse the obvious error. After Lazzeri came up and singled, Tiger Manager Bucky Harris rushed out of his dugout to protest. However, Nallin upheld his decision and allowed the game to continue with the orally corrected batting order. Thereupon Harris lodged a formal protest with the league.

American League President Will Harridge upheld Detroit's protest on August 12 and ordered the game to be replayed on September 8. The replayed game resulted in a 7–7 tie that was called due to darkness. In view of the no-decision contest, the game was forced to be replayed again the very next day.

The Tigers won the replay of the replay but the incident created a problem regarding lifetime statistics for players who appeared in the various makeup games. The individual stats for the season included those of the makeup games. However, it was decided not to give participating players credit under "games played" by one game since the league had decided to consider the tie game official and the resulting Tiger victory a single game.

The player most affected by this was Lou Gehrig, who was in the midst of his historic 2,130 consecutive games played streak. It wasn't until 1937 that the American League reversed its original decision and credited Gehrig with participating in two games and not just one.

When the Yankees clinched the 1932 American League flag on September 13, Joe McCarthy became the first manager in major league history to win pennants in both leagues. Meanwhile, over in the National League that year, some interesting developments unfolding that would bear on events that would take place in the World Series.

"Marse Joe" had been watching the NL pennant race all season long with great interest. He was hoping that the Cubs would win it so that he could have an opportunity to whip them and their manager, Rogers Hornsby. He still believed that Hornsby had greased the skids for him in Chicago two years earlier when the job was taken away from him.

However, Hornsby had gotten himself into hot water during the 1932 season supposedly by "borrowing" money from several Cubs players fraudulently. The Chicago newspapers had accused the manager of using the money to either bet on the horses or to share in some joint ventures with the players. Although Commissioner Kenesaw Mountain Landis subse-

7. Back on Top Again (1932)

quently cleared him after an investigation, Hornsby was dismissed as manager of the Cubs. The team had already played 97 games and was in second place at the time. Hornsby's replacement was Charlie Grimm, who happened to be a good friend of McCarthy's.

One of Grimm's first moves was to repair his shaky infield that had been severely weakened by an injury to its regular shortstop, Billy Jurges. Thereupon Grimm obtained the former Yankee Mark Koenig from the Pacific Coast League to fill the slot. Koenig had been shipped out there after a couple of uneventful years in Detroit. It turned out to be a great move for the Cubs, as Koenig was an even better player now than when he was in New York. He proved to be a steadying influence on the Cubs' infield and even helped them win some key late season games with his timely hitting. In 33 games Koenig batted a hefty .353 after coming east from the PCL.

"He made it possible for us to win the pennant," declared Grimm after the season ended. "He was a real life saver."[8] The Cubs won 37 of their last 57 games under Grimm to finish four games in front of the Pirates.

What rankled the Yankees was the fact that when it came to dividing up their Series shares, the Cubs only voted Koenig a quarter of a share. When the word got out, the Yankees were not the least bit bashful about lashing out in the press at the Cubs' players. Moreover, they couldn't wait to tell them so to their faces when the Series got underway.

The Yankees came into the Series as heavy favorites after finishing 13 games ahead of the Athletics. Offensively, the team led the American League in walks with 766, in on base percentage at .376 and in runs scored with 1,002. Gehrig set the pace for the Yankees by batting .349, hitting 34 homers and driving in 151 runs. Ruth was not far behind with a .341 batting average, 41 home runs and 137 runs batted in.

Lazzeri had one of his best years yet. He batted an even .300, hit 15 homers and drove in 113 runs. McCarthy's reservations about Tony's durability were not borne out by his 1932 season in the pinstripes. Evidently the injuries he had suffered in the previous season were of no consequence. He appeared in 141 games and came to bat 510 times.

Another holdover from the glory days of Murderer's Row, 33-year-old Earle Combs also had a spectacular season, hitting .321 and scoring a remarkable 143 runs. Rookie Johnny Allen's 17–4 record gave him the league lead in winning percentage. Lefty Gomez had another vintage season with a 24–7 mark while Red Ruffing went 18–7 and George Pipgras was 16–9. All in all, the club was operating on all cylinders as the Series approached.

The Cubs countered with some solid hitters but all lacked consistent power. JoJo Moore was their top home run producer with only 13. Left fielder Riggs Stephenson at .324 was their leading batsman but he was primarily a singles hitter with only four homers. He was also their top RBI man at 85.

The pitching staff was led by Lon Warneke, whose 22 wins and 2.37 earned run average were tops in the National League. Veteran right-hander Guy Bush won 19 games that season, and both Pat Malone and Charley Root posted 15 victories each.

When the Series opened in New York on September 28, the venom that existed between the two competing franchises was totally out in the open. The Cub players, who had to pass through the Yankee dugout to reach the field, were greeted with silence until Mark Koenig made his way up the narrow steps.

Some of his former teammates called out to him: "Hello, Mark! How are you, boy?" Then in a booming voice that could not be mistaken, the Babe roared: "Who are those cheapskates with you, Mark?"

The mortified Koenig and all of the Cub players heard the taunt plainly. Soon other Yankee players joined in: "How does it feel to be with a lot of crumb bums like that when you've been on a real ball club?"

"Nickel nursers!"

"If it hadn't been for Koenig, you wouldn't have won the pennant, you misers!"⁹ The Cubs did not respond but once the game began, they let loose a barrage of their own, particularly at Ruth.

The Cubs took a 2–0 lead off starter Red Ruffing in the first inning and Guy Bush retired the first nine Yankees in order. However, the home team exploded for three runs in the fourth to take the lead, aided by a two-run homer from Gehrig. The Yankees ultimately drove Bush from the mound in the sixth with a five-run outburst and prevailed, 12–6. The Yankees continued their verbal onslaught as the Cubs' starter left for the showers. Ruffing fanned ten Cubs along the way as he went the distance.

In Game Two, the savage derision from both benches continued unabated as Lefty Gomez out-dueled Lon Warneke, 5–2. Ben Chapman's run-producing single in the third gave the Yankees a lead they would not relinquish. Both Chapman and another Series newcomer, Bill Dickey, knocked in a pair of runs to seal the victory. Gehrig had three hits and scored two runs in the victory to give New York a two-games-to-none lead as the teams headed to Chicago.

Ruth continued to be the object of the Cubs' wrath as some 49,986 fans jammed Wrigley Field for Game Three. George Pipgras opposed Charley Root in a game that was destined to go down in history as one of major league baseball's most memorable. Despite being derided unmercifully by the Cub benchwarmers and their fans, the Bambino uncorked a three-run homer in his first time at bat to give the New Yorkers a quick 3–0 lead.

With one down in the bottom of the third, Kiki Cuyler belted one into the right field stands that ignited a Cub rally. Riggs Stephenson singled to right and after Johnny Moore forced him out at second, player-manager Charlie Grimm lined a double to right that even the speedy Chapman could not run down. Moore scored all the way from first base, leaving the home club down by only one run.

The Cubs were undaunted as they pecked away to tie the score, 4–4, in their half of the fourth inning. The taunting of Ruth reached a fever pitch when he missed a shoestring catch of a liner hit by Billy Jurges in the run-tying fourth. Making up for a costly error that he had made earlier in the game, Jurges got two bases on the hit. Ever the jokester, Ruth doffed his hat to the crowd as play continued.

Immediately after Lazzeri made a spectacular catch of a high twisting pop fly off the bat of Billy Herman, he kicked Woody English's grounder as Jurges raced across the plate with the tying run.

As the Yankees came to bat in the top of the fifth, it was Ruth's turn to take center stage for his extraordinary brand of heroics. While there exists to this day a number of versions of what happened next, John Drebinger's account of the game in *The New York Times* may be the most authentic:

> A single lemon rolled out to the plate as Ruth came up in the fifth and in no mistaken motions the Babe notified the crowd that the nature of his retaliation would be a wallop right out the confines of the park.
>
> Root pitched two balls and two strikes, while Ruth signaled with his fingers after each pitch to let the spectators know exactly how the situation stood. Then the mightiest blow of all fell.
>
> It was a tremendous smash that bore straight down the center of the field in an enormous arc, came down alongside the flagpole and disappeared behind the corner formed by the scoreboard and the end of the right field bleachers.
>
> It was Ruth's fifteenth World Series home run and easily one of the most gorgeous. The crowd, suddenly unmindful of everything save that it had just witnessed an epic feat, hailed the Babe with a salvo of applause.
>
> Root, badly shaken, now faced Gehrig, and his feelings well can be imagined. The crowd was still too much excited over the Ruth incident to realize what was happening when Columbia Lou lifted an enormous fly high in the air. As it sailed on the wings of the lake breeze the ball just cleared the high flagpole, and dropped in the temporary stands.
>
> Grimm, the player-manager of the Cubs, called time. Consolingly, he

invited Root to retire to the less turbulent confines of the clubhouse, and ordered Pat Malone to the mound."[10]

Paul Gallico, writing for the *New York Daily News*, also saw Ruth's turn at bat very much the same way. His description of Ruth's circling of the bases, which John Drebinger omitted, is a classic: "The Babe ran around the bases gesticulating at the Cub dugout, mocking them, teasing them and holding up three fingers. Oh, my New York constituents, how your hearts would have warmed had you seen the Babe, thus confounding his enemies, thus making his run."[11]

Earle Combs, who was watching the Cubs in their dugout, described the scene thusly: "There they were—all out on the top step and yelling their brains out." When Ruth hit it out, Combs said, the Cub players "fell back as if they were being machine-gunned."[12]

Ruth's description of how he felt when he hit Root's delivery is also worth recalling: "As I hit the ball, every muscle in my system, every sense I had, told me I had never hit a better one, that as long as I lived nothing would ever feel as good as this one."[13]

The Bambino was also honest about whether he had actually called the home run: "I didn't exactly point to any spot, like the flagpole. I just sorta waved at the whole fence, but that was foolish enough. All I wanted to do was give the thing a ride ... outta the park ... anywhere. Every time I went to bat the Cubs on the bench would yell 'Oogly googly.' It's all part of the game, but this particular inning when I went to bat there was a whole chorus of 'Oogly googlies.' The first pitch was a pretty good strike and I didn't kick. But the second was outside and I turned around to beef about it. As I said, Gabby Hartnett said, 'Oogly googly!' That kinda burned me and I said 'All right, you bums. I'm gonna knock this one a mile. I guess I pointed, too."[14]

Both Ruth and Gehrig contributed a pair of home runs in the game that the Yankees won behind Pipgras and Pennock. Gehrig had gotten hold of one in the third inning, and then followed Ruth's spectacular homer in the fifth with one of his own deep into the right field bleachers.

The back-to-back clouts stood up as the margin of victory as the Yankees, after trading runs with the Cubs in the ninth, prevailed 7–5. The Cubs, who at the very least had hoped to get back into the Series with a victory, were devastated by the drama that had unfolded in their own ballpark. The Yankees on the other hand could not contain themselves with delight in their dugout.

Did Ruth call his fifth inning home run? Root said he didn't but his catcher, Gabby Hartnett, said he did. It was Root's contention that if Ruth had pointed to an anticipated home run landing spot, he would have knocked him down with his next pitch.

Gehrig also said that Ruth did indeed point to some distant location in the right field stands, but Grimm said he didn't. In fact, the next day Gehrig was quoted as saying: "What do you think of the nerve of that big monkey calling his shot and getting it?"[15] Of course, "Larrupin' Lou" was on deck as usual when the Bambino delivered his dramatic home run.

Manager Joe McCarthy, who usually never missed anything that went on during a ball game, wasn't sure himself. "Tell you the truth," he said, "I didn't see him point anywhere at all. But maybe I turned my head for a moment."[16]

Years later, the two principals, Ruth and Root, met on the Hollywood set where they were making the motion picture *Pride of the Yankees* following Lou Gehrig's death. Also there was the former Brooklyn Dodger slugger Babe Herman, who portrayed Gehrig at home plate when the movie's long shots were being filmed. Herman later said that Root turned to Ruth at one point and asked: "Say, Babe, you didn't really call your shot that day, did you?" Herman said that Ruth laughed and told Root: "Of course not. But it made a hell of a story, didn't it?"[17]

It's almost irrelevant but this remarkable event's place in major league baseball lore is assured. In July of 2002, MasterCard sponsored the compilation of the 30 most memorable moments in major league baseball history. Members of the media, baseball executives and baseball historians selected the list. Their choice for the most memorable moment in baseball history? Ruth's "called shot" took the honors.

Despite spotting the home team a 4–1 lead in the first inning of Game Four thanks largely to a three-run home run by Frank Demaree, the Yankees stormed back to defeat the Cubs by a lopsided score of 13–6. In so doing, the New Yorkers had chalked up their third consecutive World Series sweep.

Bush, who started the game for the Cubs, in an apparent attempt to intimidate Ruth, hit the slugger on the arm. Of the five batters that the Chicago right-hander faced, he was only able to register one out and had to be replaced by Lon Warneke.

"Poosh 'Em Up" had his best day ever in a Series game by blasting a pair of two-run homers to lead the 19-hit attack. To demonstrate the kind of power Lazzeri had to either field, one of his home runs reached the left field bleachers while the other one was deposited into the right field bleachers. So a game that was tied at 5–5 after six innings turned into a 13–6 runaway for the Yankees, as they scored four times in both the seventh and ninth innings.

Tony's wife, Maye, and their son, Tony, Jr., in 1932. (National Baseball Hall of Fame Library, Cooperstown, N.Y.)

Even Earle Combs, whose distinguished major league career was rarely associated with the long ball, cleared one over the fence with a solo shot. It was the center fielder's one and only home run in 16 World Series games.

7. Back on Top Again (1932)

As a matter of fact, the "Mail Carrier" only hit 58 homers in 1,454 regular season games.

Much to Joe McCarthy's delight, his revenge against his former employers was indeed sweet. His team had simply demolished the Cubs by scoring 37 runs on 45 hits in the four-game set. Lazzeri went 5-for-17 in the four games to post a .294 batting average. He also drove in five runs and scored another four as well.

Gehrig capped off his incredible season with an average of .529 in the Fall Classic, which included three home runs, nine runs scored and eight runs batted in. Ruth hit .333 as did Joe Sewell. In fact, the Bambino's pair of homers was to be his last in World Series competition.

Earle Combs and his .375 average also helped the Yankees establish yet another new record of consecutive Series victories at twelve. And Bill Dickey, who had pulled even with Mickey Cochrane in any discussion of who the best catcher in baseball was at the time, batted .438.

Outfielder Riggs Stephenson led the Cubs by hitting .444 while shortstop Billy Jurges, who had replaced Mark Koenig after Game One, was next at .364.

If anyone was happier than Joe McCarthy, it had to be Colonel Jacob Ruppert. The Yankees had resumed their perch on top of the baseball world once again, a post they truly believed no one else should occupy.

Another major development that the Yankees had nurtured since the hiring of Joe McCarthy was the farm system that was to form the nucleus of their present and future successes. The purchase of the Newark Bears of the International League late in 1932 was the first building block in that expansion. Colonel Ruppert, who originally had been against that purchase, was persuaded to buy the team by an attorney named Max Steuer. Even Ed Barrow was unaware of the deal until after it was consummated.

However, once Barrow got on board with the acquisition, it was his belief that Newark was to represent the crown jewel of the budding Yankee farm system. And he believed that there was no better man to run the system than one George Weiss. Although Ruppert had never heard of him, Barrow had known of Weiss' work over the years beginning when Joe Dugan was the third baseman on the high school baseball team that Weiss coached.

Weiss later made a successful independent professional ball club out of that team and called it the Colonials. He eventually bought the New Haven franchise in the Eastern League and ultimately moved on to take over the Baltimore team of the International League.

Weiss learned his lessons well. With his knowledge of the success that Branch Rickey had built up in his creation of a much-admired farm system for the Cardinals, Weiss was able to present an intriguing plan to the Yankees that would soon be the envy of all of major league baseball.

Weiss' plan was to take the players that Yankee scouts had signed and place them on teams where the Yankees would have a vested interest. He argued that it would better for the ball club to bring them along under managers and coaches familiar with their system and theirs alone. He felt that it would do far more for the Yankees to have these players develop within their own system rather than to play on teams where the managers and coaches would not necessarily have the best interests of the parent organization in mind.

In time, the best prospects would wind up in Newark as their final destination before heading up to the Bronx Bombers. The managers of the teams the Yankees began to acquire were mostly former players from Yankee farm clubs. With the acquisition of Kansas City of the American Association, the Yankees now had both Newark and Kansas City as major stops for players eventually capable of playing in the big leagues.

Weiss was a rather drab, detail-oriented man who seemed to have no social relationships outside of baseball. He only appeared to care about his wife and a small, select group of friends.

Other adjectives used to describe him from time to time during his career included shy, cold, humorless, frugal and nasty, particularly at contract time with players. Racist was another charge leveled against Weiss, who did not put an African-American player into a Yankee uniform until nine years after Jackie Robinson played in his first major league game. He also could not abide the press: "To hell with newspapermen, you can buy them with a steak," he once uttered contemptuously.[18]

Joe McCarthy, who was unfamiliar with most of the players that Weiss was developing in the Yankee farm system, had little to do with moving players along after each season. However, he had everything to do with their selection to the big ball club following the close of training camp in St. Petersburg, when it was time to go north with a 25-man roster. It was a system that would indeed pay huge dividends for the Yankees in the years that followed.

8

Runners Up (1933–1935)

Tony Lazzeri was 29 years of age and coming off one of his best years in the majors in 1932. With seven big league seasons behind him, "Poosh 'Em Up" had every reason to believe that 1933 would add not only to his personal laurels but also to those of his World Champion Yankee teammates as well. However, there were some, particularly those among the reporters following the ball club, who thought that he might have lost a step or two and wrote about it.

During spring training, Lazzeri got off to what for him had been the norm — a slow start. A young reporter, assigned to cover the Yankees for the *New York Daily News,* apparently was out to make a name for himself. He proceeded to attack Lazzeri almost daily in his reports from St. Petersburg, where the Yankees were in training. Not only did the young man criticize Lazzeri's ability but he went so far as to write that the second baseman's days with the Yankees were numbered because he was probably washed up anyway.

The Yankees were playing an exhibition game in St. Petersburg one afternoon and Lazzeri came to bat in the eighth inning with the bases loaded. He promptly belted one out of the park to clear the bases. Veteran sportswriter Bill Slocum reported: "In the eighth inning, Lazzeri hit a ball out of the park, sending home Combs, Koenig, Ruth and the young man from the *Daily News.*"[1] The last eight words never ran; the newspaper edited them out. Frank Slocum years later had this to say about it: "He [Bill Slocum] always wished his paper had printed that."[2]

The Yankees were basically the same team in 1933 that had won it all a year earlier. Lou Gehrig was still in the midst of a long consecutive game streak at first base. Lazzeri was firmly entrenched at second and backed up by a former National Leaguer, utility infielder Doc Farrell. The ball club had tried to either trade or sell Frank Crosetti during the spring, but he hung on and impressed Joe McCarthy enough to win back the shortstop job. Joe Sewell continued to start at third base while Lyn Lary would come off the bench to replace both he and Crosetti on occasion.

Babe Ruth, Earle Combs and Ben Chapman continued to patrol the outfield with the 22-year-old rookie Dixie Walker and fifth-year man Sammy Byrd in reserve. Bill Dickey was counted upon to do the bulk of the catching again and another fifth-year player, 28-year-old Arndt Jorgens, spelled him at times during the season. Jorgens, who had come up to the Yankees in 1929, would go on to spend his entire ll-year big league career with the Yankees as Dickey's backup.

Lefty Gomez, now considered the best left-hander in the American League, led a pitching rotation that again included right-handers Red Ruffing and Johnny Allen as well as a rookie southpaw, 26-year-old Russ Van Atta. The veterans Herb Pennock and Wilcy Moore were still around to fill in as relievers and spot starters. However, 34-year-old George Pipgras was sold to the Red Sox in May after eight productive seasons in New York.

Newcomers to the staff included: a Harvard man, 23-year-old right-hander Charlie Devens, who had pitched in one late season game for the ball club in 1932; a 29-year-old rookie right-hander, Don Brennan; 6'4" Walter "Jumbo" Brown, a 26-year-old right-hander who weighed close to 300 pounds; and still another veteran right-hander, Danny MacFayden, the 1932 mid-season acquisition from the Red Sox.

Later in the season, the club would acquire a 35-year-old journeyman right-hander, George Uhle. A former ace for the Indians and Tigers, he had won over 20 games three times during his long career. With the Yankees, he was penciled in to be used primarily out of the bullpen.

Early in the season it appeared that the race would turn into a three-tiered affair among the Yankees, Athletics and Senators. Both Philadelphia and Washington had finished in second and third places respectively in 1932. However, the A's were damaged by some winter transactions they had made with the Red Sox that had not panned out for them. Mr. Mack's ball club soon fell out of contention. In fact, Philadelphia, a perennial contender, would be hard-pressed to finish third that season and, eventually, only seven games over .500 at that.

The Yankees were rolling along at close to a .700 clip into the month of June when the bottom completely fell out from under for them. Ruth and Gehrig became mired in prolonged slumps and their pitching went south as well. Astonishingly, the New Yorkers dropped some 30 points in the standings in just eight days.

It was becoming more and more evident that Ruth's abilities were beginning to deteriorate rapidly. Obviously, this lack of consistency from a man who had been the greatest player in baseball history for two decades was having a negative effect on his team's overall performance.

Rookie player-manager Joe Cronin had his Washington ball club breathing down the Yankees' necks. With future Hall of Famers Goose Goslin and Heinie Manush leading the way offensively, and pitchers Earl Whitehill and Alvin "General" Crowder nearly unbeatable, the 26-year-old Cronin had his high-flying Senators in first place by June 24.

Gomez would wind up with a record of 16–10 in 1933 as compared to the 24–7 mark he had posted the year before. However, all things considered, he had actually pitched better in 1933, as his earned run average would attest — 4.21 in 1932 vs. only 3.18 in 1933. The difference was in the lack of run support he received.

When asked to explain why he wasn't winning as regularly as he had in the past, Gomez quipped: "I'm throwing as hard as I ever did. The ball's just not getting there as fast."[3]

Ever the flake, Lefty delighted in constantly tweaking Lazzeri. "Poosh 'Em Up" was no slouch himself when it came to displaying a keen sense of humor. One day Gomez was pitching against the powerful Athletics, whose lineup included such devastating hitters as Mickey Cochrane, Al Simmons and Jimmie Foxx. Each slugger was capable of hitting one out at any time. With Simmons at bat, Bill Dickey gave the signal for Gomez to throw a curve ball. Lazzeri, who spotted the sign, yelled out: "No. No."

Gomez promptly shook off the sign but Dickey repeated it. Lazzeri again called out: "No. No."

Thereupon, Gomez delivered a fastball that Simmons quickly deposited far into the left field stands for a home run. While Lazzeri stood at second in total silence, Gomez inquired of his fellow San Franciscan: "What the devil was the idea of shaking me off the curve?"

To which Lazzeri deadpanned: "Can't a guy talk to himself? You're the one who is pitching the ball game."[4]

It wasn't long before the ever-playful Gomez would get revenge. Lefty started a game in which he was quickly reached for three hits to load the bases. When the ball was returned to him, Gomez looked around to survey his fielders and called Lazzeri over to the mound. When Tony got to his side, Gomez surprised him with this invitation: "You're such a smart baseball dago, do you want to pitch?"[5]

One of the premier events in major league baseball in 1933 was the institution of the annual All-Star Game. It was the brainchild of *Chicago Tribune* Sports Editor Arch Ward, who suggested it as an adjunct to the Century of Progress Exposition. The fair was being held in the Windy City that year. When Ward proposed the idea, he and just about everyone else thought it would be strictly a one-shot event.

The suggestion caught on immediately and a date of July 6 was selected because it was a day in which eastern teams traveled west and vice versa. The game was to be held at Comiskey Park, which was chosen over Wrigley Field by virtue of a coin toss. Managers and fans were invited to select the teams. The former manager of the Giants, John McGraw, was picked to manage the National League while the venerable Connie Mack was selected to pilot the American League squad.

A total of 18 players were picked to represent each league in a game that was billed as the "Game of the Century." The Yankees sent six players—the most from any team—to Chicago. They included Ben Chapman, Bill Dickey, Lou Gehrig, Lefty Gomez, Tony Lazzeri and Babe Ruth.

A crowd of 49,200 fans attended the spectacle in which Gomez started for the American League against the National League's choice, Bill Hallahan of the Cardinals. Ever mindful of the big stage that he was always on, Babe Ruth did not disappoint. With a man on in the bottom of the third, the Bambino cracked a homer off of Hallahan, the first one ever to be hit in the game's history. He also made a spectacular catch of a ball hit by the Reds' Chick Hafey in the eighth to help preserve a 4–2 win for the American League. The Cardinals' Frankie Frisch also hit a home run that day and went down in history as the first National Leaguer to do so in All-Star competition.

For some reason best known to Mr. Mack, Mickey Cochrane and Bill Dickey rode the bench for the entire game as Rick Ferrell was used exclusively behind the plate. Even future Hall of Famers like Tony Lazzeri and Jimmie Foxx never got into the game. Charlie Gehringer and Lou Gehrig were kept in the game by Mr. Mack and held down the second and first base positions respectively for the entire nine innings. Pitcher Hal Schumacher of the Giants was the only player not to participate in the contest for the National League.

The game itself was a tremendous success among the fans and proved to be the forerunner of a much-anticipated annual tradition. Some of the future 24 Hall of Famers who were there that afternoon in 1933 could not have possibly foreseen what the game would become in the years to follow. Joe Cronin was one. Fifty years later he said: "Although much is being made today of the fact that we played in the 1933 All-Star Game, we also considered it a great honor then because we thought it would be the one and only All-Star Game."[6]

As the regular season wore on in 1933, it was evident that the Yankees were not nearly as strong as they had been in 1932. On August 3, Lefty

Grove of the A's shut them out. It marked the first time in 308 consecutive games that the New Yorkers were unable to score a run.

Two weeks later, Gehrig broke Everett Scott's consecutive game record by appearing in his 1,308th straight game. Ironically, Gehrig was in the Yankee dugout the day that Scott's record ended. When "The Iron Horse" set the new record, Joe Sewell was his teammate. As a member of the Indians, Sewell had shattered Scott's mark of 1,103 consecutive games earlier.

Unable to catch the high-flying Senators, the Yankees sent Babe Ruth to the mound on the final day of the season as a promotional stunt to attract fans into Yankee Stadium. Once again the Bambino, who loved center stage in any capacity, did not let the fans down. After not starting a game in three years, the Bambino pitched a complete game victory over his former club, the Red Sox, 6–5. Fittingly, the Yankee victory that day came as a direct result of the Babe's 34th home run of the year.

Although attendance was down for the Yankees, the 728,000 fans that did come to the Stadium in 1933 represented the tops in the major leagues. And it was safe to say it was the aging Bambino that most of them had come to see.

The Senators topped the Yankees by seven games to win the pennant. The boy manager, 27-year-old Joe Cronin, had his players adopt his youthful fighting spirit as they hustled on every play. However, they were no match for the more experienced Giants, who beat them in five games to win the World Series.

Ruth's power continued to decline; his 34 homers represented his lowest total in nine years, when he only appeared in 98 games. In fact, Foxx smacked 48 in 1933 to win the home run crown easily for the second year in a row. When asked about "Double-X's" power, Lefty Gomez retorted: "He has muscles in his hair."[7]

The Babe's runs-batted-in total was also down, from 137 a year earlier to 103 in 1933. He also barely hit over .300, finishing up at .301 or 40 points less than his 1932 average. These were numbers that almost any big leaguer would have loved to chalk up, but they were not acceptable for Ruth.

Overall Gehrig had an excellent year, hitting 32 home runs, posting a .334 batting average and driving in 139 runs. Although Lazzeri's batting average had dipped six points to .294, he still managed to hit 18 home runs for the third time in his career and drive in 104 runs. It also marked the sixth time in his eight seasons in the big leagues that Lazzeri had driven in over 100 runs.

While Gomez's 16 wins led the pitching staff, Ruffing's nine were only half of what he had won in the previous season. Between the pair, a shortfall of 17 victories resulted from 1932 to 1933.

Johnny Allen at 15–7 was a bright spot that appeared to bode well for the future. However, his short fuse was getting him pegged as a bad actor. Even Gehrig, who seldom criticized anyone let alone a teammate, remarked that whenever the rookie right-hander lost a game, he considered it "a personal conspiracy against him."[8]

"Marse Joe" McCarthy planned to revamp his personnel drastically in order to get the ball club back to where he and Yankee management thought it should be. Rebuilding the team for the 1934 season would begin with the removal of some veteran players from the roster.

Among the first to go were Herb Pennock and Joe Sewell. The classy Pennock was released unconditionally and caught on with the team from whence he had come — the Red Sox. The 40-year-old left-hander had served the Yankees well during his final years in New York, serving as a pitching coach without a portfolio to some of the youngsters on the staff. However, as much as McCarthy liked and respected Pennock, he knew it was time for the Yankees to sever their ties with him after eleven highly productive seasons.

Pennock pitched only occasionally for Boston in 1934 and left the majors for good after the season ended. "The Squire of Kennett Square" retired to his farm, where he had always raised silver foxes as a hobby. An excellent horseman and horticulturist, Pennock was also a master of hounds. The same grace and style that he exhibited in his daily life was what he brought to the mound during his 22-year career in the majors. Herb Pennock was voted into the Hall of Fame in 1948.

Sewell, on the other hand, left the game altogether after being cut by the Yankees following the 1933 campaign. The release of Sewell meant that the Yankees needed a third baseman and that player appeared to be none other than Tony Lazzeri when the season began. Lazzeri, now 30, was certainly no stranger to the position, having played there at times throughout his eight-year Yankee career.

Initially replacing Lazzeri at second was Don Heffner, who had been purchased over the winter from Baltimore of the International League. The 23-year-old rookie came to New York with a reputation as a magician with the glove. After four seasons in Baltimore, scouts reported that his hitting had improved to a point whereby he could be expected to hit big league pitching.

Tabbed to be the new shortstop for the Yankees was a 1931 Dartmouth College graduate, Robert "Red" Rolfe. The 25-year-old Rolfe, an English major at Dartmouth, was coming off two seasons in with the International

League's Newark ball club following a year in Albany of the Eastern League. "The luckiest thing I ever did was sign with the Yankees," he said. "When you're with really great players, they pull you along."[9]

The result of the changes that McCarthy was instituting meant that Frank Crosetti found himself on the bench alongside veteran utility infielders Lyn Lary and Jack Saltzgaver, who had been recalled from Newark.

As training camp opened in St. Petersburg in 1934, *The New York Times* reported: "Lazzeri will have no serious rival for third, because it is generally agreed that Tony can play the position and it likewise is recognized that Lazzeri's batting power guarantees that Tony will be found at one position or the other when the bell rings."[10]

Myril Hoag, a 26-year-old outfielder, had rejoined the club from a one-year exile in Newark. He had played briefly for the Yankees in 1931 and 1932 but McCarthy wanted him to get more playing time. Since it was impossible for him to obtain many at-bats with the Yankees at the time, he was able to play regularly for the Bears.

Hoag had the smallest feet in the majors. He wore a size-four shoe on his right foot and four-and-half on his left. Because of his strong arm, the Yankees once had seriously considered making a pitcher out of him but never did. However, later in his career he did pitch in one game for the Browns and in two others for the Indians. His totals in four innings of pitching were not that bad — three hits, one walk and no runs allowed.

Among the pitchers added to the staff in 1934 was 24-year-old Jimmy DeShong, a right-hander who had seen some service with the Athletics two years earlier. Also brought in to bolster the group was 26-year-old Johnny Murphy, another right-hander and a graduate of Fordham University. Murphy, who had always been a starting pitcher, was about to be turned into one of the greatest relief pitchers of all time by Joe McCarthy.

Initially it looked like the Yankees' stiffest competitors would once again be the defending league champion Senators. Then, too, the Red Sox were supposed to be in the hunt after having been strengthened by some off-season deals. The attention paid to the Tigers, now led by the fiery player-manager Mickey Cochrane, was negligible. However, with strong seasons from right-handers Tommy Bridges and Lynwood "Schoolboy" Rowe, Detroit would claw its way into the American League lead by July as the Yankees' early grip on first place subsided.

The Bambino was showing signs of wear-and-tear at the plate and even more so in the field. Gehrig and Dickey were having their usual productive years but Lazzeri was not contributing the way he was expected to. It wasn't the pitching that led to their demise in 1934 but rather the poor run production, which was now well off from previous seasons. From a league-leading 927 runs scored in 1933, the Yankees were only able to produce 842 in 1934.

Ruth started to take himself out of the lineup more and more. "Marse Joe" was forced to call upon Myril Hoag and a 26-year-old rookie from Newark, George Selkirk, to spell him. The manager only put the Babe in the lineup when he asked him to and took him out when he requested it as well. The relationship between the two men, never that good to begin with, grew considerably colder as the year wore on.

Had it had been another player, McCarthy would have seated him firmly on the bench. But this was the "Sultan of Swat" he was dealing with. Therefore, he had earned the right to play himself out of the lineup and off the club entirely for his extraordinary past performances for the Yankees.

Ruth spoke only when spoken to when it came to communicating with his manager. Meanwhile, he would tell the press and some of his teammates about how bad things really were on McCarthy's watch. "Marse Joe" just kept his veteran right fielder on a long leash as he patiently waited for the day when he would finally be gone.

Selkirk, who had spent some eight seasons in the minor leagues, had a great eye at the plate. During his career, he was able to draw two walks in a single inning no less than four times. However, as the player who looked to the fans like he was pushing Ruth out of a job in 1934, his popularity was not that high in his rookie year.

On July 23, Earle Combs crashed into the concrete bleacher wall in St. Louis' Sportsman's Park and nearly killed himself. A skull fracture and torn shoulder put the center fielder out for the rest of the season and virtually ended a fine career. The mishap was a big blow to the team, more so because they feared for Combs' life rather than just for the loss of the veteran center fielder for the balance of the year.

The services of the famed baseball physician, Dr. Robert F. Hyland, were called upon and he immediately treated Combs, who was in a coma for hours. Not only did the good doctor bring him around but he also operated on his torn shoulder so capably that Combs would return to duty the following season.

Due to the loss of Combs, McCarthy was now compelled to mix and match in the outfield. He also shifted Lazzeri back to second from third, inserted the line- drive hitting Rolfe at the hot corner and returned Crosetti to shortstop. To further weaken the team's fortunes, an injury to Johnny Allen forced the pitcher out of the starting rotation as well.

With six weeks left to go in the season, the Yankees suffered a dev-

8. Runners Up (1933–1935)

astating Sunday doubleheader loss to the Tigers at a jam-packed Yankee Stadium. Mickey Cochrane's surprising ball club featuring Schoolboy Rowe, Tommy Bridges, Hank Greenberg and Charlie Gehringer, among others, was convinced it would win the pennant if they took both games.

The Yankees never recovered from the double dip losses. Detroit moved on to win the American League flag, as the team had convinced itself that it could. In fact, the New Yorkers had to fight off a challenge for second place from the onrushing Indians.

The Tigers finished in front by seven games in 1934 led by their pitching aces, Bridges and Rowe, who posted nearly half of the team's 101 victories between them. Offensively, Detroit rode the crest of first baseman Hank Greenberg's 26 homers, 139 runs batted and .339 batting average, as well as Charlie Gehringer's .356 BA and 127 RBI.

Lou Gehrig wound up having another of his patented monster years by winning the league's Triple Crown with a .363 average, 49 homers and 165 RBI. Unbelievably though, Cochrane, who hit 43 points lower, had 47 fewer home runs and 89 fewer RBI, was voted the American League's Most Valuable Player award.

To make matters worse for the Yankees that season, Ruth only hit .288, drove in but 84 runs and produced just 22 home runs. Any other player in the big leagues would have been overjoyed to put up such numbers but this was not just any other player. These totals were the lowest that the Bambino had posted since his unproductive 1925 season when he only played in 98 games. And 1934 was by far his worst year of the 15 he had spent in a Yankee uniform. It was also destined to be his last in the pinstripes.

Lazzeri also had his least productive season with the bat since 1931; he batted only .267 while hitting 14 homers and driving in just 67 runs. The latter number would represent his lowest RBI total throughout his entire Yankee career. Nearly lost in the shuffle was Lefty Gomez's sensational 26–5 mark and 2.33 ERA to go along with Gehrig's career year. Both seemed wasted among the multitude of poor Yankee player performances.

While the Tigers lost the World Series to the Cardinals in an exciting seven game set, Detroit was still the prohibitive favorite to repeat as American League champions in 1935. What to do with Ruth and the rest of the ball club was uppermost in the minds of the Yankee hierarchy and they set out to address both issues immediately.

Ruth, who still believed that the Yankee managerial job should have been his, went directly to Colonel Ruppert after the season ended and practically demanded the position. All he got from the owner was an offer to gain some experience by going down to Newark to run the Bears in 1935.

"No," he said. "I won't go to Newark or any other minor league club. Why should I? I'm a big leaguer. Why should I go to the minors?"

Ruppert shrugged. "I think you are foolish," he said.

"Maybe. But that's the way I feel about it."

"Then I can do nothing for you," Ruppert said.[11]

It was evident that the Babe Ruth era was over in New York, at least as far as the Yankees were concerned. Following the 1934 World Series at which he was a spectator, Ruth went on a barnstorming tour of the Orient with a group of other big leaguers, including Gehrig and Gomez. The Babe eventually circled the globe and came back to New York by way of Europe.

Upon his return, Ruppert and Barrow told the Bambino that they had agreed to give him a provisional contract for 1935. It called for a nominal sum of money and was based upon the stipulation that he would get in shape during spring training so he could return to his old form. If those conditions were met, the club would offer him terms that both parties would agree upon.

The Babe not only refused to sign the deal but also stated emphatically that he and not McCarthy should manage the Yankees. He still truly believed that he deserved the post. Moreover, he went so far as to declare that he would never wear the Yankee uniform again unless he was given the job.

Firmly in McCarthy's corner and believing that they were dealing fairly with Ruth, both Ruppert and Barrow obtained waivers on him from every American League team and he was sent to the Boston Braves on February 25, 1935. The Yankees didn't even request compensation from Emil Fuchs, a former New York magistrate who controlled the National League's Boston franchise at the time.

Fuchs had been vying with the youthful and wealthy owner of the Red Sox, Tom Yawkey, for the attention of the fans in Beantown. Up to then he had brought in "name" but "has-been" players like Rogers Hornsby, George Sisler, Casey Stengel, Christy Mathewson, Hank Gowdy, Rabbit Maranville and Johnny Evers to bring in customers. None of this had worked and the ball club never finished above seventh place while he owned the team. However, the chance to obtain Babe Ruth, especially for no compensation, was an opportunity that Judge Fuchs could not refuse.

The Braves gave Ruth a couple of titles that were actually meaningless—assistant manager to Bill McKechnie and club vice president. Neither "position" had any clout and the Babe knew it. They were simply window dressings that were designed to appeal to the team's low fan base.

The Bambino flouted his team's spring training rules and became, as always, a law unto himself. The result was a complete fiasco for Fuchs and the Braves. Although he hit six home runs, including three in his last game in Pittsburgh on May 25, balls dropped all around him in the outfield and his average dipped down to .181. The experiment ended before it really ever began as Judge Fuchs went on to lose over a million dollars as the ill-fated owner of the National League's franchise in Boston.

As far as the Yankees were concerned, they would go in to battle for the first time since 1920 without Babe Ruth in the trenches with them. The volatile Ben Chapman had replaced the scholarly Earle Combs in center field. Combs had been reduced to a part-time player, particularly after his near-fatal injury late in the 1934 season.

The unpopular George "Twinkletoes" Selkirk, who continued to be booed lustily for having the temerity to replace the Bambino, including wearing his Number Three, would now patrol right field. Selkirk's nickname had been pinned on him for his unorthodox running style. Several players were to share left field for the Yankees in 1935 with future PGA golfer Sammy Byrd and Myril Hoag getting the lion's share of the playing time.

The players used to call Byrd Babe Ruth's caddy or his legs, as the Georgia native would frequently replace the Bambino in the outfield or as a pinch runner in previous seasons. A veteran of eight years in the majors when he left after the 1936 season to become a professional golfer, he actually went on to win a number of prestigious tournaments.

The infield appeared to be set with Lou Gehrig, Tony Lazzeri, Frank Crosetti and Red Rolfe in place, in much the same way as they had finished the prior season. After holding out at the start of spring training, Lazzeri ultimately signed for a figure that the press could only speculate about. *The New York Times* in their February 28 edition indicated that the "veteran second baseman" had been a holdout "but whether he gained anything by delaying acceptance of his contract could not be learned. The terms, which induced the Coast Italian to capitulate, were not revealed. Speculation, however, placed his salary at about $10,000 for the season."[12]

Ten days later, James P. Dawson in *The New York Times* wrote: "The veteran Tony Lazzeri was out cavorting about third base in a manner which indicated he will be tried at Joey Sewell's vacated perch in the infield. Johnny Saltzgaver, candidate for the post, did not don a uniform, although he is in town."[13]

On March 24 the newspaper reported that "Tony Lazzeri [was] getting accustomed to things at his old stomping ground, second base, and Frank Crosetti operating at third base. In virtually all the infield workouts up to today Lazzeri had performed at third.

"There was no particular significance to this arrangement, it was said. McCarthy plans to open the season with Don Heffner at second base. This

From left to right, Joe DiMaggio, Frank Crosetti and Tony Lazzeri, all of whom hailed from San Francisco, as the start of the 1937 Yankees' season. (National Baseball Hall of Fame Library, Cooperstown, N.Y.)

means that Lazzeri will have no serious rival for third, because it is generally agreed that Tony can play the position and it is likewise recognized that Lazzeri's batting power guarantees that Tony surely will be found at one position or the other when the bell rings."[14]

Lefty Gomez, Red Ruffing, Johnny Allen and a second-year man, 26-year-old Johnny Broaca, formed the basis of a solid rotation. Johnny Murphy and the veteran right-hander Pat Malone, whom McCarthy had managed with the Cubs, were key in the bullpen. And although there were a number of good catchers in the majors at the time, there was none better than Bill Dickey in 1935.

The pennant race was almost a reproduction of the year before. The Yankees broke out fast, alternately knocking the Indians and White Sox out of first place. However, the New Yorkers faded quickly in June and July; Gomez did not pitch well and Gehrig struggled with the bat.

McCarthy, Barrow and Ruppert were extremely unhappy. They blamed much of the club's lack of success on the Far East barnstorming trip that Gehrig and Gomez had taken with Ruth. Though the team stayed on top through June and most of July, the defending champion Tigers took over sole possession of first place late in the month and remained there for the rest of the season.

"Marse Joe" was forced to replace Combs in center field with Chapman at mid-year while using Hoag and a 28-year-old rookie, Jesse Hill, in left field. Crosetti was not getting the job done at shortstop so McCarthy had to call up a pair of journeymen infielders from the minors, 32-year-old Nolen Richardson and 29-year-old Blondy Ryan, to spell him late in the year. However, neither one was able to help much.

Lazzeri's numbers were an improvement over 1934 and he got most of the playing time at second. However, Don Heffner and Jack Saltzgaver were now receiving ample time at the keystone sack as well.

The players gave it all they had and McCarthy drove them hard, but they were just not equal to the task. Gomez went from his superb season the year before to a below average 12–15 mark in 1935. Ruffing failed to pick up the slack; he could do no better than post a 16–11 record. Gehrig's batting average fell by 34 points and his home run production was down by 19 despite a late surge — too late to make a difference.

Though the race was tighter than in 1934, when the Tigers won eight less games, the Yankees won five less themselves and finished three games out. In looking back at the season, McCarthy was convinced there were at least five or six games the club could have won that could have actually propelled to the pennant. This year, though, belonged to Detroit under player-manager Mickey Cochrane. They would win the pennant once again and also become the World Champions by beating the Cubs in six games.

The Yankees lost the race primarily because of their inconsistent pitching, a power outage and poor fielding, all of which were characteristics of the team when they were winning championships. After three consecutive runner up finishes, some of the New York writers took to labeling the manager "Second Place Joe," much to McCarthy's consternation.

The fact was that in five years of managing the Yankees, "Marse Joe" had won only one pennant and had never finished below second in the other four years. All it meant to him was that his team had lost out four out of those five years. They might just as well as have finished last as far as he was concerned. But help was on the way in the person of a 22-year-old outfielder from the San Francisco Seals named Joseph Paul DiMaggio.

The young man batted .340 while hitting in an unequaled 61 consecutive games in 1933. He followed up that exemplary season with a .341 batting average in 1934 and a resounding .398 mark in 1935. DiMaggio tore up the Pacific Coast League that year. But it was his 61-game hitting streak in 1933, much like Tony Lazzeri's 60-homer season for Salt Lake in 1925, that had captured the attention of the baseball world.

DiMaggio injured his knee while exiting a taxi in 1934 and that nearly prevented the Seals from concluding a huge financial deal for his services in the big leagues. Previously inundated with offers from a host of major league ball clubs, the Seals found only one team — the Yankees — failed to lose interest.

Yankee scouts Joe Devine and Bill Essick begged Ed Barrow to purchase the youngster. While Barrow trusted their judgment, he only agreed to the sale for after an orthopedist selected by the Yankees checked out DiMaggio's knee and bestowed his medical approval.

Part of the deal was to allow DiMaggio to spend another year in San Francisco and test out the once-balky knee. The young man passed that trial with flying colors. He played a complete, unimpeded 1935 season and posted that marvelous .398 mark with 270 base hits, among them 48 doubles, 18 triples and 34 home runs.

Not lost on the Yankees at the time was DiMaggio's Italian heritage. By teaming DiMaggio fellow Italian-Americans and San Franciscans Tony Lazzeri and Frank Crosetti, the ball club concluded that his attraction as the newest kid on the block could produce astonishing results for them at the box office. This would be true not only at Yankee Stadium turnstiles but in virtually every city in which this talented prospect would appear and where the Yankees would obtain a share of the proceeds.

Joe DiMaggio was soon riding in an automobile heading for St. Petersburg in the spring of 1936 with the likes of Lazzeri and Crosetti. The San Francisco connection was indeed alive and well.

So now as Joe McCarthy sat in front of the fire at his Gates Circle home in wintry 1935–36 Buffalo, he could only speculate on what lay ahead for him and the New York Yankees. Little did he know that he and his team were about to embark upon a period of success like no other team in baseball history had ever enjoyed.

9

Return to Paradise (1936–1937)

It was Tony Lazzeri's idea to take Joe DiMaggio with him and Frank Crosetti on the long car trip from San Francisco to St. Petersburg in the spring of 1936. "Poosh 'Em Up" didn't want the youngster to take the long and arduous train trip to Florida from the Bay Area, as DiMaggio had originally planned. Besides, Tony had just bought a brand-new roadster and felt that the trip would be much more comfortable for the valuable new Yankee rookie.

Then, too, Lazzeri didn't know Joe well. He thought the trip would provide a good way for all concerned to get to know each other. Lazzeri had heard all of the accolades and wanted to get to know his new teammate better.

According to Joseph Durso, author of *DiMaggio: The Last American Knight*, Joe was a kid who rarely got excited. So to Tony that kind of temperament closely resembled his and Crosetti's. The so-called hot Italian temper didn't go with the three Romans of the Ruppert legion.[1]

DiMaggio was yet another Italian youngster from the Bay Area sandlots who had made it all the way up to the big time. And just as Lazzeri had bonded with Crosetti three years earlier, so too was Lazzeri resigned to becoming responsible for the well-being of the newest kid off the streets and playgrounds of San Francisco.

Although he was well aware of Joe's accomplishments with the Seals and the local sandlots before that, Tony had never seen him play. There was a gap of some ten years in their ages. Lazzeri was now 31 and a veteran of ten years in the majors. Joe, at 21, was coming off three sensational years in the Pacific Coast League with the Seals.

Purchased by the Yankees for $25,000 and five players, the ball club knew that DiMaggio was a risk physically. Nonetheless, the feeling persisted among club management that he could play effectively despite his previously injured knee. With the natural tools that he possessed, DiMaggio was a ball player the Yankees could not pass up.

There were, of course, other considerations that the club's hierarchy had taken into account. The Yankees had become the prototypical representatives of urban America. Now with three Italian-Americans on their roster — all of whom were key position players — the team symbolized what the big cities of the United States were in 1936 — multi-ethnic, complex and offering a wide variety of religious and economic backgrounds.

The St. Louis Cardinals, on the other hand, were the antithesis of the Yankees. Their roster typified the small towns and farms of a more rural part of the nation. The dust-covered, baggy uniforms of the "Gashouse Gang" featuring the likes of Dizzy Dean, Pepper Martin and Rip Collins were in sharp contrast to the clean, unassuming stylishness of the Yankee pinstripes.

Joe McCarthy, who never missed a chance for "one upsmanship" with the opposition, liked to dress his club in uniforms that were cut at least a size bigger for each man so that the players would appear larger and more powerful. Always a stickler for decorum, the manager demanded that his team shave before coming to the ballpark. "This is your job. Shave before you come to work," Marse Joe would command.[2]

Teams like the Yankees were now starting to be populated by sons of immigrant families from southern and eastern Europe. Consequently, attendance was burgeoning at games where the DiMaggios, Lazzeris, Greenbergs and the like were now occupying prominent positions in the lineups. This fact of life was now being reflected in ticket sales.

While the numbers of big leaguers from German and Irish stock waned, players of Italian, Polish and Jewish descent began to intensify. The only notable exception time was the complete absence of African-Americans. It would be another ten years before Branch Rickey, in a development that would change the face of the game forever, would break the color barrier with the historic signing of Jackie Robinson.

As far back as 1923, *The Sporting News* took note of the changes that were taking place in the game: "Except the Ethiopian (i.e. black), the Mick, the Sheeney, the Wop, the Dutch and the Chink, the Cuban, the Indian, the Jap or the so-called Anglo-Saxon — his nationality is never a matter of moment if he can pitch, or hit, or field."[3]

The players now coming into baseball from the new breed often ran into ethnic slurs. Some bench jockeys would not hesitate to call Hank Greenberg and other Jewish ballplayers "Christ-killers."[4] Even the newspapers of the day would refer to Tony Lazzeri, Joe DiMaggio and others of Italian ancestry as "Dagos."[5]

As prominent a figure as DiMaggio would become in major league baseball, even he would be unable to escape the kind of innuendos and outright barbs that Lazzeri had faced throughout his life. In an article that appeared in the most prominent magazine of its day—*Life*—that would come out three years after he arrived in the big leagues, DiMaggio was portrayed thusly: "Although he learned Italian first, Joe, now 24, speaks English without an accent and is otherwise adapted to United States mores. Instead of olive oil or smelly bear grease, he keeps his hair slick with water. He never reeks of garlic and prefers chicken chow mein to spaghetti."[6]

In a story titled "Viva Italia," sportswriter Dan Daniel called attention to the influx of Italian-American major leaguers in this manner: "This surely is Italy's year," he wrote. "Italy finally has invaded baseball with a bang. The time was when it was considered an oddity for any club to have an Italian ballplayer."[7]

Daniel—a Jew whose real surname was Moskowitz—went on to say in his piece that for a team to have two Italians in their lineup (Lazzeri and Crosetti) "was considered phenomenal or bizarre, according to ... the manner in which your psychology responded to the invasion of baseball by the sons of immigrants from Europe."[8] According to Daniel, the exploits of DiMaggio, Lazzeri and Crosetti "have intrigued Italians all over the country" and "have established in every city visited by the Yankees ... a new school of fans."[9]

In addition to Lazzeri, Crosetti and DiMaggio, other Italian-American ball players cited in Daniel's article would go on to have outstanding careers in the game, including Ernie Lombardi, Gus Mancuso, Zeke Bonura, Tony Cuccinello, Cookie Lavagetto, Phil Cavaretta and Dolph Camilli.[10]

Noted baseball enthusiast and distinguished professor Lawrence Baldassaro, in his article "Before Joe D: Early Italian Americans in the Major Leagues," pointed out that by 1936 Italian-American baseball players had arrived in the majors not only in numbers but also in the statistics they were producing on the field. For example, of the leading 32 batting averages in the National League, Italian-Americans claimed six. Also three players—Mancuso, Camilli and Lombardi—were to be accorded Most Valuable Player votes in the National League and two others—DiMaggio and Bonura—were to garner MVP votes in the American League that season.[11]

Professor Baldassaro also noted in his article that in spite of these achievements, the media throughout the decade of the '30s continued to characterize Italian-American players by their nationality. The 1936 edition of "Who's Who in the Major Leagues" very nearly all the time identified Italian-American ballplayers by their ethnicity while other players were not characterized by their cultural backgrounds.

Ernie Lombardi was described as "one of numerous Italians who won major league renown." Lazzeri was called "the lanky Italian" and DiMaggio "the giant Italian." Noted sports cartoonist Willard Mullin portrayed Lazzeri, Crosetti and DiMaggio as "The Three Musketeers from 'Frisco" who sang "Oh, the miners came in '49, the wops in '51."[12]

According to Professor Baldassaro, two of the typical adjectives used to depict Italian-American ballplayers were "fiery" and "colorful." It is his contention that such appellations were code words indicating the popular view of Italian-Americans as hot-blooded and temperamental. He also wrote that Dan Daniel in his aforementioned "Viva Italia" article described Italians as an "agile race, a sturdy, enduring and durable people, quick to learn and aggressive to the highest degree." Professor Baldassaro also pointed out that a later piece, written in 1939 by Frederick Lieb in *The Sporting News*, called pitcher Italo Chelini a player "whose hot Italian blood gets him trouble."[13]

When Lazzeri, Crosetti and DiMaggio set out for the Yankees' training base in St. Petersburg, Tony felt the driving could be shared equally. Tony started out as the driver for the first four or five hours and turned the chore over to the "Crow," who also put in about the same amount of time. It was then that Tony motioned to Joe to take the wheel. "All right," said Lazzeri "It's your turn."

"I'm sorry," Joe said. "I can't drive."

Lazzeri and Crosetti looked at each other.

"Let's throw the bum out and leave him here," Tony said.

DiMaggio settled himself more comfortably in the back seat. "Get going," he said with a laugh. "I got a date with the Yankees."[14]

None of the three San Franciscans could ever be accused of being blabbermouths. One day during the season, Jack Mahon, a sportswriter for International News, said he saw the trio sitting in the lobby of the Hotel Chase in St. Louis.

"I came down in the elevator," he said, "and the three of them were sitting there, watching the guests coming and going. I bought a paper and sat down near them, and after a while became aware of the fact that none of them had a word to say to the others. Just for fun, I timed them, to see how long they would maintain their silence. Believe it or not, they didn't speak for an hour and twenty minutes. At the end of that time, DiMaggio cleared his throat. Crosetti looked at him and said, 'What did you say?'

"And Lazzeri said: 'Shut up. He didn't say nothing.'

"They lapsed into silence and at the end of ten more minutes I got up and left. I couldn't stand it anymore."[15]

When the trio first arrived at the clubhouse at Huggins Field in St. Petersburg, the rest of the Yankee players were gawking at DiMaggio as if he were some kind of curiosity. Tony was now Joe's self-appointed guardian and took him around and introduced him to each of the players. DiMaggio, although stoic, was pleasant enough as he shook hands with each man. Only one Yankee — Red Ruffing — said anything to him: "So you're the great DiMaggio!"[16] Joe was taken aback by the pitcher's greeting and Lazzeri gave Ruffing a cold stare.

Years later, DiMaggio said of the incident: "I didn't know, of course, what a needler Charlie [Ruffing] was," he recalled. "When I put out my hand to shake his, he just stared at me dead-panned. Then he turned away from me. I was scared anyway, at meeting the Yankees all in a bunch like that, and Charlie really gave me a shock. I didn't say anything and neither did Tony, but Tony looked as though he felt like taking a punch at him."[17]

Tony also brought DiMaggio into Joe McCarthy's office and left him there while the two had a brief talk. When DiMaggio came out, the newspapermen swarmed all over him. Again it was Lazzeri who introduced each of them to the newest Yankee.

The New York Times in their March 3, 1936, edition commented on the activities in the Yankee camp in this fashion: "Peppiest of the lot seemed to be the veteran Tony Lazzeri, here in perfect condition and ready to fight in defense of his second base job. The eyes of the fans were riveted on the sparkling Joe DiMaggio, California's latest gift to the big leagues. He responded with a couple of drives into left field, which disappeared among the waving palms."[18]

It became increasingly evident to all concerned that with DiMaggio now in tow, Lou Gehrig was going to play second fiddle again just as he done in years past with Babe Ruth. However, Gehrig had no problem with it, just as he hadn't with Ruth. "It's a pretty big shadow," he used to say about Ruth's presence. "It gives me lots of room to spread myself."[19]

But DiMaggio's cast a shadow of a different sort. Gehrig marveled at how DiMaggio eased into his role minus the strut that the Bambino had displayed in all those years.

Lazzeri was also one who did not crave attention from the press and the adulation of the fans as his career was to begin to take shape. He never did. Tony simply did not require the kind of clamor or publicity that Ruth had always commanded and that Gehrig sometimes received during his ten seasons with the ball club.

Lazzeri was the most solid player on the team and the one his teammates looked up to. He was the one the players turned to in times of crisis. This was the case even though Gehrig had actually been a Yankee a little longer.

Although Tony was a veteran of eleven years in the big leagues, he had changed less than any player who had been around that long. He still had the mark of a "busher" on him with an enthusiasm for playing the game that few others possessed. He wasn't like some of the kids who came out of the tank towns with their brakeman's haircuts and mail order clothes. Rather he was big-town guy with all of the street-smart traits one acquired by coming off the playgrounds of a city like San Francisco.[20]

What set Lazzeri apart from the others was his craftiness on the field. This point was continually emphasized in anecdotes circulating around major league baseball regarding his quick-thinking and baseball instincts. In one game during the 1936 season, Lefty Gomez was on the hill against the Athletics in Yankee Stadium, nobody was on base and an A's batter hammered one directly to the pitcher. Gomez fielded it and threw it to Lazzeri at second base. Tony barely got the throw and was puzzled and rather confounded by what the southpaw had just done. He went to the mound to ask him why he did it.

"Tony, only yesterday I read a very interesting story in *The Sporting News* rating you as one of the brainiest infielders in the history of the American League," declared Gomez. "I did not doubt this rating. But I said to myself, 'How am I going to test Tony and find out for myself?' So when the ball was hit to me, with the play at first base, I said, 'Here's a chance to make that test.' "So I threw the ball to you, eager to find out what a really brainy second baseman could do with it." Lazzeri walked back to his position more baffled than ever.[21]

According to author Joseph Durso, Gomez was now rooming with fellow San Franciscan, DiMaggio. The team distinguished between the three Italians by calling Lazzeri "Big Dago," Crosetti "Little Dago" and DiMaggio just "Dago."[22]

Lazzeri's leadership on the field was unquestioned. And he continued to look out for DiMaggio at all times as well. In a game played on May 19, 1936, in Cleveland, the Indians were attempting to stop a five-game slide against the Yankees. The home team was naturally quite uptight. During the course of the game, the much-heralded Yankee rookie slid into the Indians' second baseman Billy Knickerbocker attempting to break up a double play. Knickerbocker threw the ball directly at Joe's head but missed.

DiMaggio, oblivious to what was going on, simply looked around to see if he had been called out or safe. Knickerbocker advanced toward Joe in a menacing way in an effort to goad him into a fight. It was Tony Lazzeri, followed by Joe McCarthy, who led a charge out of the Yankee dugout toward second base to protect the team's precious new commodity.

The umpires quickly moved in to restore order and no further action resulted. However, a strong message had been delivered: don't mess with the new Yankee.

Well before the season opened, the so-called experts picked the Yankees to finish third in the American League. The reasoning was that the Tigers were at least as strong as they were in 1935 when they won the pennant and the World Series and the New Yorkers had won only one league flag since 1928. Then, too, the Yankees were coming off three second place finishes under "Marse Joe" McCarthy. Someone evidently forgot to tell the Yankees how things should develop because once the season got underway, they broke out of the gate rapidly.

Before long there was little doubt that they would regain what they believed to be their rightful position — first place in the American League and a berth in yet another World Series. With Joe DiMaggio in their lineup in left field, Ben Chapman in center following Earle Combs' retirement and George Selkirk in right, the Yankee outfield was the best that it had been since Babe Ruth, Combs and Bob Meusel patrolled it. Now a Yankee coach, Combs was assigned the task of working closely with DiMaggio and instructing him on all of the nuances that he would encounter in the vast Yankee Stadium outfield.

The infield was probably the best in the game with Gehrig at first, Lazzeri at second, Crosetti at short and Red Rolfe over at third. The pitching staff was bolstered by the additions of two veteran right-handers, Bump Hadley from Washington and Monte Pearson via Cleveland. Pearson had been obtained from the Indians along with another right-hander, Steve Sundra, in a swap for the temperamental Johnny Allen, with whom McCarthy was having problems.

Mainstays like Lefty Gomez, Red Ruffing, Johnny Broaca and Walter "Jumbo" Brown filled out the rotation while the bullpen was in good hands with Johnny Murphy and Pat Malone, whom McCarthy had had with him in Chicago. The Yankee skipper changed the game forever when he became the first manager to split up his pitching staff into starters and relievers. Thus ended a period of 15 years in which all pitchers in the major leagues performed both tasks. "Marse Joe" had rarely used his bullpen during his years in Chicago and almost never in New York until the 1936 season.

Few catchers could hold a candle to Bill Dickey, behind the dish or at bat. Dickey, who never played another position during his 17-year career, was about to record the highest batting average for a receiver in major league history—.362. The 1954 Hall of Fame inductee never thought about anything but his work behind home plate. His handling of the Yankee pitching staff and its success over the years can never be minimized. "A catcher must want to catch," he said once.[23]

Colonel Jacob Ruppert was very disappointed in Gomez's less-than-scintillating 12–15 season. In fact, he tried to cut the lefthander's salary from $20,000 to $7,500. "Goofy" told him in his own inimitable style: "You keep the salary, I'll take the cut."[24]

Gomez, whose automobile license plate read GOOF, had an assortment of nicknames that he collected throughout his 14 years in the big leagues. These included "El Goofo," "Goofy," "Singular Senor," "The Happy Hidalgo," "Yankee Doodle Zany," "The Gay Castillian," and "The Gay Caballero."

The defending champion Tigers would provide only token competition to the Yankees in 1936 and then for only a short period of time. Detroit was destined to finish a distant nineteen and a half games off the pace behind New York. The Athletics, who had provided the Yankees with their most troublesome opponent for many years, were only a shadow of their former selves and would actually finish last in 1936, losing no fewer than 100 games in the process.

At no time was the A's fall from grace more evident than on May 24, 1936, when the Yankees crushed them, 25–2, in Philadelphia's Shibe Park. It was also a record-breaking game for Tony Lazzeri, who recorded the best day offensively he would ever lay claim to during his Hall of Fame career. The 33-year-old had now been relegated to hitting eighth in the powerful Yankee lineup after a decade in which he had hit no lower than sixth.

Yet on this day Lazzeri would show the world that he was far from done. He pounded out three home runs, two of them with the bases loaded—in the second and fifth innings respectively—and a third with two men on in the seventh. He also missed a fourth home run by inches in the eighth. He had to be content with a triple that scored two runners for a record eleven runs batted in, a mark that has never been broken in the American League.

Lazzeri's initial grand slam came off a 21-year-old right-hander, George Turbeville, who had walked the bases loaded. The South Carolinian tried to slip a 3–1 pitch past "Poosh 'Em Up" but the Yankee second baseman made it disappear over the right field fence.

Red Bullock, a 23-year-old left-hander, was Lazzeri's next victim in the fifth inning. In an almost *déjà vu* scenario, the young southpaw also had walked the bases full before Tony drilled it out of the reach of the A's outfielders.

Lazzeri led off the seventh inning and worked the count to 2–2 against another lefty, Woody Upchurch. Lazzeri bounced the next pitch off the roof of the left field stands and circled the bases for his third home run to give him nine RBI for the game at that point.

In the eighth inning with Upchurch still on the mound and two on, Lazzeri crushed a line drive that struck the top of the left field wall for a triple and his record tenth and eleventh runs batted in. A faster runner might have given him his fourth home run on the day.

To ice the cake during the rout, the Yankees hit three other home runs. And none other than the other two San Franciscans on the ball club supplied them. Rookie Joe DiMaggio smacked one and Frank Crosetti, not usually considered a slugger during his major league career, hit the other two.

In a doubleheader against the A's just the day before, Lazzeri had walloped three home runs, one in the first game and two more in the second. It took 66 years before that mark of six home runs in three games was matched. Alex Rodriguez of the Texas Rangers did it when he hit his sixth homer in three games on August 19, 2002, to tie the American League record originally set by "Poosh 'Em Up."

Since Lazzeri had hit another round tripper in the game before the doubleheader, the seven home runs that he had blasted in four consecutive games set a league record, as did the five he had hit in two consecutive games. These four games for Lazzeri gave notice that he was on his way to a much better season than the two previous so-so campaigns.

Following the eleven-RBI game, beat writer James P. Dawson of *The New York Times* wrote: "Lazzeri was almost mobbed when his triple gave him a new American League mark for runs batted in and at the conclusion of the game he had to fight his way through a cluster of autograph seekers, without police aid by the way, after 8,000 wildly enthusiastic fans suppressed the disappointment of being unable to see him in a chance to improve upon his mark."[25]

On June 14, McCarthy pulled off a trade that he felt would solidify his team even more. He sent Ben Chapman to Washington even up for Jake Powell. On the face of it, it appeared the Senators benefited far more than the Yankees in acquiring the talented Chapman. Although the swap drew heavy criticism from the press and fans alike, McCarthy didn't see it that way at all.

Chapman, though a natural, was not "Marse Joe's" kind of player. He was flaky, a hothead and argumentative, while the tough-minded, hard-nosed Powell did everything asked of him without question. Jake was immediately placed in left field as McCarthy moved DiMaggio to center, where he had more range than Powell and was to roam for the rest of his fabulous career. Coach Earle Combs, who had patrolled those pastures for 12 years, would see to it that DiMaggio would get to know every nook and cranny out there.

DiMaggio's popularity was awesome, particularly among the Italian-American fans that flocked to every ballpark in the league where he was scheduled to appear. In many ways it was similar to the hero-worship that "Poosh 'Em Up" had garnered a decade earlier. There were parties and dinners given in his honor just like Lazzeri had been accorded. Gifts awaited him wherever he went. DiMaggio's arrival in American League cities in 1936 was truly a "happening."

By the month of August, most of the teams in the American League had folded their tents and seemed to be playing out the string as the Yankee juggernaut rolled on. New York clinched the flag by September 9 to set a league record for the earliest date ever. The second place Tigers finished a distant nineteen and one-half games back.

The Yankees were a hitting machine in 1936. They scored 1,065 runs, the second highest total by a major league team in the twentieth century. They also set records for RBIs and total bases that still stand. Bill Dickey led the team in hitting in 1936 with that historic—for catchers—.362 average, while league MVP "Larrupin' Lou" Gehrig was not far behind at .354. The highly regarded DiMaggio lived up to his hype by batting .323, hitting 29 homers and driving in 125 runs. Gehrig's career-high 49 home runs led the league while the team as a whole hit an even .300, including 182 homers.

Lazzeri the only holdover besides Gehrig from Murderers Row, had his best season in five years, playing in 150 games, batting .287, hitting 14 home runs and driving in 109 runs. Red Rolfe, George Selkirk and Jake Powell also hit over .300. In addition to Gehrig, Lazzeri and DiMaggio, Dickey and Selkirk also drove in over 100 runs. The offensive numbers that season were truly astonishing and compared favorably to those put up by the 1927 squad.

The pitching, on the other hand, was not quite on a par with the club's hitting prowess, although the staff did allow the fewest runs in the AL. Red Ruffing won 20 games while newcomer Monte Pearson, who had been obtained from Cleveland after the previous season, was just one behind at 19. Bump Hadley chipped in with fourteen wins and Lefty Gomez added another thirteen, decidedly sub par for him. Even the perennial relievers, Johnny Murphy and Pat Malone, won twelve games each. Overall the Yankee relief corps turned in 21 saves, far more than any other team in the league.

After a hiatus of thirteen years, New York City was the setting of yet another "Subway Series," as the Yankees faced off against the neighboring Giants. Manager Bill Terry's Polo Grounders had finished five games in front of both the Cubs and Cardinals that year. The great lefthander with the dazzling screwball, Carl Hubbell, who was coming off a sensational 26–6, 2.31 earned run average season, led the Giants. Offensively, the 27-year-old future Hall of Famer Mel Ott and his 33 home runs and 135 runs batted in set the pace for the National Leaguers.

The first game of the Series was played at the Polo Grounds during intermittent rainfalls. The 33-year-old Hubbell dueled the 32-year-old Ruffing and both went the distance. The Yankees drew first blood when George Selkirk homered off Hubbell in the top of the third. The Giants tied it in the home half of the fifth when shortstop Dick Bartell smacked one of Ruffing's offerings into the left field stands.

Powell touched up Hubbell for base hits in his first three trips to the plate, but beyond that and Selkirk's solo home run, the remainder of the Yankee lineup was unable to solve Hubbell. The screwballer fanned eight and allowed just three other hits besides Powell's three and Selkirk's home run.

The home team pushed over another run in the sixth to take the lead for good, breaking it open with four in the eighth to win 6–1. Amazingly, not one Giant outfielder had a chance in the game.

In Game Two, attended by President Franklin D. Roosevelt, the Yankees roared back and set a World Series record by scoring 18 runs with every man in their lineup delivering at least one hit. Lazzeri cracked a grand slam homer — only the second player in Series history to do so — while Dickey socked one with two on. Both players knocked in five runs each in the 17-hit attack to establish a new Series record, one of which was already held by "Poosh 'Em Up." Lazzeri was the first player in 16 years to hit a World Series bases-loaded home run. Elmer Smith of the Indians had accomplished a similar feat in the 1920 World Series against the Dodgers.

Hal Schumacher, who started for the Giants, was chased after only two innings, and the Yankees ran off to a 9–1 lead after only three innings. Lefty Gomez gave up only six hits as he pitched the entire game, an 18–4 victory that tied the Series at a game apiece. This was the famous game in which Gomez ignored a hitter as he watched an airplane fly overhead, while Manager Joe McCarthy seethed silently on the Yankee bench.

Moving across the Harlem River to Yankee Stadium for the next three games, Freddie Fitzsimmons started for the Giants against the ex–Senator

Bump Hadley in Game Three. Although the Giants pounded out eleven hits, they were only able to score one run. The Yankees won it, 2–1, to take the Series lead, two games to one.

The Yankees jumped out to an early 1–0 lead in the bottom of the second when Gehrig smacked one into the right field seats. After Jimmy Ripple of the visitors tied the game with a home run in the top of the fifth, Frank Crosetti broke the tie by singling Powell home in the bottom of the eighth. Hadley went eight innings for the victory while the ex–Cub Pat Malone saved it for him by shutting down the Giants in the ninth.

Hubbell was Terry's choice to start Game Four while McCarthy countered with the former Indian, Monte Pearson. Gehrig reached Hubbell for a two-run homer in the bottom of the third to give the Yankees a 4–0 lead after three innings. Crosetti, who had doubled, scored on a single by Red Rolfe. Pearson pitched all the way and the Yankees were now up by a commanding three games to one.

The Giants, however, did not roll over and die. They came back in Game Five to win, 5–4, in ten innings. Schumacher pitched all ten innings while Ruffing, who started for the Yankees, gave way to Malone after six innings.

The Giants went up 3–0 in the first inning by virtue of three RBI singles, but the Yankees narrowed the gap single runs in the second and third innings. The Giants picked up another run in the top of the sixth to go ahead briefly. However, the Yankees came back to tie it in the bottom half of the sixth with a run of their own.

The game remained tied at 4–4 until the tenth inning, when the Giants tallied the go-ahead run. Malone was charged with the loss when Jo Jo Moore's double, Dick Bartell's sacrifice bunt and a sacrifice fly by player-manager Bill Terry won it for the Giants, 5–4. Schumacher, who pitched heroically throughout, and the Giants were victorious when pinch runner Bob "Suitcase" Seeds, who represented the tying run, was thrown out trying to steal second in the bottom half of the tenth.

Returning to the Polo Grounds for Game Six, Freddie Fitzsimmons started for the Giants against Lefty Gomez. Neither pitcher was particularly sharp; Fitzsimmons pitched into the fourth and Gomez lasted until the seventh. The Yankees led 6–5 going into the ninth and broke it wide open with a seven-run flourish from five hits and four walks. The Yankees were champions of the world once again thanks to a second 17-hit salvo.

It was the last appearance as a player for future Hall of Famer Bill Terry. The Giants manager who claimed that the Yankees had bought themselves a cripple when they purchased Joe DiMaggio changed his tune after seeing the young man in action against his Giants. "That club has everything," Terry exclaimed. "They're the toughest club I've ever faced. I always heard that one player could make the difference between a lousy team and a winner, and I never believed it. Now I know it's true."[26]

Lazzeri and Gehrig tied for the RBI lead in the series with seven each. Gehrig had now boosted his RBI totals in Series play to 31 in 25 games. Powell, the mid-season acquisition from the Senators, led all batters with a .455 average and ten hits.

Rolfe, who batted .400, also had ten hits while the much-heralded rookie DiMaggio hit .346. The lone shining light for the Giants was Hubbell, whose performance in Game One had snapped the Yankees' twelve-game winning streak in World Series competition.

Colonel Jacob Ruppert could not contain his joy and neither could Ed Barrow, who set out to join scout Paul Krichell on a hunting trip. Meanwhile, Manager Joe McCarthy was acclaimed as the number one manager in all of baseball. The Yankees, the team literally within walking distance of the Giants, clearly owned the "braggin' rights" in New York in 1936.

The success of the 1936 New York Yankees would prove to be the forerunner of the most amazing record in professional sports. For from then on to 1964, the club would win 22 American League pennants and 16 World Series, the most protracted period of domination in the history of professional sports in this country.

Apparently all was not well in the Tony Lazzeri household that winter, however. Tony and his wife, Maye, were apparently experiencing difficulties in the thirteenth year of their marriage. The problems boiled over into a suit for divorce that Tony himself had filed and then withdrew on December 8. An Associated Press story simply stated that "the Yankees' second baseman, at home with Mrs. Lazzeri and their 5-year-old son, said 'It's all a big mistake.'"[27]

To anyone's knowledge, the couple remained together for the rest of Tony's life since there was never any hint that the subject of separation or divorce surfaced again. At least no public pronouncement on the matter was ever made concerning the Lazzeris and their private life together.

When Tony Lazzeri arrived in New York City on February 2, 1937, he settled his wife and son in at the Concourse Plaza Hotel in the Bronx just a block away from Yankee Stadium and the club's offices. Tony was in town to attend the Baseball Writers Association Dinner and to receive their annual award as the most outstanding player of the past season. Also scheduled to receive a plaque at the same dinner was former Giants infielder Travis Jackson, for being a player whose contributions over the years had been most beneficial to the game of baseball.

Lazzeri told the press at the dinner that he was by no means satisfied with the contract that General Manager Ed Barrow had mailed out to him over the winter. He believed his play warranted a substantial increase over the $12,000 he had been making since 1931. He had a meeting with Barrow the next day to discuss the situation at length.

At the dinner, Tony said happily that Myril Hoag, the fleet-footed Yankee reserve outfielder who had suffered a serious head injury the previous season in Detroit, had recovered completely. He also told those covering the event that Hoag, a neighbor of his from nearby Davis, California, was set to fight for a regular berth come spring training. Lazzeri also reported that his fellow San Franciscans, Joe DiMaggio and Frank Crosetti, were in excellent shape and primed to start the season in their quest for a second consecutive World Series championship.

Tony let it slip that he and Yankee management were about $4,000 apart in their negotiations to date. The 33-year-old second baseman ultimately signed a new contract on February 6, 1937. It would be the last contract he would sign with the Yankees.

When asked about the terms of the new deal, it was reported that the club's owner, Colonel Jacob Ruppert, said in the presence of Lazzeri: "We compromised—but Tony got the better of it."[28] Although neither side would disclose the final figure, reporters speculated that Tony received another $1,000 a season to raise his annual salary to $13,000. It was a far cry from the $4,000 he was seeking, but all he really wanted to do was play baseball, and to do that he had to sign a contract.

Now in his twelfth season with the Yankees, Lazzeri was showing signs of slowing down. His reflexes were not as quick as they used to be and, to make matters worse, 22-year-old Joe Gordon was making a name for himself across the Hudson River in Newark with the AAA Bears. Gordon had been a shortstop but Joe McCarthy converted him into a second baseman. A right-handed hitter with above average power, Gordon would, in time, prove to be a slick fielder around the bag as well.

Tommy Henrich, who was a rookie right fielder with the Yankees in 1937, admired Lazzeri immensely. In his book, *Five O'Clock Lightning*, Henrich wrote of him: "Lazzeri typified the Yankee emphasis on toughness and a professional attitude. He was an epileptic, but you'd never know it. On the field he was as tough as any of the rest of us, or tougher.

"He said he had been looking forward to the challenge of playing the Indians in what was still an important series at that stage of the season. He felt the Indians had approached the games with a defeatist attitude, and Lazzeri, always the competitor, was disappointed that Cleveland didn't give the Yankees more of a battle. The Indians finished in fifth place."[29]

9. Return to Paradise (1936–1937)

Someone else might have paid little attention to Joe Gordon during the club's training camp in St. Petersburg in 1937. Not Lazzeri. An hour after Gordon arrived in camp, there was Tony showing the young man who was destined to take his job the little tricks of playing the bag. Tony even taught Joe how to break his wrist (baseball jargon for getting snap into one's swing) when batting.

Normally Lazzeri would have left a rookie alone if he didn't seek his advice. In this case, the relationship between Lazzeri and Gordon was idyllic. Joe had been highly touted as a natural and Tony could have easily ignored him, but Lazzeri was determined to see to it that Gordon succeeded.

Harold Burr, writing in the March 1939 issue of *Baseball Digest*, described the scene of two years earlier thusly:

> And there's Tony Lazzeri and Joe Gordon. The old Yankee second baseman loves baseball passionately. Even today, after twelve years steadily in the big leagues on hard infield dirt, the Terror of Telegraph Hill still insists that he has several more years left to him. He was always a throwback to the old warrior days of give-and-take. John McGraw and Hank Chance would have liked Tony Lazzeri at the midway.
>
> But Tony kept up with the changing times. If a rookie didn't want his advice, he would leave him severely alone and he was a relentless bench jockey. He could have ignored the rookie [Gordon] and nobody would have censured him for it. Gordon had rushed up through the Yankee farms to a fanfare of trumpets. On all sides he was hailed as a natural. In his old courageous heart Lazzeri knew that the arrival of Gordon doomed him and his fat World Series checks that might have kept coming in for years if Gordon had failed. But Tony saw to it that he didn't fail.[30]

The Yankees were established as overwhelming favorites to repeat in 1937 and rightly so. After breaking camp in late March and heading north, the team took about a month into the season before it got untracked.

The Tigers and White Sox stayed close to the Yankees for a while but Detroit was devastated by a season- and career-ending injury to its great catcher, Mickey Cochrane, on May 25 at Yankee Stadium. "Black Mike," as he was called, had run the count to three balls and one strike against Bump Hadley when the next pitch sailed up and in tight.

Cochrane evidently lost sight of the ball in his line of vision. The ball struck his temple and he went down unconscious. With his skull fractured in three places, he remained that way for ten days before regaining consciousness. He never played again.

Yet even if the Tigers had the benefit of Cochrane in their lineup all year long, there was little likelihood that they would have caught up to the

Yankees that season. The New Yorkers had moved into first place two days before the Cochrane beaning and never looked back. Although Cochrane recovered, he had played in his last major league game.

The Yankees' thundering herd never slowed down in 1937, not with the kind of career years that most of their players were having. Despite injuries to George Selkirk — a broken collarbone — and Jake Powell's illness for much of the year, the rookie Henrich and the veteran Myril Hoag stepped up their games as they flanked DiMaggio in right and left fields respectively.

Hoag had languished on the team's bench for five years before getting his big break and he made the most of it by hitting .301. The left-handed hitting Henrich, beginning a fabulous career with the Yankees at the age of 24, batted a resounding .320 in the 67 games in which he appeared. He was a very dangerous clutch hitter throughout his career and would later be nicknamed "Old Reliable" by famed Yankees broadcaster Mel Allen.

"Joe D" was on his way to another mammoth year by leading the league in home runs with 46, batting .346 and driving in 167 runs. Lou Gehrig was not to be outdone by the second year man as he hit .351, banged out 37 homers and drove in 159 runs. George Selkirk hit 18 home runs and drove in 78 runs and would have done better if injuries hasn't limited him to 78 games.

Lou Gehrig and Frank Crosetti continued to be as good defensively as always. Red Rolfe, now an All-Star, had firmly established himself as the best third baseman in the American League now. Rolfe, who would enjoy a ten-year career with the Yankees, never played again after serving in the military in World War II. He later managed the Tigers from 1949 to 1952 before returning to his alma mater, Dartmouth College, where he coached the baseball team from 1954 to 1967. The field there was later named for him.

Only Lazzeri slipped from what he had once been, with a career-low .244 batting average coming off only 109 hits in 1937. Although he hit 14 home runs, he only managed to drive in 70 runs, the second lowest total in his twelve-year run with the Yankees. Bill Dickey had his usual solid year with a .332 batting average, 29 home runs and 129 runs batted in.

The pitching was superb as Lefty Gomez compiled one of his best years ever. He posted a 21–11 won-lost mark while amassing the American League's lowest earned run average, 2.33, as well as its highest number of shutouts, six. Red Ruffing was 20–7 and a rookie right-hander, Spud Chandler, up from Newark, and veterans Bump Hadley and Monte Pearson, shored up the starting rotation.

Johnny Murphy, with 13 victories and ten saves, was now being called

"The Fireman" for his ability to put out fires for the ball club at any time during a game. He was being recognized as the game's premier reliever. "Grandma" was now saving so many games for Gomez that the newspapers began referring to the "Gomez-Murphy wins."[31]

Although suffering through his worst season yet as a Yankee, Lazzeri refused to give in to the constant reports that he was going to be replaced by Joe Gordon at the earliest possible opportunity. He continued to play hard and displayed his greatness, if only at times, during the regular season.

Returning from the club's first western road trip, Lazzeri complained to sportswriter Frank Graham about his lack of hitting. Graham recalled that Tony "was the only one who had gumption enough to grumble."[32] Graham claimed the other players just sat there in the clubhouse holding their heads.

"I can't get a hit to save my life," Tony said. "Even when I do get hold of a ball, I hit it on a line right at somebody."[33]

An injury to his throwing hand in late August shelved Lazzeri not only for the remainder of the month but also most of September. After nine days on the bench, the veteran second baseman unleashed a bombshell of a statement to *The New York Times*. Lazzeri told the newspaper that he intended to retire as a player after the season ended provided he could get a job as a manager, preferably in the American League. Obviously, the remark left the door wide open for Yankee management to move swiftly with their plans to bring Joe Gordon up permanently in 1938 to replace Lazzeri.

Tony's retirement had long been rumored. The ball club felt that his skills had eroded to the point where it had become necessary for Manager Joe McCarthy to rest him occasionally. Now with the injury to his right hand, the press speculated about his future with the Yankees, and Lazzeri himself decided it was time to discuss the matter openly with the press.

In the September 5, 1937, edition of *The New York Times*, a staff correspondent quoted Tony Lazzeri as saying: "I will see Mr. Barrow after the World Series and discuss the situation with him. They all have to quit some time and if my days are done I want to quit playing without delay.

"The idea of being an emergency man doesn't appeal to me and I would not be attracted by a proposition to manage a minor league club. If there is no manager's job for me in the major leagues, I'll retire from the game and keep myself occupied with some other line."[34]

Of course, Tony had no idea what occupation he would be attracted to once his baseball career came to an end. Although he still had his boilermaker's union card, he surely had not planned to return to the foundry life. Baseball was all he knew and all he cared about. He was certain that someone would be calling to inquire about his services.

Lazzeri also took the occasion to deny that he had been offered the managerial position of the Cleveland Indians if and when Steve O'Neill, its popular skipper, left. Newspaper reports had bandied Tony's name about in connection with that job during the season and he used this interview to quell such unfounded speculation.

An incident that took place late in the campaign shows that Lazzeri had not lost his sense of humor. In a meaningless game played at Philadelphia's Shibe Park on September 29, 1937, Tony decided to pull a prank on Athletics outfielder "Indian Bob" Johnson, also a fan of the practical joke. Johnson, the team's top slugger, had hit at least 21 home runs in his first nine seasons in the big leagues and was one of the American League's most feared batters.

It has been said that Tony worked on the prank for about two weeks before it took place. He doctored a baseball by pounding it with a bat, soaking it in soapy water and rubbing dirt into it before coating it with white shoe polish to make it resemble an ordinary baseball. The result was that the ball was as "dead as a doornail"; it would look like a regular baseball when thrown but drop like a dead weight when hit.

On the day of the game, the Yankees had already clinched the pennant and were twelve games ahead of the second place Tigers. The A's were playing out the schedule en route to another disastrous seventh place finish, a distant 46½ games behind the frontrunning Yankees. The game itself was considered so unimportant that neither manager, Joe McCarthy or Connie Mack, showed up for it.

In an inning when Johnson was due to bat, Lazzeri ran out to second base with the doctored ball in his pocket. As "Indian Bob" stepped into the batter's box, Tony went out to the mound and switched balls with pitcher Kemp Wicker. Wicker promptly grooved a pitch right down the middle and Johnson took a huge swing at the ball, hitting it as solidly as he could. Instead of towering into the outfield, the ball was fouled off the grandstand screen with a thud as the bewildered Johnson stood at home plate. The players in both dugouts and the crowd howled with laughter.

Here's Tommy Henrich's version of what happened next, from his book:

> Our bat boy, Timmy Sullivan, retrieved the ball immediately and brought it back to our dugout without giving the home plate umpire, Bill Summers, the chance to decide whether to keep the ball in the game.
>
> Billy Werber, the A's third baseman, comes charging out of the dugout and starts arguing about the ball. Johnson, in the meantime, turns to Sum-

mers and asks in disbelief, 'What was that?' The ball just didn't look right to Johnson, and Werber smelled something fishy.

Summers quickly puts two and two together and calls out to Lazzeri at second base, "Give me the ball."

Lazzeri gets the look of innocence on his face and says, "What ball?" Tony didn't have it. The batboy had it in the dugout.

Then we found out what Summers suspected: Lazzeri was guilty of conspiracy. Before the game he had taken a ball and rubbed it with soot from the ground below Yankee Stadium so that it was black. By the eighth inning, with darkness creeping in, no hitter was going to be able to see a black baseball until the pitch was past him, and that's exactly what happened.

Summers didn't count the pitch. To make matters worse for him, he had to write a report to the league office.[35]

Twenty-five years later, Summers claimed that he immediately knew what had happened, because he saw the ball stuck in Lazzeri's pocket when Lazzeri turned around. Summers said that he ruled the foul ball a valid strike even though Wicker had clearly thrown an illegal pitch by using a tampered baseball. Thereupon, he overruled the protests of Johnson and his teammates to protect Lazzeri and the American League.

Nevertheless, *The New York Times* contradicted Summers' rendition in its game report on the following day:

> Tony Lazzeri and the left-hander Kemp Wicker, whose pitching had the protection of a 16-hit assault on enemy hurlers in the opener, were the parties to the comedy which promises to bring censure or penalty from President Will Harridge of the American League. As Bob Johnson opened the eighth inning, Wicker tossed up a muddied ball instead of the shiny new ball put into play by Umpire Johnny Quinn.
>
> Johnson fouled off the pitch back of the plate amid a guffaw from the 4,425 fans and dignified silence from the umpires. The game was held up, the foul strike was ruled out by Quinn, and on a suggestion from the Athletic' bench, Umpire Bill Summers ran out to Lazzeri and extracted the ball that should have been play from the veteran's pocket.
>
> It all passed off innocently enough, as viewed from the stands, and the crowd had a good laugh, although the umpires seemed to be doing some snappy criticizing on the field.
>
> Between games, however, it developed that an official report will be made of the incident. Umpire Quinn will call to [American League] President Harridge's attention a violation of the rule covering tampering with the ball."[36]

The *Times* article brings into question certain details presented as fact, particularly by Bill Summers. It appears that he was not the home plate umpire that day — Johnny Quinn was. Summers worked the second game of the twin bill behind the plate, not the opener. Summers apparently also didn't immediately recognize what had really occurred, at least not until the A's bench suggested he check Lazzeri's pocket for the real ball. Also, the foul ball that Johnson hit did not count as a strike. Quinn voided the pitch as soon as he figured out that it had been made with a doctored ball.

It also appears that the umpires did not cover for Lazzeri. Quinn stated that he would file a report with the American League office to indicate that Lazzeri broke the rule about tampering with a game ball. Since no follow up article in the *Times* ever appeared indicating that Lazzeri had been punished for the offense, there is no reason to believe that "Poosh 'Em Up's" prank was ever considered enough of a violation to warrant a censure.

When all was said and done in the 1937 regular season, the Tigers were again runners up to the Yankees, this time by another large gap—13 games. The New York club's 102 victories matched the total they had posted in the previous season. The Yankees featured three 100-RBI men in their lineup: Joe DiMaggio with 167; Lou Gehrig with 159; and Bill Dickey with 133 for a whopping total of 459 for the trio. For Gehrig it would mark the last great year the "Iron Horse" would turn in before falling victim to amyotrophic lateral sclerosis.

For the second successive year, Bill Terry's Giants, who had edged out the Cubs by two games in a tight National League race, would provide the opposition in the World Series. Just as in the 1936 series, both club's aces—Lefty Gomez (22–11) for the Yankees and Carl Hubbell (22–8) for the Giants—were the starting pitchers in Game One, this time at Yankee Stadium. Hubbell was narrowly getting the best of Gomez, 1–0, going into the bottom of the sixth. It was then that all hell broke loose and the Yankees' vaunted "Five O'clock Lightning" struck for seven runs to rout the Giants' "Meal Ticket." Tony Lazzeri put the icing on the cake with a bases empty homer off Al Smith to nail down the 8–1 win.

In Game Two at the Stadium, the Yankees won again, 8–1, behind Red Ruffing. Rookie Cliff Melton (20–9) had started for the Giants and was sent to the showers in the sixth when the Yankees added four runs to the two they had scored in the fifth. The home club logged on two more in the eighth to complete the rout. Selkirk drove in three of the Yankee runs while good-hitting pitcher Ruffing helped his own cause by getting two hits himself—one a two run double—and three runs batted in.

When the Series shifted to Polo Grounds for Game Three, Monte Pearson (9–3) opposed Hal Schumacher (13–12) of the Giants. The Yankees pecked away at Schumacher for one run in the second, two more in the third and singletons in the fourth and fifth before Melton relieved him in the sixth. The big hit was a triple by Bill Dickey, as neither team home-

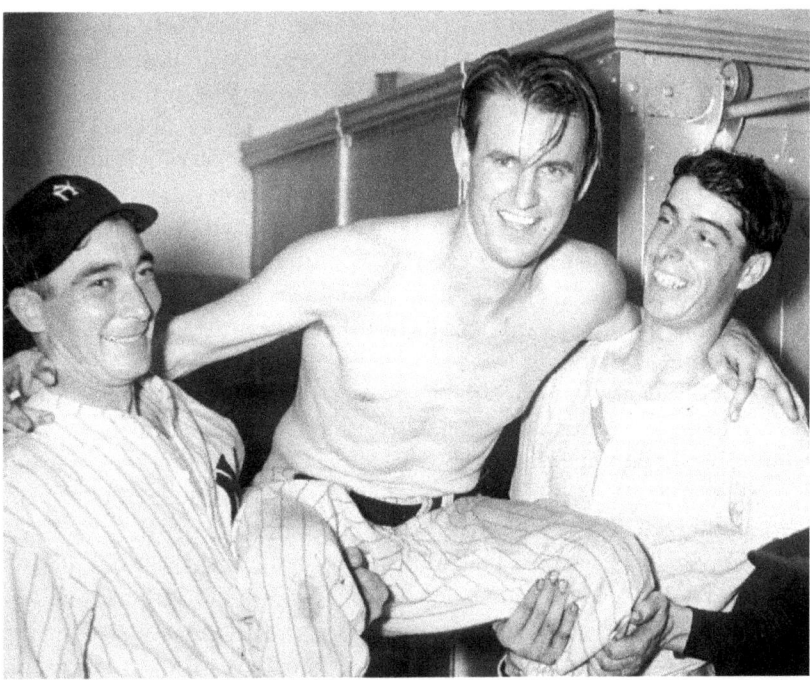

Still another San Francisco connection, from left to right, Tony Lazzeri, Lefty Gomez and Joe DiMaggio celebrate the Yankees' 1937 World Series victory over the neighboring Giants. (Transcendental Graphics, Mark Rucker)

red for the second game in a row. Joe McCarthy had to call on Johnny Murphy to bail out Pearson in the ninth after the Giants loaded the bases.

Now down three games to none, the Giants sent Hubbell out to start against Bump Hadley (11–8). The screwballer did not let his ball club down; he pitched the Polo Grounders to a complete game 7–3 win. The Giants erupted for six runs in the second inning, as the Yankees brought in Ivy Andrews to relieve Hadley. Center fielder Hank Leiber began the rally for the Giants with a base hit. Later in the same inning, he capped it off with a two-run single.

It was the last World Series game in which future Hall of Famer Hubbell would ever pitch. He surrendered a ninth inning home run to Gehrig, which marked Gehrig's last four-bagger in a World Series.

The Yankees dispatched their ace, Gomez, out to try to wrap up the Series. The left-hander came through with a complete game 4–2 win at the Polo Grounds. For Gomez, it brought his Series pitching record to a perfect 5–0. Melton, who started for the Giants, lasted through five innings and was tagged with his second loss of the Series.

Myril Hoag had given the Yankees a brief 1–0 lead when he rapped out a solo second inning home run. Mel Ott proceeded to lift the Giants into a temporary 2–1 lead by hitting a two-run homer in the bottom of the third.

The Yankees tied it in the fifth when Lazzeri smacked a leadoff 485-foot triple over Leiber's head. Gomez, normally a notoriously bad hitter, lined a hit off of second baseman Burgess Whitehead's glove as Lazzeri raced home with what proved to be the winning run. Thereupon the visitors took a lead that they would not relinquish. Gehrig doubled Gomez home with an insurance run and the southpaw kept the Giants at bay for the rest of the game.

The Series victory gave the Yankees a record sixth world championship to break the tie they had shared until then with the Athletics. Overall the "Bronx Bombers" hit a sub-par .249 in the Series, but Lazzeri's .400 led all batsmen. It appeared as if he was certain that his days with the team were numbered and he willed himself to go out in a flourish.

"Poosh 'Em Up's" fine play in the Series both offensively and defensively did not escape the notice of the Cubs' owner, Phil Wrigley. Following a meeting between Wrigley and Ed Barrow, the Yankees approached Lazzeri on his willingness to accept a release and make his way to Chicago.

Tony, reluctant to leave New York but knowing full well that Joe Gordon was to be the Yankees' second baseman in 1938, agreed. The club promptly secured waivers on the twelve-year veteran and an unconditional release was mailed to him at his home in Millbrae, California, by Colonel Ruppert.

Along with the release, Ruppert wrote:

> My Dear Tony: We have received word from a reliable source that you have a chance to sign with a major league club either as a coach or assistant manager. With this in mind, the New York club is hereby granting you your unconditional release. All American and National League clubs have waived claim to your services.
>
> While we are taking this step with keen regret, we are doing it in keeping with the promise we made to you some time ago, in appreciation of your long and faithful service.
>
> Wherever your future endeavors may lead, please believe that the best wishes of the Yankee organization and myself will follow you. As soon as this letter reaches you, please wire acknowledgement. With every good wish for your health and happiness of your family and yourself, Jacob Ruppert, President.[37]

In point of fact, the Cubs signed Lazzeri to a generous contract plus a bonus. "What I really am trying to do," Wrigley admitted, "is to capture some of that Yankee spirit I admire so much. It seems to me that for a long time Lazzeri has typified that spirit, and I am sure he can impart it to our players."[38]

With Lazzeri's departure, only Lou Gehrig remained from the fabled 1927 Murderers' Row team.

Regardless of the circumstances leading up to Tony Lazzeri's release, Yankee fans and followers of the game in general were taken by surprise. Many felt Lazzeri would get a reprieve because he led both teams in batting in the World Series. Nonetheless, the Yankees and Tony himself had made up their minds to turn the page. The time had come to move on from his illustrious career in New York.

Or had it? On October 18, owner Phil Wrigley announced to the press that Lazzeri had accepted an invitation to come to Chicago for a conference relative to his signing on with the National League team. However, Lazzeri, from his home in Millbrae, California, proclaimed, "it's all news to me."[39]

In his statement, Wrigley declined to say whether Lazzeri would be offered the Cub manager's job in 1939, the year after Charlie Grimm's contract ran out. Although Tony agreed with the owner that he was not slated to take over as the team's manager any time soon, it appeared that he was going to play some hardball with his new club.

"I have no intention right now of going east," he said from his California home. "I don't know a thing about what Wrigley says. It's all news to me. Besides, why should I leave? I like to play golf around here. Don't you think I deserve it?"[40]

At the same time other rumors began to circulate. One had Lazzeri receiving an offer from St. Louis Browns' owner Donald Barnes to manage their ball club. The situation regarding Steve O'Neill's status as manager of the Indians and Tony's possible interest in that job once again surfaced. And finally, player-coach Gabby Hartnett, the Cubs' second in command, was mentioned in trade talks with the Boston Bees, whereby he would become the manager in Boston, and leave an opening for Lazzeri to take over as Grimm's right-hand man in Chicago.

Wrigley, who had never met Lazzeri but had admired his aggressiveness and intelligence from afar, finally got to sit down with him in Chicago on October 28. After a brief one-hour meeting, Tony signed a one-year contract with the ball club as a player-coach. Wrigley, determined to get his Cubs back into the World Series, believed that Lazzeri would be a catalyst to help lead them there. He said that "Poosh 'Em Up" was joining the ball with Charlie Grimm's enthusiastic approval.

"This is just what I wanted," Lazzeri said. "I will be ready to play any time the Cubs need me, and I want to learn about this coaching business. It's a great opportunity. It will add a lot to my baseball future and gives me a start toward reaching my goal, a managing job.

"It will seem kind of strange not to be with the Yankees again. Twelve years is a long time to spend with one club. But I feel just like I'm starting all over again. I get a kick out of that."[41]

Lazzeri had indeed moved on from his long Yankee and American League career. Although he and his wife, Maye, who had accompanied him on the trip, had planned to stay in Chicago for two days, they left that same evening. A celebration in San Francisco in his honor as well as his now-former Yankee teammates, Joe DiMaggio and Frank Crosetti, awaited them.

At Lazzeri's departure from New York, *New York Times* columnist Arthur Daley wrote that Tony Lazzeri was "a truly great performer, a long ball hitter and a money player almost without equal. He was truly the pivot on which Yankee pennant hopes spun."[42]

Teammates like Frank Crosetti told writer Harry Jupiter of the *San Francisco Chronicle*: "Tony was a great man, not just a great player. A leader and a great ballplayer with the guts of a burglar. There was nothing he couldn't do."[43]

10

The End Draws Near (1938–1943)

As someone who was accustomed to playing regularly throughout his major league career, Tony Lazzeri must have known in his heart of hearts that he was destined to become nothing more than a utility infielder with the 1938 Cubs. For the previous six seasons, Billy Herman had been firmly entrenched as that club's second baseman. The future Hall of Famer had batted well over .300 in five of those seasons.

Herman did not wield the kind of power that Lazzeri was capable of delivering, nor was he capable of driving in runs the way that the ex–Yankee could. Batting in the second spot behind the club's reliable leadoff man, third baseman Stan Hack, he was expected to do the little things to help the Cubs score runs—sacrifice bunt, hit-and-run, or just about anything he could do to move the runners along. Billy Herman had delivered in those areas consistently well.

More to his advantage was the fact that he was also five years Lazzeri's junior and at 29 he was just reaching his peak. Herman was also coming off a year in which he batted .335 while "Poosh 'Em Up" had experienced his poorest regular season ever in the big leagues.

Although Tony would have his moments with the Cubs in 1938, he only played in 54 games and batted .267 that season. Most of the games in which he started, however, had him at shortstop and not second base. And his starts usually took place when the ball club's regular shortstop, Billy Jurges, needed a breather. Lazzeri played in seven games at third (where his fielding average was a rather anemic .833), once in the outfield and only four games at his regular second base position.

One of the games in which Lazzeri demonstrated his old spark left took place early in the campaign against the Brooklyn Dodgers in Wrigley

Field. Playing shortstop and hitting cleanup on the afternoon of May 12, Tony was a perfect four-for-four with a walk. He also drove in five runs as the Cubs went on to win the ball game that day by a score of 9–5.

Such performances, though, were few and far between and Lazzeri, like the rest of his teammates, went through a rather tempestuous season in 1938. But through it all, he remained always the professional, never displaying any outward signs of bitterness toward the organization for his predicament.

Though Tony Lazzeri had left New York, he remained enormously popular in the city where he had contributed so much to the success of the Yankees over the previous 12 years. So although he was now in Chicago, he maintained a presence in the city with an advertisement for a breakfast cereal called Huskies.

Long before famous athletes were to be seen everywhere in television commercials, they were incorporated into comic strip ads that appeared in each week's colorful Sunday newspaper "funnies" section. Many of the athletes would be chosen from the ranks of the Yankees due to their continuing success as champions of the baseball world.

Stars like Lou Gehrig, for example, who would tout a popular cigarette brand of the day, was featured as a hero in a comic strip story that would be drawn with a fictitious adventure theme. The superstar would ultimately emerge in some heroic manner. All would be attributable to the particular product he would be promoting in the hopes that readers would be enticed into buying it.

In Tony Lazzeri's case, he appeared as the hero of a strip in the May 15, 1938, edition of the *New York Daily News*, which at the time was the most widely circulated daily newspaper in the country. In this particular strip, Lazzeri was depicted as an individual who would single-handedly run a bloodthirsty jungle beast out of town simply because he ate his Huskies every morning.

However, while Lazzeri wore a Cub uniform that season, all was not well between Cub ownership and its once-popular manager, Charlie Grimm. It all came to an unpleasant head after the 81st game of the season on July 20 when "Jolly Cholly" was abruptly let go despite having managed the team to a respectable 45–36 record.

The winning record was not good enough for Phil Wrigley, who replaced Grimm with still another favorite of his, 37-year-old National League all-star catcher Gabby Hartnett. The Hall of Famer-to-be guided the Cubs to a marvelous 44–27 record during the remainder of the season, leading them into the World Series once again. None of this appeared to have any particular relevance to Tony Lazzeri, who continued to play as sparingly under Hartnett as he had under Grimm.

10. The End Draws Near (1938–1943)

For the first time in 13 big league seasons, Lazzeri, as a member of the 1938 Cubs, wore a uniform other than the Yankee pinstripes. (National Baseball Hall of Fame Library, Cooperstown, N.Y.)

Lazzeri did play a significant role in the famed "Homer in the Gloamin'" game at Wrigley Field in the waning days of the season. The game took place on Saturday, September 28, and the Cubs' opponents were the front-running Pittsburgh Pirates, who were faltering at the time. Meanwhile the Cubs had won eight straight and 17 of their previous 20 games.

Going into the contest, the second of a three-game series, Chicago was a slim half-game behind the Pirates after breathing down their necks for the previous two and a half months. With the Corsairs up, 5–3, in the bottom of the eighth, Ripper Collins led off the inning for the Cubs with a single, his third hit of the afternoon. Although the Pirates' starter, Bob Klinger, had pitched a fine game up until then, his manager, Pie Traynor, felt that his pitcher was spent. Traynor opted to replace Klinger with a sidearming fast baller named Bill Swift.

After Swift walked Billy Jurges, the pitcher's spot was due up so Hartnett called upon Lazzeri to pinch-hit. With runners on first and second and nobody out, Tony was asked to bunt them over into scoring position. His first attempt to do so trickled foul, as did his second try. With the bunt sign taken off, Lazzeri was given a sign to hit away.

"Poosh 'Em Up" promptly drilled the next pitch on a line to right field where Paul Waner was unable to flag it down. Collins scored to pull the Cubs within one run of the Pirates. Meanwhile, Billy Jurges made it all the way to third as Lazzeri pulled up at second with a ringing double. There was still no one out.

With the tying and potential go-ahead runs in scoring position, Hartnett did not want to take a chance on Lazzeri's lack of speed so he sent in reserve outfielder Joe Marty to run for the 13-year veteran. A few years earlier in his career, no one would have dared to replace Tony with a pinch runner. However, the ravages of time had slowed Lazzeri down to the point where such a move had to be made.

Traynor then ordered Stan Hack, the Cubs' best hitter that year, to be intentionally walked to fill the bases and set up a potential force play at any base. Billy Herman spoiled Traynor's plans by slapping a single through the infield to score Jurges with the tying run.

At the same time, Marty ignored third base coach Red Corrigan's sign to hold up and the pinch runner raced for home. However, Waner ran the ball down and made a great throw to nail Marty at the plate. It was a reckless play on Marty's part since there were still none out and he could have scored easily thereafter either on a sacrifice fly or groundout.

Traynor then called for his ace reliever, Mace Brown, to come in and preserve order. The right-hander, who was having a sensational season winning 15 games, all in relief, did just that. Brown induced the next Cub batter to hit into a double play ball to end the rally with the score tied at 5–5.

As the darkness descended rapidly upon the playing field, it was

10. The End Draws Near (1938–1943)

becoming increasingly difficult to see. The umpires got together and conferred on just how much longer they would allow the game to continue. Plate umpire George Barr informed both managers that they would permit the game to go on for just one more inning. The Cub pitching staff was already strained to the limit and the home club wished to avoid playing a Sunday doubleheader to end the season.

The Pirates were held scoreless in the top of the ninth, coming up with just a lone single for their efforts. With two out and none on in the bottom half of the inning, player-manager Hartnett remained his team's last hope. Brown got ahead in the count 0–2 with two consecutive curveballs.

However, Hartnett got good wood on the third pitch — yet another curve — and barely deposited it into the darkening left-field bleachers to earn Chicago a 6–5 win that the press would label "The Homer in the Gloamin.'" The bedlam that took place thereafter engulfed Hartnett, who had to fight his way through the swirling, hysterical mob that had poured onto the field. Only help from his players and the ushers allowed the manager to escape without injury into the dugout.

In their book *Baseball, Chicago Style,* veteran sportswriters Jerome Holtzman and George Vass claimed that many in the crowd and some players had lost sight of the ball in the dusk, that is everyone but Hartnett. "A lot of people told me they didn't know the ball was in the bleachers," Hartnett said. "Well, I did. I knew the minute I hit it.

"I swung with everything I had and then I got that feeling, the kind of feeling you get when the blood rushes out of your head and you get dizzy."[1]

The victory allowed Chicago to slip past Pittsburgh into first place by a half-game. The Cubs would hang onto their newfound lead as the season ended with their tenth straight win to make them National League champions for 1938.

As fate would have it, none other than Joe McCarthy's Yankees were to provide the opposition for the Cubs in the upcoming World Series. McCarthy loved nothing better than to stick it to the Cubs whenever he could for letting him go in 1930. He and his team were primed to do it once again, just as they had so gleefully in 1932.

New York had once again waltzed in nine and one-half games ahead of the second place Red Sox to capture the American League flag for the third year in a row. Rookie Joe Gordon, who had supplanted the popular Lazzeri, had a superb first year, hitting .290 (ten points better than his previous season in Newark), slamming 25 home runs, driving in 97 runs and stealing 31 bases.

Shortstop Frank Crosetti led the league in steals with 47, while third baseman Red Rolfe batted .311. Although Gehrig showed signs of slowing down, he still managed to hit 29 homers, drive in 114 runs and hit .295, his lowest average in 11 seasons.

Now in his third season in the South Bronx, "Jolting" Joe DiMaggio had another banner year for the New Yorkers with 140 RBI, 32 homers and a .324 batting average. Second year man Tommy Henrich (22 home runs and 91 RBI) and George Selkirk (10 homers and 62 RBI) more than held their own in left and right field respectively. The team's now-perennial all-star catcher, Bill Dickey, continued to roll along by contributing 27 home runs, 115 runs batted in and a .313 batting average.

Red Ruffing with 21 victories and Lefty Gomez with 18 led the Yankee pitching staff, while Monte Pearson added another 16 wins. Second year man Spud Chandler posted an additional 14 victories and "Grandma" Johnny Murphy continued to bolster the bullpen by saving 11 games and winning eight others.

Murphy got his nickname from his teammates because of his orderly and fastidious demeanor on the mound. Whenever a Yankee starter was in trouble, Murphy would get the call and the players on the bench would chant, "Here comes Grandma!" Only he didn't pitch like "Grandma" because he remained cool in critical situations with good stuff and a wicked curve ball. He was also just wild enough to put some fear into opposing batters when he felt it was required.

The Cubs had next to no firepower in their lineup as evidenced by first baseman Ripper Collins, who led the team with a mere 13 homers. The North Siders were paced by third baseman Stan Hack, who hit .320 and led the National League in steals with just 16.

The only other player to top .300 for Chicago was a semi-regular outfielder and former American Leaguer named Carl Reynolds. Reynolds batted .302 but managed to hit only three home runs. Thirty-seven year old player-manager Gabby Hartnett was the only other regular to hit as many as ten home runs for the Cubs that season.

Not a single player knocked in over 100 runs for the Cubs in 1938. In fact, outfielder Augie Galan, with just 69 runs batted in, led the club in that category. DiMaggio, who was the Yankees' leading producer of runs batted in, had 71 more than Galan.

The Chicago pitching staff was anchored by right-hander "Big Bill" Lee, who recorded 22 victories that year. He also led the National League in both earned run average with 2.66 and in shutouts with nine. Clay Bryant, another righty, contributed 19 wins while veteran Charlie Root with eight saves did most of the relieving.

10. The End Draws Near (1938–1943)

Dizzy Dean tried to come back from a severe toe injury that he had suffered in the 1937 All-Star game, and he had hurt his arm. The veteran, though only 27 years old, had come over from the Cardinals in April and, to everyone's surprise, won seven of eight decisions as a spot starter. Just three years earlier he had led the major leagues in victories with 30, the last pitcher to win that many until Denny McLain won 31 for the Tigers 34 years later.

In many ways the 1938 World Series was shaping up like a repeat of the 1932 classic. While the 1932 Cubs replaced Rogers Hornsby with Charley Grimm in late August that season, the 1938 scenario had Grimm being dismissed in favor of Hartnett in late July. Meanwhile, Joe McCarthy guided the Yankees for the duration. All that remained from the original script was for the Yankees to sweep the Cubs again and indeed they did.

In Game One at Wrigley Field, Bill Dickey led the Yankees offensively, going 4-for-4 — all singles — against the starter, Bill Lee, who was outpitched by Red Ruffing in a complete game 3–1 win. Dickey scored one run and drove in another as the Yankees jumped out to a one game to none header.

Dizzy Dean got the call to start for the Cubs in Wrigley Field against Lefty Gomez in an emotion-packed Game Two. The Cubs were up 3–2 after seven innings thanks to a gutsy performance by Dean, who had pitched aggressively and yielded but three hits. Changing speeds and using his guile and experience, he kept the Yankee hitters off balance throughout his tenure on the mound. Joe McCarthy lifted Gomez for a pinch-hitter in the top of the eighth when the New Yorkers rallied for two runs against Dean.

George Selkirk got the Yankees' fourth hit of the game when he led off the inning with a single. Two force-out ground balls almost let Dean off the hook but Frank Crosetti, of all people, drove one of Dean's offerings into the left field stands with Myril Hoag on first base.

The Crow's two-run homer gave the Yankees a 4–2 lead. Crosetti was an implausible choice for the rally; he had hit only nine home runs in the entire season — the lowest total of any Yankee regular.

Dean struck out Red Rolfe to end the eighth but he was unable to survive the ninth. After Tommy Henrich singled, New York struck for two insurance runs thanks to a home run by "The Yankee Clipper," Joe DiMaggio. Reliever Johnny Murphy held the Cubs scoreless in both the eighth and ninth innings to preserve the 6–3 victory. For the winning pitcher, Gomez, it marked his sixth and final victory in World Series competition against nary a defeat.

It was the Gomez-Murphy perfecta all over again. When the eccentric southpaw was asked how he felt before a game, he would reply: "It isn't important how I feel. What's important is how Murphy feels."[2] The win sent the Yankees home with a commanding two games to none lead.

Rookie Joe Gordon set the pace in the Yankees' victory in Game Three at New York. He rapped a bases-empty home run in the fifth and added a two-run single in the sixth. Gordon's home run was the first hit off starter Clay Bryant, who was replaced in the sixth inning. The home team won it, 5–2, behind a complete game performance by Monte Pearson.

A sweep now appeared inevitable as the starters in Game One — Red Ruffing and Bill Lee — were called upon once again by their respective managers in Game Four. The usually light-hitting Crosetti continued to amaze everyone again by driving in four runs with a double and a triple to help not only ice the game but also clinch another world championship for the Yankees.

Lee could not get past the third inning as the home team recorded an easy 8–3 win. Ruffing pitched his second complete game victory of the Series, while both Gordon and Dickey, each with six hits in 15 at-bats, shared the team lead in batting at .400.

Lou Gehrig, who had worn out Cub pitchers with three home runs and eight RBI back in 1932, was now but a shell of his former self this time around. He neither hit a home run nor drove in a single run in the 1938 Series, but rather produced only four singles in 14 at-bats. As history would later prove, the illness that would take his life in a few short years was already beginning to take its toll on his body.

Nevertheless, Gehrig's legacy was that he had become the first to play for a World Championship team in three consecutive years. The 1938 World Series was to be the last for Gehrig and teammate Gomez.

Oddly enough, the leading World Series hitters average-wise in 1938 were from the Cubs — Stan Hack at .471 (8 for 17) and the youthful Phil Cavaretta at .462 (6 for 13). However, of the team's 33 base hits, only seven were for extra bases. The absence of the long ball surely did not help their cause. Although their pitching was what got them there to begin with, it was no match for the Yankee bats.

Tony Lazzeri, who had been a non-factor for the Cubs for most of 1938, continued in that same vein during the World Series. He appeared in only two of the games, primarily as a defensive replacement. In his only official time at bat, he was sent up to pinch-hit for Billy Jurges in the ninth inning of the final game of the Series. Ironically, after working the count full, he hit a grounder to — of all people — his successor, Joe Gordon, who threw him out at first base.

The New York Times did not lose sight of the Lazzeri-Gordon "con-

10. The End Draws Near (1938–1943)

frontation" and reported it as follows: "Youth and age, experience and inexperience faced each other at the Yankee Stadium in a drama that was not lost on veteran baseball followers or the players themselves. For the first time Tony Lazzeri came face to face with Joe Gordon in action — and youth was served.

"It happened in the ninth inning. Lazzeri, a World Series participant for the first time as a member of a cast other than the Yanks, came out of the Cubs dugout in the ninth inning to bat for Jurges with one out. The veteran worked the count to three and two, then rolled to Gordon and was thrown out by the man who succeeded him as Yankee second baseman."[3]

Following the Series, it had become readily apparent to the thirteen-year veteran that if he wished to continue playing, Chicago was not where he should be. There was no doubt in Lazzeri's mind that he could still play, but where and for whom?

About a month later, Tony telephoned Phil Wrigley from his California home asking the Cubs' owner if he could secure his release in case he wanted to "go shopping." "He was informed that he could," Wrigley said, "when he was signed after leaving the New York Yankees. He was told he would be able to obtain his release any time he had an opportunity to better himself."[4]

However, Wrigley insisted that he wouldn't "be surprised if he's still with us next season."[5] Lazzeri did admit at the time that he had no immediate prospects but hoped to do some more playing in the majors.

On the occasion of his 34th birthday (December 6, 1938), Lazzeri sent Wrigley the following wire: "Am making formal request for release; appreciate same." Wrigley responded: "Granted."[6]

Tony claimed to have received "four or five offers" to play with major league teams and expected to accept one within the next week. What he wanted to do, he said, "is play — none of this sitting on the bench for me."[7]

The New York Times in its December 7, 1938, edition indicated that the "taciturn [Lazzeri] did a lot of sitting last season. During the opening weeks of the campaign he filled in brilliantly at shortstop and second base. From then on, he was used sparingly and, for the most part, was not particularly effective.

"He signed with the Cubs in 1937, after his release from the Yankees. Reports immediately blossomed that he was in line for the Cub managership, but catcher Gabby Hartnett took that job when Charlie Grimm was dismissed in July and it was said that Lazzeri was not considered for the post."[8]

All that was known about Lazzeri's future in baseball at the time was that his old Salt Lake City manager, Oscar Vitt, had sought his services as a coach for the Indians, whom he was now managing. Oddly enough, five days after the article in the *Times* ran, Tony announced that he had accepted a one-year contract to play for the Brooklyn Dodgers. After negotiating over the telephone with the club's owner, Larry MacPhail, Lazzeri had agreed to a deal that he said would return him not only to the New York area but also to playing second base on a regular basis in 1939.

"Mr. MacPhail and I were in complete accord on the matter," he declared. "He understood what I wanted and I told him I was certain I could produce for him. This is the break I have been waiting for." He added that he thought he "was good for many years as a player."⁹

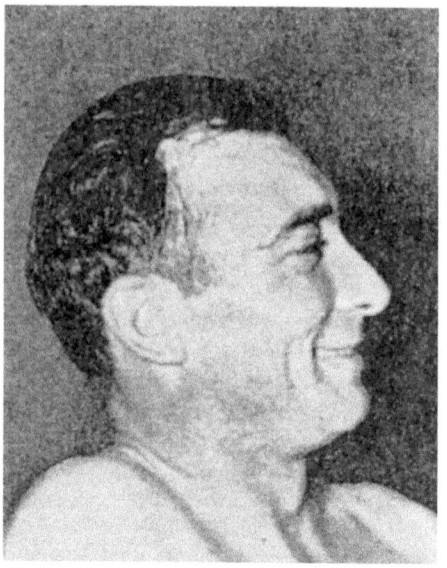

Tony Lazzeri was considered washed up as a player at the age of 33 following 1938 season. (*Baseball Magazine*)

Lazzeri was energized by the fact that he would be returning to the city where he continued to be immensely popular and where he had enjoyed his greatest successes. He was also going to be reunited with a former Yankee teammate, Leo Durocher, who had been named manager of the Dodgers in the off-season to replace Burleigh Grimes. Durocher was also the club's regular shortstop and with Lazzeri on board the pair would seemingly form the double play combination for Brooklyn in 1939.

Yet when Tony arrived at the Dodger training camp base in Clearwater, Florida, he found some things brewing that troubled him. The most prominent issue was Durocher's idea to try out the much-heralded rookie, Pete Reiser, at second base.

Reiser was an outfielder by trade who could occasionally play some infield, notably third base, but he had never played second base.

Durocher also had a second year player, Pete Coscarart, a natural second baseman, also available if the Reiser experiment were to fail. The Dodgers were loaded with outfielders so there was no other place for Reiser to play on an everyday basis. When he demonstrated that he wasn't going to work out at second and there was not enough outfield work for him to remain with the club, "Pistol Pete" was returned to the minor leagues.

10. The End Draws Near (1938–1943)

As heady as Lazzeri's return to the city where he had enjoyed some marvelous seasons appeared to be, play in the borough of Brooklyn did not come close to equaling his previous triumphs. First of all, he was forced to share the second base assignment with Coscarart, who seemed to be a particular favorite of Durocher's. Lazzeri appeared in 14 games and recorded eleven hits in 39 times up, including three homers, two doubles, six runs batted in and a .282 mark before coming down with a sudden attack of tonsillitis.

Lazzeri was sidelined for several days; the club left him behind in Brooklyn when it went to Boston. Lazzeri received a mysterious wire on May 13 from the team's secretary, John McDonald, informing him that he had been released. McDonald indicated to the press that the move had been contemplated for several days and that the decision was made unilaterally by Durocher. It was now clear that Pete Coscarart was to be the regular Dodger second baseman, at least for the foreseeable future.

Tony was flabbergasted. Reached at his apartment while he was convalescing from the tonsillitis attack, he declared: "I got a telegram only about 20 minutes ago. It was a surprise to me. I thought I was doing all right and expected to join the club in Chicago. I don't know what I am going to do, except I'll stay in New York for a week or so. This tonsillitis will keep me here for awhile."[10]

Lazzeri was not unemployed for long. The arch rival Giants, still managed by Tony's former nemesis Bill Terry, asked him to join them. Now a second division team in the National League, the Giants had a rookie, Burgess Whitehead, playing second base for them. The ball club's former regular second sacker, Alex Kampouris, backed him up. Both Whitehead and Kampouris were fair to poor with the bat and it was felt that Lazzeri could help offensively, that is if he had anything left. Tony got into 13 games for the Giants, hitting .293 on the strength of 13 base hits, including a home run and eight RBI.

However, a funny thing happened on the way to "Poosh 'Em Up's" resumption of his playing career. The Toronto Maple Leafs of the International League contacted him about taking over their now-vacant position of manager. An ex–St. Louis Browns player, Jack "Slug" Burns, had filled the post.

A last-place team in the rebuilding process, the Maple Leafs represented an opportunity for Tony that he simply could not resist. He had always said he wanted to stay in the game either as a coach or manager when his playing days were at an end. Ever the realist, he knew full well that as he approached 35, he would probably never have the opportunity to play regularly in the big leagues again. And riding the pines was not a viable option.

On June 19, Lazzeri officially took over the reins of the Toronto ball club and, while the team remained solidly entrenched in last place for the balance of the season, club management seemed pleased with his performance. President Don Ross said he was "satisfied" that Lazzeri had done "everything possible" with the material at his disposal. On September 12 Ross announced that Tony would once again manage the Maple Leafs in 1940.

Ever the competitor and always ready for a challenge, Lazzeri even inserted himself into the lineup as a relief pitcher in the nightcap of a doubleheader against the Montreal Royals on August 20. Replacing his starter in the second inning with two men on, none out and seven runs already in, "Poosh 'Em Up" retired the side in order and thereafter had only one bad inning—the sixth, when he allowed four runs—en route to a 13–4 defeat of his pitching-short ball club.

Dario Lodigiani, a fellow San Franciscan and a member of the Maple Leafs that season, considered Tony Lazzeri a fine manager. "He knew the game inside and out," said the former Athletics and White Sox infielder. "We had a fair team but we lacked consistent pitching and that doomed us to last place again. Looking back at it there's no doubt in my mind that Tony would have been a successful major league manager had he been given the chance. He was great with the players."[11]

Lodigiani, who roomed with Lazzeri, was well aware of Tony's epileptic condition. "It never affected him during a ball game though," he said, just as Mark Koenig had stated some years earlier when he roomed with Tony. "The only time I saw evidence of it was once when we were in Newark to play the Bears," Lodigiani said. "The game had been rained out and a few of us, including Tony, had gone to a movie. While we were walking back to the hotel, Tony had a seizure. I'll never forget it. We brought him under the cover of an entrance to a shoe store. The attack was over in a matter of minutes. That's the only time I remember seeing him like that."[12]

When the season ended in 1940, the Toronto ball club had even more troubles off the field than on it. There was some doubt that the team would be allowed to continue to exist in the International League. Changes had to be made and Tony Lazzeri was among the first of many.

Arthur Leman, secretary-treasurer of the Maple Leafs, issued a statement on November 7 announcing that Lazzeri had been let go as manager: "In view of the uncertainty regarding Toronto continuing in the International League in 1941, Tony Lazzeri's contract as manager has not been renewed. Lazzeri severed his connection with the Toronto ball club with absolute goodwill and under an arrangement, which was entirely satisfactory to all parties concerned.

10. The End Draws Near (1938–1943)

"Because of the uncertainty mentioned above, the Toronto Baseball Club, Ltd., has not as yet engaged a manager for next year, nor has it approached the Toronto Harbor Commission for renewal of its lease."[13]

Despite the doomsday implications of Leman's statement, the president of the International League, Frank Shaughnessy, told the Associated Press that he knew nothing of any uncertainty about Toronto remaining in the league. "As far as our headquarters are concerned," he said, "we have heard nothing to make us think the Maple Leafs would not be in the league next year, and I'm confident Toronto will find its way clear to continue."[14]

The contradictory statement by Shaughnessy seemed to be totally at odds with reality. Be that as it may, all Tony Lazzeri knew was that he didn't have a job — again. As 1941 rolled around, he was determined to get back into baseball in one capacity or another. Now 38 but still feeling that he had something left as a player, he signed a contract with his home town San Francisco Seals to play once again in the Pacific Coast League, where he had last been in uniform in 1925.

The New York Times, which had always been well disposed toward Tony, was almost gleeful in reporting on his return to the game. In its January 25, 1941, edition, the newspaper covered it thusly:

> Tony Lazzeri, the original "poosh 'em up" man of baseball signed his contract with the Seals today, paving the way for what may be the final and one of the most unusual chapters of his long and brilliant playing career.
>
> Reared in this city and a "boy wonder" product of its playgrounds, Lazzeri traveled practically around the baseball world to arrive as a member of the San Francisco team for the first time in twenty years.
>
> He returns this season as the second baseman, 38 years old and, perhaps, in the creaky bones class.
>
> Lazzeri's batting power, at least, is far less diminished than his speed. He drives a golf ball close to 300 yards, which may or may not be important, but if hiking from three to six miles daily over a course will strengthen the legs, Lazzeri has been building endurance.
>
> As a Yankee star from 1926 to 1937, Lazzeri played in six world series. After spending the 1938 season with Cubs and the next with Brooklyn and the Giants, Lazzeri served as non-playing manager of Toronto last year. He will celebrate his twentieth season in organized baseball by getting back into active competition.[15]

Tony was indeed in great shape. And after not playing baseball regularly for the past couple of years, he was delighted to be doing it once again for his hometown of San Francisco, which he had only seen almost 15 years earlier as a visiting player.

Lazzeri knew this would only be a temporary solution to his desire to stay in baseball. He had a taste of managing and he enjoyed it. He longed for another chance and an offer did come his way.

The Portsmouth, Virginia, ball club of the Piedmont League contacted him about their managerial job for the upcoming season and Tony eagerly accepted it. The assignment was for a team low in the pecking order beneath the major league and AAA levels. However, it represented the only opportunity to manage that was to come Lazzeri's way and that's all the former big leaguer cared about.

After a rather uneventful season below the Mason-Dixon line, the Wilkes-Barre club of the Eastern League got in touch with Tony and signed him on to become their manager in 1943. The job itself was to his liking but the relationship with club management proved to be a stormy one.

Shortly after the season ended, he was asked to resign. At first "Poosh 'Em Up" resisted and vowed to fight to keep his job. On January 11, 1944, he said: "If they want to get rid of me, they'll have to throw me out."[16]

Lazzeri contended that he had no idea that the club wanted him to retire from his post until the club's secretary, Mike McNally, asked him to resign. He told the United Press that he did not know why the team wanted him to retire. "If they wanted to be nice about it, they could have informed me sooner," he said. "Now the winter meetings are over. All the 1944 jobs have been filled."[17]

He was absolutely right on that score. There were not going to be any jobs available for him either then or later. For Tony Lazzeri, one of the all-time greats in the history of major league baseball, it appeared that no organization had an opening for him in any capacity in a game that he loved beyond all else.

11

Retirement and the Final Exit (1944–1946)

As "Poosh 'Em Up" Tony Lazzeri had correctly surmised, not a single job offer was on the table for him in organized baseball for the 1944 season. Now 40 years of age, he had finally come to the realization that it was indeed over for him as a player.

Moreover, no one was beating a path to his door to provide him with a job either as a player, coach or manager. So for the first time in nearly 20 years, he found himself at home in the Bay Area without the slightest hint of a job in professional baseball.

What to do? He wasn't skilled at any trade or vocation that he could turn to like some other former ballplayers. Many of them had worked regularly at something or other in their off seasons and could fall back on such jobs once their careers had come to an end. Not so with Tony Lazzeri. If he did anything at all, it was to tee it up on the golf course. Consequently, he had acquired no special work skills that he could fall back on when the time for retirement arrived.

Tony had not been inside a boiler plant since the last time he had worked there with his father as a teenager. And what's more, that was the farthest thought from his mind at this point in his life. All that he ever knew or cared about was baseball. No matter that he still had his old boilermaker's card. It was never an option that he would turn to once his playing days ended.

One certainty was that Lazzeri's popularity had never diminished in his hometown of San Francisco. This was not only because of his prowess in the game of baseball, but also because he had never strayed far from where he had first honed his skills. It occurred to him that it might not be a bad idea to open a business where he could draw people in to see him personally and talk about his exploits on the diamond. What better place to hold court than in a saloon and that's exactly what he did.

The bar business turned out to be precisely what the doctor ordered for Tony Lazzeri. Although he could never be accused of being a blabbermouth, he was capable of talking at length with his patrons about the game that he loved and his storied experiences in it.

Be that as it may, it always rankled him that, more often than not, many of his customers would resurrect the famous duel that he had with Grover Cleveland Alexander in the seventh game of the 1926 World Series. "Funny thing," he said at the time, "but nobody seems to remember much about my ball playing except that strikeout. There isn't a night goes by but what some guy leans across the bar and brings up the old question. Never a night."[1]

It was actually going to take something as tragic as his premature death in 1946 at age 42 before the successes of his career would be written for the world to see. Unfortunately, it would take that same untimely event to acknowledge what a tremendous career that Tony Lazzeri had put together in baseball.

On that fateful day — August 7, 1946 — Tony was alone in his Millbrae, California, home. His wife, Maye, and his brother-in-law, Louie Servente, had just returned from a vacation trip when they found Tony's lifeless body at the foot of a staircase in their home.

At first it was assumed that Tony had suffered an epileptic seizure and fallen down the stairs to his death. However, an autopsy revealed that he had actually experienced a heart attack, which caused his fall. Coroners determined that he had died some 36 hours earlier and listed the official cause of death as the heart attack.

The New York Herald-Tribune, in its obituary published on August 9, 1946, said that Maye and Louis "found him slumped at the foot of a landing near the entrance to his home. Apparently [he] had struck his head against a banister in slipping or falling in the home. A coroner's office said he had been dead for thirty-six hours, and said death might have been caused by a heart attack."[2]

The newspaper went on to cite several important events in the Hall of Famer's baseball life:

> Somewhat like Fred Merkle and Heinie Zimmerman, "Poosh 'Em Up" Tony Lazzeri was a first-class ballplayer tenaciously remembered for a famous moment when he failed to come through. The taciturn Italian held three major league records for slugging home runs, but whenever his name was mentioned a fan was sure to say: "Remember the time old Pete Alexander struck him out in the 1926 World Series."

11. Retirement and the Final Exit (1944–1946)

Two years later, again in the World Series, again with the bases full, Lazzeri faced Alexander and belted a double for three runs, but such was the peculiar drama of the earlier time that, as Lazzeri bemoaned, nobody ever seemed to forget it.

A baseball crowd always wonders what an infielder says to a pitcher when he goes over to the mound in a tense moment. Lefty Gomez reported what Lazzeri said to him once in such a crisis when the bases were full. "You got us into this, you so-and-so, by walking two guys. Now get us out of it."

Lazzeri was more than a playing asset to the Yankees. Great crowds of Italians used to turn out to watch him and it was from their urging when he was at the plate that he got the "Poosh 'Em Up" handle.[3]

Funeral services for Lazzeri were held at St. Paul's Church in San Francisco on August 10, 1946, and entombment followed at the Sunset Mausoleum in nearby Berkeley.

The baseball world was stunned over the sudden turn of events for a living legend like Tony Lazzeri who, up until only three or four years earlier, was still playing and managing.

Red Smith, the renowned sports columnist for the *New York Herald-Tribune* who adored "Poosh 'Em Up" and his style of play wrote the following in acknowledgement of his passing

> It was a shock to read in the reports of Lazzeri's death that he was not yet forty-two years old. ... One would have guessed Lazzeri's age a good deal higher because his name and fame are inextricably associated with an era which already has become a legend — the era that is always referred to as the time of "the old Yankees."
>
> You can't think of Tony without thinking also of Babe Ruth and Bob Meusel and Herb Pennock and Waite Hoyt and Lou Gehrig and Mark Koenig and Benny Bengough and Wilcy Moore, all of whom have long gone from the playing fields for what seems a long time.
>
> They chose Lazzeri Player of the Year after one of his closing seasons. They could just as well have made it Player of the Years, for in all his time with the Yankees there was no one whose hitting and fielding and hustle and fire and brilliantly swift thinking meant more to any team.[4]

Another distinguished sportswriter of the day, Arthur Daley of *The New York Times*, defined the meaning of Lazzeri's life and times in this manner

> The grim-visaged Californian from San Francisco's Telegraph Hill was a truly great performer, a tremendous long-ball hitter, a money player almost without equal and one of the smartest athletes ever to patrol the diamond. It's ironic, perhaps, that his name is in the Hall of Fame at Cooperstown, but only in a left-handed way. It rests there on the plaque devoted to Grover

> Cleveland Alexander because one of Aleck's claims to immortality was that he fanned Lazzeri with the bases full in the seventh and deciding game of the 1926 World Series....
> The lad from the Golden Gate was essentially a "a ball player's ball player." He evoked infinitely greater admiration from the other athletes than he ever did from the fans. It was not only his mechanical proficiency which caught their eyes. It was also his hair-trigger brain. Tony was one of the fastest thinkers baseball ever has had.
> And now "Poosh 'Em Up" is gone. He left a mark on baseball that never will be forgotten, even if part of his memory will contain one of his rare failures.[5]

Despite his records and the achievements of the teams he played on, Tony Lazzeri was denied entry into the Hall of Fame every year that his name was brought up for possible induction. Teammates already in the Hall included Babe Ruth, Lou Gehrig, Joe DiMaggio, Red Ruffing, Waite Hoyt, Bill Dickey and Lefty Gomez. Meanwhile Lazzeri remained outside looking in. All sorts of speculation has persisted as to why this injustice continued, but the fact remains that it did for no less than 52 years after he played his last major league game and for 45 years following his death.

A movement to get "Poosh 'Em Up" in Cooperstown began when a group of dedicated fans in the Bay Area under the direction of a local restaurateur named Kevin Johnson refused to take "no" for an answer anymore. After several years of petitioning the 18-man Hall of Fame Veterans Committee for Lazzeri's induction into the Hall, their dreams were finally realized in 1991. Enshrinement in Cooperstown at long last became a reality for Tony Lazzeri in the same year that Rod Carew, Ferguson Jenkins, Gaylord Perry and Bill Veeck were also given their due recognition — 1991.

"It was long overdue," said his longtime teammate and double play partner, Frank Crosetti, at the time.

> I don't know why they kept him out so long. He not only was a great ball player, he was a great man. He was a leader. He was like a manager on the field.
> Players should wait their turn to be in the Hall of Fame. Second basemen like Red Schoendienst and Bobby Doerr. They're both in the Hall of Fame, but they played after Tony. He should have gone in ahead of them.
> He was tremendous player, a great clutch player. He had ice water in his veins. He wasn't a big person, but he was thick through the chest.
> He took a lot of pride in his defense. I remember one time a ball went through his legs because he didn't get his glove down. The next time the ball came to him he got his glove down so far that when he brought it up, big chunks of dirt flew off of it. I can still see that to this day.
> He took me in hand when I went with the Yankees. Before the season I went over to his house to talk to him. He told me what to do. I looked up to him like a big brother.[6]

11. Retirement and the Final Exit (1944–1946)

In a letter to the Hall of Fame endorsing his enshrinement, Frank Crosetti's predecessor at shortstop, Mark Koenig, wrote:

> I was Tony's teammate from 1926 through 1929 with the New York Yankees. During that time we won three American League Championships and two World's Championships. Tony Lazzeri was a major reason that we were so successful.
>
> In addition to his remarkable hitting, Tony was a marvelous second baseman and a team leader. Tony hit for power and average and was an outstanding clutch player. It would be hard to overstate his importance to the Yankees of that era.
>
> As a basis for comparison, I had the good fortune to play with both Charlie Gehringer and Billy Herman as well as Lazzeri during my career. Both Gehringer and Herman are quite rightfully in the Hall of Fame and having seen all three of them for extended periods I can assure you that Tony was unquestionably on their level as a batter and as a second baseman.
>
> Not only was Lazzeri an exceptional all-around player, he was a very fine individual of outstanding character. I have often wondered why he has not yet been elected to the Hall of Fame and I hope that my comments may have some effect towards his election. It would be a very fitting reward for his career and a great tribute to his memory. I sincerely hope that he will get this recognition from the Veterans Committee.[7]

Ellsworth "Babe" Dahlgren, the man who replaced Lou Gehrig at first base for the Yankees following the conclusion of the Iron Horse's consecutive games played streak, also wrote to Veterans Committee on Lazzeri's behalf:

> I played against Tony Lazzeri in 1935 and 1936 while I was with the Boston Red Sox and was his roommate in spring training in 1937. I am writing to say that I strongly feel that he ought to be in the Hall of Fame.
>
> Tony was an outstanding player, a very fine fielder and, of course, a great power hitter. He was also one of the most respected players in the league, especially by his teammates. You couldn't help but like and admire Tony; with all that he had accomplished in his career it had never gone to his head.
>
> He was tremendously helpful to the younger players on the team in many ways. In my opinion, Tony was as valuable on the Yankees as anyone they ever had. He helped Joe DiMaggio immensely when Joe first came up.
>
> As a player, Tony was a great performer in the clutch. He drove in over 100 runs seven times with a lot of home runs. His knowledge of the game was just outstanding.
>
> When you consider everything that Tony did in his career it is a mystery to me as to why he isn't already in the Hall of Fame. Having known him as both a ball player and as a person there is no doubt in my mind that he deserves to be in the Hall of Fame and I very much hope that he will be elected.

> P.S. Tony was a generous guy off the field and had a heart as big as a watermelon![8]

In a 1989 interview with columnist Harry Jupiter of the *San Francisco Examiner*, "The Yankee Clipper" himself, Joe DiMaggio, summed it up: "Tony belongs in the big Hall of Fame in Cooperstown. He was great, one of the best I ever saw."[9]

In that same article, teammate Lefty Gomez told Jupiter: "He was the guy who taught us what it meant to be a big leaguer. He taught us what it meant to be a Yankee. What was expected of us, and how to behave."[10]

Samuel Pond "Sad Sam," Jones, a pitcher known for his sharp-breaking curveball and sorrowful countenance who spent 21 seasons in the American League with the Indians, Red Sox, Yankees, Browns, Senators and White Sox, remembered "Poosh 'Em Up" this way: "Tony was a very witty guy, full of fun. Quiet, but always up to something. A real nice guy. And a great second baseman, too. He was an awful strong fellow. He had real big muscles on him. He could hit a ball as far in right field as he could in left. How they can keep leaving him out of the Hall of Fame is beyond me."[11]

It all came to fruition at long last for Tony Lazzeri in 1991 when he was posthumously inducted into the Major League Baseball Hall of Fame in Cooperstown, New York.

Appendix A: Career Statistics

Birth Name:	Anthony Michael Lazzeri
Born on:	December 6, 1903
Born in:	San Francisco, California
Batted:	Right
Threw:	Right
Height:	5'11½"
Weight:	170
Nickname:	"Poosh 'Em Up"
Major League Debut:	April 13, 1926

Batting—Regular Season

Year	Club	League	Pos	G	AB	R	H	2B	3B	HR	RBI	BA
1922	Salt Lake	PCL	1B-3B	45	78	9	15	4	3	1	8	.192
1923	Peoria	I.I.I.	2B	135	436	63	108	22	7	14	—	.248
1923	Salt Lake	PCL	SS	39	130	25	46	7	1	7	21	.354
1924	Lincoln	Western	INF	82	316	65	104	18	3	28	—	.329
1924	Salt Lake	PCL	SS-3B	85	293	51	83	15	3	16	61	.283
1925	Salt Lake	PCL	SS-2B	197	710	202	252	52	14	60	222	.355
1926	New York	AL	2B	155	589	79	162	28	14	18	114	.275
1927	New York	AL	SS-2B	153	570	92	176	29	8	18	102	.309
1928	New York	AL	2B	116	404	62	134	30	11	10	82	.332
1929	New York	AL	2B	147	545	101	193	37	11	18	106	.354
1930	New York	AL	2B-3B	143	571	109	173	34	15	9	121	.303
1931	New York	AL	2B-3B	135	484	67	129	27	7	8	83	.267

Appendix A

Year	Club	League	Pos	G	AB	R	H	2B	3B	HR	RBI	BA
1932	New York	AL	2B	142	511	78	154	28	16	15	113	.301
1933	New York	AL	2B	139	523	94	154	22	12	18	104	.294
1934	New York	AL	2B-3B	123	438	59	117	24	6	14	71	.267
1935	New York	AL	2B	130	477	72	130	18	6	13	63	.273
1936	New York	AL	2B	150	537	82	154	29	6	14	109	.287
1937	New York	AL	2B	126	446	56	109	21	3	14	70	.244
1938	Chicago	NL	INF	54	120	21	32	6	1	5	23	.267
1939	B'klyn-NY	NL	INF	27	83	13	24	2	0	4	14	.289
1939	Toronto	IL	INF	39	97	19	22	4	2	1	20	.227
1940	Toronto	IL	INF	13	17	0	3	2	0	0	0	.176
1941	San Fran.	PCL	INF	102	315	40	78	22	3	3	39	.248
1942	Portsmouth	Pied.	INF	98	310	32	75	13	3	2	40	.242
1943	Wilkes-Barre	EL	INF	58	181	25	49	11	1	3	21	.271
Major League Totals				1740	6297	986	1840	334	115	178	1191	.292

Batting — World Series

Year	Club	League	POS	G	AB	R	H	2B	3B	HR	RBI	BA
1926	New York	AL	2B	7	26	2	5	1	0	0	3	.192
1927	New York	AL	2B	4	15	1	4	1	0	0	2	.267
1928	New York	AL	2B	4	12	2	3	1	0	0	0	.250
1932	New York	AL	2B	4	17	4	5	0	0	2	5	.294
1936	New York	AL	2B	6	25	4	5	0	0	1	7	.200
1937	New York	AL	2B	5	15	3	6	0	1	1	2	.400
1938	Chicago	NL	PH	2	0	0	0	0	0	0	0	.000
World Series Totals				32	112	16	28	3	1	4	19	.250

Miscellaneous Batting Statistics — Regular Season

		Base running Statistics			Common Hitting Ratios	
	Team	SB	CS	SB%	AB/HR	AB/K
1926	Yankees	16	7	.696	32.7	6.1
1927	Yankees	22	14	.611	31.7	7.0
1928	Yankees	15	5	.750	40.4	8.1
1929	Yankees	9	10	.474	30.3	12.1
1930	Yankees	4	4	.500	63.4	9.2
1931	Yankees	18	9	.667	60.5	6.0
1932	Yankees	11	11	.500	34.0	8.0
1933	Yankees	15	7	.682	29.1	8.4
1934	Yankees	11	1	.917	31.3	6.8
1935	Yankees	11	5	.686	36.7	6.4
1936	Yankees	8	5	.615	38.4	8.3
1937	Yankees	7	1	.875	31.9	5.9
1938	Cubs	0	0	.000	24.0	4.0
1939	Dodgers	1	0	1.000	13.0	5.6
1939	Giants	0	0	.000	44.0	7.3
Totals		148	79	.652	35.4	7.3

Fielding — Regular Season

Team	POS	G	PO	A	E	DP	FP
1926 Yankees	2B	149	298	461	31	72	.961
	SS	5	9	14	3	2	.885
	3B	1	0	0	0	0	.000
1927 Yankees	2B	113	213	398	18	60	.971
	SS	38	58	115	10	15	.945
	3B	9	10	12	1	0	.957
1928 Yankees	2B	110	236	331	26	56	.956
1929 Yankees	2B	147	368	467	27	102	.969
1930 Yankees	2B	77	184	245	13	39	.971
	3B	60	90	113	11	12	.949
	SS	8	16	24	2	8	.952
	1B	1	3	0	0	1	1.000
	OF	1	1	0	0	0	1.000
1931 Yankees	2B	90	216	288	22	52	.958
	3B	39	39	53	4	4	.958
1932 Yankees	2B	134	362	405	17	70	.978
	3B	5	2	7	0	0	1.000
1933 Yankees	2B	138	338	407	25	71	.968
1934 Yankees	2B	92	218	265	12	52	.976
	3B	30	36	51	6	7	.935
1935 Yankees	2B	118	285	329	19	72	.970
	SS	9	18	25	3	4	.935
1936 Yankees	2B	148	346	414	25	88	.968
	SS	2	2	4	0	0	1.000
1937 Yankees	2B	125	251	382	22	64	.966
1938 Cubs	SS	25	33	54	5	11	.946
	3B	7	6	4	2	0	.833
	2B	4	8	17	0	1	1.000
	OF	1	2	0	0	0	1.000
1939 Dodgers	2B	11	28	36	6	9	.914
	3B	2	1	2	0	0	1.000
1939 Giants	3B	13	11	21	4	1	.897
Position Totals	2B	1,456	3,351	4,445	263	808	.967
	3B	166	195	263	28	24	.942
	SS	87	136	236	23	40	.942
	OF	2	3	0	0	0	1.000
	1B	1	3	0	0	1	.989
Overall Totals		1,712	3,688	4,944	314	873	.966

Miscellaneous Items of Interest

All-Star Team: 1933 American League

Top 10 MVP Award Balloting: 1926 AL 10th; 1928 AL 3rd; 1932 AL 8th

Batting Average: 1928: .332 — AL 5th; 1929: .354 — AL 4th

On Base Percentage: 1928: .397 — AL 9th; 1929: .430 — AL 4th; 1932: .300 — AL 10th

Slugging Percentage: 1928: .535 — AL 7th; 1929: .561 — AL 8th; 1932: .506 — AL 9th; 1933: .486 — AL 7th

On Base Percentage Plus Slugging Percentage: 1928: .932 — AL 7th; 1929: .991— AL 5th; 1932: .905 — AL 8th; 1933: .869 — AL 7th

Games: 1926: 155 — AL 2nd; 1927: 153 — AL 2nd

At-Bats: 1926: 589 — AL 9th; 1927: 570 — AL 8th

Hits: 1929: 193 — AL 10th

Total Bases: 1926: 272 — AL 9th; 1927: 275 — AL 6th; 1929: 306 — AL 8th

Triples: 1926: 14 — AL 5th; 1930: 15 — AL 5th; 1932: 16 — AL 2nd; 1933: 12 — AL 7th

Home Runs: 1926: 18 — AL 3rd; 1927: 18 — AL 3rd; 1929: 18 — AL 6th; 1933: 18 — AL 5th

Runs Batted In: 1926: 114 — AL 2nd; 1927: 102 — AL 8th; 1929: 106 — AL 8th; 1930: 121— AL 9th; 1932: 113 — AL 8th; 1933: 104 — AL 8th

Bases on Balls: 1927: 69 — AL 7th; 1931: 79 — AL 9th; 1932: 82 — AL 9th; 1933: 73 — AL 10th; 1936: 97 — AL 5th

Strikeouts: 1926: 96 — AL 1st; 1927: 82 — AL 3rd; 1928: 50 — AL 9th; 1930: 62 — AL 4th; 1931: 80 — AL 3rd; 1932: 64 — AL 7th; 1933: 64 — AL 8th; 1935: 75 — AL 5th; 1936: 65 — AL 8th; 1937: 76 — AL 5th

Stolen Bases: 1926: 16 — AL 6th; 1927: 22 — AL 3rd; 1931: 18 — AL 4th; 1933: 15 — AL 5th; 1934: 11— AL 9th`

Extra Base Hits: 1926: 60 — AL 7th; 1927: 55 — AL 10th; 1929: 66 — AL 8th

Times On Base: 1927: 245 — AL 7th; 1929: 265 — AL 9th

Hit By Pitch: 1929: 4 — AL 9th

Uniform Numbers: 1926-1927-1928 Yankees: None; 1929 Yankees: 6; 1930 Yankees: 5; 1931 Yankees: 5; 1932 Yankees: 24; 1933 Yankees: 7; 1934 Yankees: 6; 1935 Yankees: 6; 1937 Yankees: 6; 1938 Cubs: 15; 1939 Dodgers: 11; 1939 Giants: 19

Appendix B: Career Highlights

- **August 1, 1925:** The New York Yankees purchase the contract of Tony Lazzeri from the Salt Lake City Bees of the Pacific Coast League. He is scheduled to join his new ball club at their spring training base in St. Petersburg, Florida in March of 1926. Lazzeri is in the midst of hitting 60 home runs and driving in 222 runs in a 197-game schedule. He also is dubbed with the nickname "Poosh 'Em Up" from his band of Italian fans.
- **October 18, 1925:** Lazzeri hits his 60th home run of the season in a 12–10 victory for Salt Lake City over Sacramento. The home run was of the inside-the-park variety in the seventh inning off right-hander Frank Shellenback.
- **October 7, 1926:** With the World Series tied at two games each, nearly 40,000 crowd into Sportsman's Park in St. Louis to see Herb Pennock of the Yankees start against Bill Sherdel of the Cardinals for the second time in the Fall Classic. St. Louis draws first blood when Jim Bottomley doubles and Les Bell singles him home in the fourth inning. Shoddy fielding by the Cardinals gives the visiting Yankees a run in the top of the fifth inning to tie the game. Both clubs score single runs—the Cardinals in their half of the seventh and the Yankees in the top of the ninth—to send the game into extra innings. In the top half of the tenth inning, Mark Koenig of the Yankees singles, takes second on a wild pitch and after being sacrificed to third, scores on Tony Lazzeri's sacrifice fly to win it for the Yankees, 3–2. Both Pennock and Sherdel go the distance.
- **October 10, 1926:** In a steady drizzle at Yankee Stadium in New York, 38,093 fans see the deciding Game Seven of the World Series. It is not known at game time if St. Louis' Grover Cleveland Alexander is sleeping off the team's victory celebration of Game Six in the bullpen. Starting

pitcher Jesse Haines of the Cardinals has a 3–2 lead over Waite Hoyt of the Yankees in the bottom half of the seventh inning. Earle Combs, Bob Meusel and Lou Gehrig each draw a base on balls to load the bases with two down with rookie Lazzeri due up. Player-manager Rogers Hornsby brings in Alexander in relief of Haines, who has developed blister on his pitching hand. With the count at 1–1, Lazzeri smacks a line drive into the left-field stands, just a few feet to the side of the foul pole. Alexander strikes Lazzeri out on the next pitch. Alexander stays in and sets the Yankees down in order until Babe Ruth picks his eleventh walk of the Series with two out in the ninth. For some reason, Ruth attempts to steal second and is thrown out for the final out, giving the Cardinals their first ever World Championship.

- **May 31, 1927:** The Yankees win a pair of games from the Philadelphia Athletics rather easily by scores of 10–3 and 18–5. Babe Ruth hits home runs in each game, running his consecutive game mark for home runs to four and sixteen all told. The A's rookie, Jimmie Foxx, hits his first major league home run off Urban Shocker of the Yankees in the nightcap. Tony Lazzeri and Mark Koenig hit home runs in the same game and Lou Gehrig has two singles to accompany a double, triple and home run that he had hit in the opener.

- **October 8, 1927:** The Pirates, who were down three games to none to the Yankees in the World Series, send their ace, Carmen Hill, to the mound. In the fifth inning, Babe Ruth's second home run of the Series drives in Earle Combs to give the New Yorkers a 3–1 lead. After the Pirates tie it up in the top half of the seventh inning, Combs leads off with a walk in the bottom half of the ninth. Mark Koenig beats out a bunt single and Ruth is passed to load the bases. Manager Donie Bush sends Johnny Miljus in to relieve Hill. Miljus responds by striking out Lou Gehrig and Bob Meusel but with two strikes on Lazzeri, he uncorks a wild pitch that scores Combs with the winning run. The Yankees win the title in a four-game sweep. Both Ruth of the Yankees and Lloyd Waner of the Pirates lead all batters with .400 averages while Ruth's seven runs batted in top all hitters in that category.

- **May 24, 1928:** A major league record of 13 future Hall of Famers take the field in the first game of a twin bill played in Philadelphia between the Yankees and the Athletics. The Yankees are in first place and the A's are second in the American League pennant race. Non-playing Hall of Famers include Herb Pennock and Stan Coveleski of the Yankees, managers Miller Huggins and Connie Mack and umpires Bill McGowan and Tommy Connolly. Earle Combs, Leo Durocher, Babe Ruth, Lou Gehrig, Tony Lazzeri and Waite Hoyt are the future Yankee inductees while Ty

Cobb, Tris Speaker, Mickey Cochrane, Al Simmons, Eddie Collins, Lefty Grove and Jimmie Foxx represent the A's in the Hall. Lazzeri sets the pace in a 9–7 win for the Yankees with three hits and six runs batted in the first game, as Grove took the loss. The A's won the second game, 5–2, behind rookie Ossie Orwell.

• **October 9, 1928:** Following a rainout of Game Four, Waite Hoyt of the Yankees and Bill Sherdel of the Cardinals received the starting nods for their respective ball clubs. The Yankees had won all three games played previously and were looking to sweep the Series for the second consecutive season. The Cardinals held a 2–1 lead after six innings. With one out in the top of the seventh, Ruth hit his second homer of the game to tie it. Gehrig promptly untied it by hitting one of his own. After Meusel singled, Grover Cleveland Alexander was brought in to face none other than his old nemesis, Tony Lazzeri. "Poosh 'Em Up" induced some semblance of revenge for his 1926 World Series strikeout at the hands of Alexander by doubling in Meusel. Lazzeri later scored the fourth run of the inning as the Yankees went on to post a 7–3 victory, aided by Ruth's third home run of the game in the eighth. The Yankees recorded their second straight World Series sweep and Ruth's .625 average has never been topped. Gehrig followed with a .545 mark that included nine runs batted in. The pair also established individual and team offensive records for hits, home runs, total bases and at-bats in a single game.

• **May 22, 1930:** In Philadelphia, the Yankees and Athletics engage in another of their patented home run binges with the Yankees winning yet another pair of games by the lopsided scores of 10–1 and 20–13. Babe Ruth hit a pair of home runs in the first game as did Ben Chapman and starting pitcher George Pipgras. The Yankees ring up nine runs in the first two innings of the second game as the A's come back to tie later it at 12–12. In the victory, Tony Lazzeri leads the Yankee assault with a four-for-four game that includes five runs scored and four runs batted in. Ruth hits a second home run in the nightcap as Gehrig hammers three out of the park while driving in eight runs. Jimmie Foxx of the A's also has two home runs and drives in six runs in the nightcap. On the afternoon, both teams produced a total of 14 homers, including what then was a record 10 in the second game alone.

• **April 2, 1931:** A 17-year-old girl named Jackie Mitchell pitches for the Chattanooga Lookouts of the Southern Association in an exhibition game against the Yankees. Babe Ruth swings wildly at two strikes from her and then watches a third strike sail by. Lou Gehrig purposely swings at three balls so as not to hit them but Tony Lazzeri refuses to be drawn into the joke. "Poosh 'Em Up" tries unsuccessfully to bunt his way on and eventually draws a walk. The young lady leaves the game as the Yankees go on to win it, 14-4. Mitchell went on to pitch for a House of David team two years later.

• **September 13, 1931:** In the first game of a doubleheader against the Tigers, Tony Lazzeri steals second base in the twelfth inning, reaches third on a groundout and steals home to give Lefty Gomez a 2–1 victory.

• **May 21, 1932:** A crowd of over 60,000 fans sees the Yankees crush the Washington Senators by scores of 14–2 and 8–0. The Senators get only eleven hits combined off of the Yankee pitchers, Herb Pennock and Johnny Allen, in the double bill. Home runs on the day include one by Babe Ruth in the opener off Lloyd Brown and he and Lou Gehrig hit back-to-back round trippers in the sixth inning off Frank Ragland. Tony Lazzeri gets six hits in seven at-bats on the afternoon, including a home run, two doubles and a triple.

• **June 3, 1932:** Lou Gehrig hits four consecutive home runs and barely misses a fifth against the Athletics in a slugfest won by the Yankees, 20–13. Tony Lazzeri hits for the cycle as both teams establish a record that still stands for extra bases on long hits in a single contest — 41.

• **August 12, 1932:** American League President Will Harridge upholds a protest by the Detroit Tigers of its August 1 game against the Yankees and orders it replayed on September 8. The Tigers protested because Tony Lazzeri and Ben Chapman's position in the original lineup was orally reversed after the lineup cards had been handed in prior to the start of the game.

• **October 2, 1932:** The Yankees sweep the Cubs in the World Series in a 13–6 game won by New York and Wilcy Moore. Tony Lazzeri leads the way with two home runs while Earle Combs chips in with a solo shot. Combs also ties a Series record with four runs scored while Bill Dickey also ties another Series record with six at-bats.

• **May 28, 1934:** In a 13–9 win over the Browns in St. Louis, Lou Gehrig hits a sixth inning home run off Paul Andrews, and follows Babe Ruth's seventh inning homer with yet another blast into the right-field seats. The back-to-back home runs off Jack Knott are the final two that the pair will combine for. The Yankees also received home runs off the bats of Jack Saltzgaver and Tony Lazzeri.

• **May 23, 1936:** In a doubleheader against the Athletics, Tony Lazzeri hits three home runs good for four runs batted in. The Yankees win both games, 12–6 and 15–1. The unhappy Shibe Park crowd of over 24,000, one of the largest in years, makes play almost impossible at times by raining down bottles, cushions and other debris into the field of play.

• **May 24, 1936:** Tony Lazzeri sets several new records by hitting two grand slam home runs, a third homer and a triple for 15 total bases as the Yankees whip the Athletics, 25–2. By hitting seven home runs in four games and six in three games, "Poosh 'Em Up" sets a new American League mark of 11 runs batted in a single game, which still stands. Joe DiMaggio has three hits, including a home run. When Frank Crosetti cranks one out, a league record is tied when nine different Yankee players score two or more runs. The Yankees walk 16 times with Ben Chapman drawing five passes.

- **October 6, 1937:** In the opening game of the World Series, Carl Hubbell of the Giants starts against Lefty Gomez of the Yankees. The Yankees score seven runs in the sixth inning coming off five singles, three walks and two errors. Tony Lazzeri homers in the bottom of the eighth to seal an 8–1 Yankee victory.
- **October 15, 1937:** The Yankees release Tony Lazzeri at his request. He later signs on as a player-coach for the Cubs.
- **February 26, 1991:** The Veterans Committee elects Tony Lazzeri and Bill Veeck to the Hall of Fame.

Appendix C: Inscription on the Hall of Fame Plaque

ANTHONY MICHAEL LAZZERI

"Poosh 'Em Up Tony"
New York, A.L, 1926–1937
Chicago, N.L., 1938
Brooklyn, N.L., 1939
New York, N.L., 1939

Feared clutch hitter with long ball power played second base with quiet proficiency on famed "murderers row" Yankee teams with Ruth and Gehrig. A .300 hitter five times with career .292 mark. Drove in over 100 runs seven times. Set A.L. Single game record with 2 grand slam and 11 RBIs. 5/24/36. Belted 60 homers for Salt Lake City (PCL) in 1925.

Notes

Introduction

1. Berkow, Ira, *Hank Greenberg: The Story of My Life*, Triumph Books, 2001, 89.
2. *New York Daily News*, July 14, 2003.
3. *Collier's*, June 17, 1950.
4. *The New York Times*, August 9, 1946.
5. *New York Daily News*, July 14, 2003.

1. The Formative Years (1903–1924)

1. *KRON Channel 4.* December 24, 2002.
2. *Ibid.*
3. *The Sporting News*, December 11, 1930.
4. Trachtenberg, Leo, *The Wonder Team*, Bowling Green State University Popular Press, 1995, 46.
5. *The Sporting News*, December 11, 1930.
6. Trachtenberg, Leo, *The Wonder Team*, Bowling Green State University Popular Press, 48.
7. Linn, Ed, *The Great Rivalry*, Ticknor & Fields, 1991, 63.
8. Graham, Frank, *The New York Yankees — An Informal History*, G.P. Putnam's Sons, 1943, 114.
9. Light, Jonathan Fraser, *The Cultural Encyclopedia of Baseball*, McFarland, 1997, 682.
10. *KRON Channel 4,* December 24, 2002.
11. *Baseball Digest*, December 1991.
12. *Ibid.*

2. The Talk of Minor League Baseball (1925)

1. *The Salt Lake Tribune,* October 3, 1993.
2. *Ibid.*
3. *Ibid.*
4. *Ibid.*
5. *Collier's,* June 17, 1950.
6. Dick Johnson and Glenn Stout, *DiMaggio: An Illustrated Life*, Walker & Company, 1995, 42.
7. Rader, Benjamin F., *Baseball: A History of America's Game*, University of Illinois Press, 2002, 138–9.
8. *Collier's,* June 17, 1950.
9. *Ibid.*
10. *Ibid.*
11. *The Salt Lake Tribune,* October 3, 1993.
12. *Ibid.*
13. *The New York Times*, August 7, 1925.

14. *Ibid.*
15. *The Salt Lake Tribune,* October 3, 1993.
16. *Ibid.*
17. *Ibid.*
18. *Ibid.*
19. *The Baseball Research Journal,* Vol. 20, 1991.

3. A Breakout Rookie Season (1926)

1. Graham, Frank, *The New York Yankees — An Informal History,* G. P. Putnam's Sons, 1943, 105.
2. *Ibid.*
3. *Ibid.*
4. *Ibid.*
5. Frommer, Harvey, *A Yankee Century,* 167.
6. Graham, Frank, *The New York Yankees — An Informal History,* G.P. Putnam's Sons, 1943.
7. *Ibid.*
8. Trachtenberg, Leo, *The Wonder Team,* Bowling Green State University Press, 1995, 150.
9. *Ibid.*
10. Graham, Frank, *The New York Yankees — An Informal History,* G. P. Putnam's Sons, 1943, 115.
11. *The Sporting News,* April 9, 1984.
12. *Ibid.*
13. *Ibid.*
14. *Ibid.*
15. Graham, Frank, *The New York Yankees — An Informal History,* G. P. Putnam's Sons, 1943, 116.
16. *Ibid.*
17. *Ibid.*
18. *Ibid.*
19. *The New York Times,* April 28, 1926.
20. *Collier's,* June 17, 1950.
21. *San Francisco Chronicle,* May 4, 1989.
22. Graham, Frank, *The New York Yankees — An Informal History,* G. P. Putnam's Sons, 1943, 119.
23. *Ibid.*
24. *Ibid.*
25. *Ibid.*
26. *Ibid.*
27. *Ibid.*
28. *Ibid.*
29. *Ibid.*
30. *Ibid.*
31. Hoenig, Donald, *Baseball America,* 1985, 157.
32. *Ibid.*
33. *Ibid.*
34. *Ibid.*
35. *Ibid.*
36. *Ibid.*
37. *Ibid.*
38. Carmichael, John P., *My Greatest Day in Baseball: Grover Cleveland Alexander,* A.S. Barnes & Company, 1945.
39. *Ibid.*
40. *Ibid.*
41. Frommer, Harvey, *A Yankee Century,* Berkley Books, 2002, 274.
42. Carmichael, John P., *My Greatest Day in Baseball: Grover Cleveland Alexander,* A.S. Barnes & Company, 1945.
43. *Ibid.*
44. *Ibid.*
45. Robinson, Ray, *The Greatest of All,* G. P. Putnam's Sons, 1968, 177.
46. Carmichael, John P., *My Greatest Day in Baseball: Grover Cleveland Alexander,* A.S. Barnes & Company, 1945.
47. Honig, Donald, *Baseball America,* Macmillian Publishing Company, 1985, 159.
48. Light, Jonathan Fraser, *The Cultural Encyclopedia of Baseball,* McFarland, 1997, 705.

4. Murderers' Row (1927)

1. *The New York Times,* March 25, 1927.
2. Dickson, Paul, *Baseball's Greatest Quotations,* Edward Burlingame Books, 1991, 118.
3. Frommer, Harvey, *A Yankee Century,* The Berkeley Publishing Group, 2002, 146.

4. *Ibid.*
5. *Ibid*, p. 134.
6. Reidenbaugh, Lowell, *Baseball's 25 Greatest Teams*, The Sporting News Publishing Company, 1988, 11.
7. Frommer, Harvey, *A Yankee Century*, The Berkeley Publishing Group, 2002, 292.
8. *The New York Evening Journal*, March 1, 1927.
9. *The New York Times*, April 13, 1927.
10. Dickson, Paul, *Baseball's Greatest Quotations*, Edward Burlingame Books, 1991, 301.
11. Mosedale, John, *The Greatest of All*, The Dial Press, 1982, 137.
12. *Ibid.*
13. *The New York Times*, June 9, 1927.
14. *The World*, June 9, 1927.
15. Dickson, Paul, *Baseball's Greatest Quotations*, Edward Burlingame Books, 1991, 274.
16. Reidenbaugh, Lowell, *Baseball's 25 Greatest Teams*, The Sporting News Publishing Company, 1988, 9.
17. Mosedale, John, *The Greatest of All*, The Dial Press, 1982, 155.
18. Trachtenberg, Leo, *The Wonder Team*, Bowing Green State University Popular Press, 1995, 69.
19. Mosedale, John, *The Greatest of All*, The Dial Press, 1982, 139.
20. *Time*, June 26, 1929.
21. Graham, Frank, *The New York Yankees — An Informal History*, G. P. Putnam's Sons, 1943, 132.
22. *Ibid.*
23. *The Boston Globe*, December 1989.
24. Dickson, Paul, *Baseball's Greatest Quotations*, Edward Burlingame Books, 1991, 166.
25. *Baseball Digest*, January 1980.
26. *Ibid.*
27. *Ibid.*
28. *Ibid.*
29. Dickson, Paul, *Baseball's Greatest Quotations*, Edward Burlingame Books, 1991, 118.
30. Graham, Frank, *The New York Yankees — An Informal History*, G. P. Putnam's Sons, 1943, 130.
31. *The New York Times*, August 19, 1927.
32. *The New York Times*, September 1, 1927.
33. Mosedale, John, *The Greatest of All*, The Dial Press, 1982, 202.
34. Linn, Ed, *The Great Rivalry*, Ticknor & Fields, 1991, 99.
35. *Ibid.*
36. Mosedale, John, *The Greatest of All*, The Dial Press, 1982, 225.
37. *Baseball Digest*, January 1980.
38. Dickson, Paul, *Baseball's Greatest Quotations*, Edward Burlingame Books, 1991, 61.
39. Frommer, Harvey, *A Yankee Century*, The Berkeley Publishing Group, 2002, 240.
40. *Ibid.*
41. Ruth, George Herman, *Babe Ruth's Own Book of Baseball*, University of Nebraska Press, 1992, 92.
42. Graham, Frank, *The New York Yankees — An Informal History*, G. P. Putnam's Sons, 1943, 136.
43. Mosedale, John, *The Greatest of All*, The Dial Press, 1982, 233.
44. *Ibid.*
45. *Ibid.*
46. *Ibid.*
47. *Ibid.*
48. *Ibid.*
49. *Ibid.*
50. *Ibid.*
51. Frommer, Harvey, *A Yankee Century*, The Berkeley Publishing Group, 2002, 274.

5. Back-to-Back Champions (1928)

1. Graham, Frank, *The New York Yankees — An Informal History*, G. P. Putnam's Sons, 1943, 138.
2. *Ibid.*
3. *The New York Times*, February 29, 1928.

4. *The New York Times,* March 3, 1928.
5. *The New York Times,* March 4, 1928.
6. *The New York Times,* March 5, 1928.
7. *Ibid.*
8. *Ibid.*
9. *The New York Times,* March 6, 1928.
10. *Ibid.*
11. Frommer, Harvey, *A Yankee Century,* The Berkeley Publishing Group, 2002, 148.
12. Creamer, Robert W., *Babe: The Legend Comes to Life,* Simon & Schuster, 1974, 316.
13. Graham, Frank, *The New York Yankees — An Informal History,* G. P. Putnam's Sons, 1943, 142.
14. Dickson, Paul, *Baseball's Greatest Quotations,* Edward Burlingame Books, 1991, 191.
15. *Ibid.*
16. Dittmar, Joseph J., *Baseball Records Registry,* McFarland, 1997.
17. *Ibid.*
18. Graham, Frank, *The New York Yankees — An Informal History,* G. P. Putnam's Sons, 1943, 142.
19. *Ibid.*
20. *Ibid.*
21. Durocher, Leo, *Nice Guys Finish Last,* Simon & Schuster, 1975, 45.
22. Graham, Frank, *The New York Yankees — An Informal History,* G. P. Putnam's Sons, 1943, 145.
23. *Ibid.*
24. *The New York Times,* August 27, 1928.
25. Graham, Frank, *The New York Yankees — An Informal History,* G. P. Putnam's Sons, 1943, 149.
26. *Ibid.*
27. *Ibid.,* p. 150.

6. Also-Rans (1929–1931)

1. Frommer, Harvey, *A Yankee Century,* The Berkeley Publishing Group, 2002, 216
2. Shatzkin, Mike, editor, *The Ballplayers,* William Morrow and Company, 1990, 947.
3. *The New York Times,* August 8, 1929.
4. *The New York Times,* March 1, 1929.
5. Graham, Frank, *The New York Yankees — An Informal History,* G. P. Putnam's Sons, 1943, 155.
6. *Ibid.*
7. Smith, Clay, "Postscripts," *Austin Chronicle,* September 17, 2003.
8. *Ibid.*
9. Dickson, Paul, *Baseball's Greatest Quotations,* Edward Burlingame Books, 1991, 184.
10. Graham, Frank, *The New York Yankees — An Informal History,* G. P. Putnam's Sons, 1943, 162.
11. Dickson, Paul, *Baseball's Greatest Quotations,* Edward Burlingame Books, 1991, 177.
12. Graham, Frank, *The New York Yankees — An Informal History,* G.P. Putnam's Sons, 1943, 162.
13. Dickson, Paul, *Baseball's Greatest Quotations,* Edward Burlingame Books, 1991, 177.
14. *Ibid.*
15. *The New York Times,* March 13, 1931.
16. Graham, Frank, *The New York Yankees — An Informal History,* G.P. Putnam's Sons, 1943, 178.
17. *Ibid.*
18. *Ibid.*
19. Orr, Jack, "The Girl Who Struck Out Babe Ruth," Sport, June 1954.

7. Back on Top Again (1932)

1. *The New York Times,* March 2, 1932.
2. *The New York Times,* March 4, 1932.
3. *The New York Times,* March 13, 1931.

4. Dickson, Paul, *Baseball's Greatest Quotations*, Edward Burlingame Books, 1991, 215.
  5. *Baseball Magazine*, June 1944.
  6. Shatzkin, Mike, editor, *The Ballplayers*, William Morrow and Company, 1990, 397.
  7. Dickson, Paul, *Baseball's Greatest Quotations*, Edward Burlingame Books, 1991, 153.
  8. *Ibid*, 184.
  9. *Ibid*.
  10. Cosgrove, Benedict, *Covering the Bases*, Chronicle Books, 1997, 50.
  11. *Ibid*.
  12. "History of the World Series—1932," *The Sporting News*.
  13. Dickson, Paul, *Baseball's Greatest Quotations*, Edward Burlingame Books, 1991, 66.
  14. *Ibid*.
  15. "History of the World Series—1932," *The Sporting News*.
  16. *Ibid*.
  17. Frommer, Harvey, *A Yankee Century*, The Berkeley Publishing Group, 2002, 229.
  18. Dickson, Paul. *Baseball's Greatest Quotations*. Edward Burlingame Books, 1991, 293.

8. Runners Up (1933–1935)

  1. *The Sporting News*, March 24, 1979.
  2. *Ibid*.
  3. Shatzkin, Mike, Editor, *The Ballplayers*, William Morrow & Company, 1990, 397.
  4. *Baseball Magazine*, June 1944.
  5. Linn, Ed, *The Great Rivalry*, Ticknor & Fields, 1991, 124.
  6. *Ibid*.
  7. Dickson, Paul, *Baseball's Greatest Quotations*, Edward Burlingame Books, 1991, 161.
  8. Reidenbaugh, Lowell, *Baseball's 25 Greatest Teams*, The Sporting News Publishing Company, 1988, 243.
  9. Dickson, Paul, *Baseball's Greatest Quotations*, Edward Burlingame Books, 1991, 213.

  10. *The New York Times*, March 1, 1934.
  11. Graham, Frank, *The New York Yankees — An Informal History*, G. P. Putnam's Sons, 1943, 200.
  12. *The New York Times*, February 28, 1935.
  13. *The New York Times*, March 9, 1935.
  14. *The New York Times*, March 24, 1935.

9. Return to Paradise (1936–1937)

  1. Durso, Joseph, *DiMaggio: The Last American Knight*, Little, Brown, 1995, 83.
  2. Dickson, Paul, *Baseball's Greatest Quotations*, Edward Burlingame Books, 1991, 177.
  3. *The Sporting News*, June 24, 1923.
  4. Berkow, Ira. *Hank Greenberg: The Story of My Life*, Triumph Books, 2001, 22.
  5. Dick Johnson and Glenn Stout, *DiMaggio. An Illustrated Life*, Walker & Company, 1995, 84.
  6. Baldassaro, Lawrence, "Before Joe D: Early Italian Americans in the Major Leagues," *Baseball Research Magazine*, January 19, 2003.
  7. *Ibid*.
  8. *Ibid*.
  9. *Ibid*.
  10. *Ibid*.
  11. *Ibid*.
  12. *Ibid*.
  13. *Ibid*.
  14. Graham, Frank, *The New York Yankees — An Informal History*, G. P. Putnam's Sons, 1943, 221.
  15. *Ibid*.
  16. *Sport Magazine*, April 1956.
  17. *Ibid*.
  18. *The New York Times*, March 3, 1936.
  19. Dickson, Paul, *Baseball's Greatest*

Quotations, Edward Burlingame Books, 1991, 153.
20. Light, Jonathan Fraser, *The Cultural Encyclopedia of Baseball*, McFarland & Company, 1997, 408.
21. *The Sporting News*, January 5, 1963.
22. Durso, Joseph, *DiMaggio: The Last American Knight*, Little, Brown, 1995, 46.
23. Frommer, Harvey, *A Yankee Century*, The Berkeley Publishing Group, 2002, 148.
24. Dickson, Paul, *Baseball's Greatest Quotations*, Edward Burlingame Books, 1991, 163.
25. *The New York Times*, May 25, 1936.
26. Frommer, Harvey, *A Yankee Century*, The Berkeley Publishing Group, 2002, 282.
27. Associated Press, December 9, 1936.
28. *The New York Times*, February 6, 1937.
29. Henrich, Tommy, *Five O'Clock Lightning*, Birch Lane Press, 1992, 24.
30. *Baseball Digest*, March 1939.
31. Graham, Frank, *The New York Yankees — An Informal History*, G. P. Putnam's Sons, 1943, 233.
32. *Baseball Magazine*, July 1937.
33. *Ibid*.
34. *The New York Times*, September 5, 1937.
35. Henrich, Tommy, *Five O'Clock Lightning*, Birch Lane Press, 1992, 25.
36. *The New York Times*, September 30, 1937.
37. Graham, Frank, *The New York Yankees — An Informal History*, G. P. Putnam's Sons, 1943, 236.
38. *The New York Times*, October 19, 1937.
39. *Ibid*.
40. *The New York Times*, October 29, 1937.
41. *Ibid*.
42. *The New York Times*, October 30, 1937.
43. *San Francisco Chronicle*, May 4, 1989.

10. The End Draws Near (1938–1943)

1. Holtzman, Jerome and George Vass, *Baseball, Chicago Style*, Bonus Books, 2001.
2. Karst, Gene and Martin J. Jones, Jr., *Who's Who in Professional Baseball*, Arlington House, 1973, 689.
3. *The New York Times*, October 10, 1938.
4. *The New York Times*, October 26, 1938.
5. *Ibid*.
6. *The New York Times*, December 7, 1938.
7. *Ibid*.
8. *Ibid*.
9. *The New York Times*, December 11, 1938.
10. *The New York Times*, May 14, 1939.
11. Telephone conversation with Dario Lodigiani, April 14, 2003.
12. *Ibid*.
13. *The New York Times*, November 8, 1940.
14. *Ibid*.
15. *The New York Times*, January 25, 1941.
16. *The New York Times*, January 11, 1944.
17. *Ibid*.

11. Retirement and the Final Exit (1944–1946)

1. *New York Herald-Tribune*, August 9, 1946.
2. *Ibid*.
3. *Ibid*.
4. *Ibid*.
5. *The New York Times*, August 9, 1946.
6. *Baseball Digest*, December 1991.
7. Johnson, Kevin, "Tony Lazzeri," 1991.
8. *Ibid*.
9. *Ibid*.
10. *Ibid*.
11. *Ibid*.

Bibliography

Aubrecht, Michael. *Who's the Greatest?* Baseball Almanac, 2002.
Baldassaro, Lawrence. *Before Joe D: Early Italian Americans in the Major Leagues.* Carbondale: Southern Illinois University Press, 2003.
Barrow, Edward G. "Tail-End to Tiptop: Rise of the Yankees." *Collier's,* June 17, 1950.
Baseball Almanac, 2002.
Baseball Reference, 2002.
Berkow, Ira. *Hank Greenberg: The Story of My Life.* Chicago: Triumph, 2001.
_____. *Red: A Biography of Red Smith.* New York: McGraw Hill, 1987.
Beverage, Richard E. "Tony Lazzeri: Baseball's First 60-Homer Man." *The Baseball Research Journal,* Vol. 20, 1991.
Bloodgood, Clifford. "Mound Conferences." *Baseball Magazine,* June 1944.
Burr, Harold C. "Not Like the Old Days." *Baseball Magazine,* March 1939.
Carmichael, John P. *My Greatest Day in Baseball: Grover Cleveland Alexander.* A.S. Barnes, 1945.
Cosgrove, Benedict. *Covering the Bases.* San Francisco: Chronicle, 1997.
Cramer, Richard Ben. *Joe DiMaggio: The Hero's Life.* New York: Simon & Schuster, 2000.
Creamer, Robert W. *Babe: The Legend Comes to Life.* New York: Simon & Schuster, 1974.
Curran, William. *Big Sticks.* New York: William Morrow, 1990.
Daniel, Daniel M. "DiMaggio, Lazzeri, Moore Deals Stand Out in Barrow's Recollection." *Baseball Magazine,* May 1950.
DeGregorio, George. *Joe DiMaggio: An Informal Biography.* New York: Stein & Day, 1983.
Dickson, Paul. *Baseball's Greatest Quotations.* New York: Edward Burlingame, 1991.
Dittmar, Joseph J. *Baseball Records Registry.* Jefferson, N.C.: McFarland, 1997.
Durocher, Leo, and Ed Linn. *Nice Guys Finish Last.* New York: Simon and Schuster, 1975.
Durso, Joseph. *DiMaggio: The Last American Knight.* Boston: Little, Brown, and Co., 1995.
Einstein, Charles, editor. *The Third Fireside Book of Baseball.* New York: Simon & Schuster, 1968.

Frommer, Harvey. *A Yankee Century.* New York: Berkley Books, 2002.
Gallagher, Mark, and Neil Gallagher. *Baseball's Great Dynasties: The Yankees.* New York: Gallery Books, 1990.
Graham, Frank. "Hitting Slumps—Their Cause and Cure." *Baseball Magazine,* July 1937.
_____. *The New York Yankees—An Informal History.* New York: G.P. Putnam's Sons, 1943.
_____. "Those Spring Training Blues." *Sport,* April 1956.
Gutman, Dan. *Baseball's Greatest Games.* New York: Viking, 1994.
Harper, John. "The Unknown Star." *New York Daily News,* July 14, 2003.
Henrich, Tommy. *Five O'Clock Lightning.* New York: Birch Lane, 1992.
Holtzman, Jerome and George Vass. *Baseball, Chicago Style.* Chicago: Bonus, 2001.
Honig, Donald. *Baseball America.* Macmillan Publishing Company, 1985.
_____. "The New York Yankees. An Illustrated History." *Crown Publishers,* 1981.
James, Bill. *The Bill James Guide to Baseball Managers from 1870 to Today.* New York: Scribner, 1997.
_____. *The New Bill James Historical Baseball Abstract.* New York: The Free Press, 2001.
Johnson, Dick, and Glenn Stout. *DiMaggio: An Illustrated Life.* New York: Walker, 1995.
Johnson, Kevin. "Tony Lazzeri." *The Baseball Index,* 2001.
Karst, Gene and Martin J. Jones, Jr. *Who's Who in Professional Baseball.* New Rochelle, NY: Arlington House, 1973.
Kofoed, Jack. "Great Dramas in Sport." *Life,* May 1932.
Light, Jonathan Fraser. *The Cultural Encyclopedia of Baseball.* Jefferson, N.C.: McFarland, 1997.
Linn, Ed. *The Great Rivalry.* Boston: Ticknor & Fields, 1991.
Macht, Norman. "Yankee Recollections." *The Sporting News,* April 9, 1984.
Mosedale, John. *The Greatest of All.* New York: The Dial Press, 1982.
Nemec, David, and Saul Wisnia. *Baseball: More Than 150 Years.* Lincolnwood, IL: Publications International, 1996.
Newhouse, Dave. "Ex-Yankee Star Mark Koenig Remembers Better Days." *Baseball Digest,* January 1979.
_____. "Yankee Hermit: Mark Koenig and His Memories." *The Sporting News,* July 5, 1980.
Orr, Jack. "The Girl Who Struck Out Babe Ruth." *Sport,* June 1954.
Rader, Benjamin F. *Baseball: A History of America's Game.* University of Illinois Press, 2002.
Reichler, Joseph L., Editor. *The Baseball Encyclopedia.* Baseball Register, 1988.
Reidenbaugh, Lowell. *Baseball's 25 Greatest Teams.* St. Louis: The Sporting News, 1988.
Ritter, Lawrence. *The Story of Baseball.* New York: William Morrow, 1983.
Robinson, Ray. *The Greatest of Them All.* New York: G.P. Putnam's Sons, 1968.
Ruth, George Herman. *Babe Ruth's Own Book of Baseball.* Rpt. Lincoln: University of Nebraska Press, 1992.
Schinder, Harold. "Bees Star Hits the Big Time." *Salt Lake City Tribune,* October 3, 1993.
Shatzkin, Mike, editor. *The Ballplayers.* New York: William Morrow, 1990.
Slocum, Frank. "Spring Training Wisecracks Live Forever." *The Sporting News,* March 24, 1979.

Smith, Red. "Alone in the Dark." *New York Herald-Tribune,* August 9, 1946.
_____. "A Man Who Knew the Crowds." *New York Herald-Tribune,* August 9, 1946.
_____. "Tony Lazzeri: Player of the Years." *Baseball Digest,* October 1946.
Spink, J. G. Taylor. *Judge Landis and 25 Years of Baseball.* St. Louis: Sporting News Publishing Company, 1974.
Stout, Glenn, and Richard A. Johnson. *Yankees Century.* New York: Houghton Mifflin, 2002.
Summers, Bill. "What I Didn't Tell During 27 Years of Big League Umpiring." *Baseball Digest,* September 1960.
Trachtenberg, Leo. *The Wonder Team.* Bowling Green, OH: Bowling Green State University Popular Press, 1995.
Werber, Bill and C. Paul Rogers III. *Memories of a Ballplayer.* Cleveland: The Society for American Baseball Research, 2001.

Index

Aldridge, Vic 62
Alexander, Grover Cleveland 1, 34–42, 49, 78–79, 82, 170–172, 179, 181
Allen, Johnny 105, 109, 118, 122, 124, 128, 137, 182
Allen, Mel 146
American Association 115
Andrews, Ivy 151
Andrews, Paul 182
Associated Press 53, 143, 167
Atlanta Crackers 47
Austin College, Stephen C. 47

"The Babe" 43, 49, 52, 54, 58–59, 67, 79–81, 84, 95, 100–101, 105, 107, 110–111, 121, 126
"Babe Comes Home" 44
"Babe Ruth's Own Book of Baseball" 62
Bacon, Daniel 6, 13
Baker, Frank 101
Baldassaro, Lawrence 133–134
"The Bambino" 43–45, 53–54, 56, 58–59, 62, 64, 75, 80–81, 83, 94, 105, 111–113, 115, 120–121, 123, 125–127, 135
Barbary Coast 5
Barber, Red 94
Barfoot, Clyde 100
Barnes, Donald 153
Barnhart, Clyde 61, 64
Barr, George 159
Barrow, Ed 3, 18–20, 24–25, 27, 29, 48, 58, 67–69, 83, 88, 90–92, 96, 100, 102, 115, 126, 129–130, 143, 147, 152
Bartell, Dick 141–142, 144

Baseball Digest 145
"Beast" 101
Bell, Alexander Graham 10
Bell, Les 36–38, 179
Bengough, Benny 25, 32, 47, 77–78, 85, 88, 171
Berger, Wally 3, 12
Berkow, Ira 1
Birmingham Barons 84
Bishop, Max 85
"Black Mike" 145
Black Sox Scandal 42
"Bob the Gob" 92
Bodie, Ping 18
Boley, Joe 85
Bonneville Park 15
Bonura, Zeke 133
Book Cadillac Hotel 30
Boston Globe 55
Boston Pilgrims 8
Boston's North End 52–53
Bottomley, Jim 78–79, 82, 179
Bowers, Frank K. 58
Brandt, William E. 72, 87, 103
Braxton, Garland 25, 32–33, 77
Brechin, Gary 6
Brennan, Don 118
Bridges, Tommy 123, 125
Broaca, Johnny 128, 137
Bronx Bombers 56–57, 59, 78, 115, 152
Brooklyn Robins 29
"The Brooklyn Schoolboy" 94
Brown, Lloyd 182
Brown, Mace 156, 158–159
Brown, Walter 118, 137
Brundidge, Harry 7, 10

195

Bryant, Clay 160
Buckingham, Hotel 33
Bullock, Red 138
Burns, Jack 165
Burr, Harold 145
Bush, Donie 60, 64, 90, 180
Bush, Guy 110, 113
"Butcher Town" 13
Byrd, Sammy 68, 84, 118, 127

California State League 15
Camilli, Dolph 133
Capitolo, Francesco 16
Carew, Rod 172
Carmichael, John 37–38
Carroll, Owen 94
"Casey at the Bat" 7
Cavaretta, Phil 133
Century of Progress Exposition 119
Chance, Hank 145
Chandler, Spud 146, 160
Chapman, Ben 96–97, 100–101, 104, 107–108, 110–111, 118, 120, 127, 129, 137, 139, 181–183
Chase, Frank 89
Chattanooga Lookouts 100, 181
Chelini, Italo 134
Chicago Tribune 40, 119
Chinatown 8
Clarke, Fred 89
Cobb, Ty 15, 29, 51, 72–74, 104, 181
Cochrane, Mickey 29, 51, 72–73, 85, 115, 119–120, 123–124, 129, 145–146, 181
Cohen, Andy 19
Coit, Lillie Hitchcock 5
Coit Tower 5
Collins, Eddie 2, 50, 72–73, 90–91, 181
Collins, Pat 25, 32, 47, 53, 77
Collins, Rip 132, 158, 160
"Columbia Lou" 111
Columbia University 45
Combs, Earle 1–2, 25, 28–29, 33, 35–36, 40, 44–45, 56–57, 60–61, 64–65, 68, 72, 77–78, 81, 85, 89, 96–97, 100, 104, 109, 112, 114–115, 117–118, 120, 123, 127, 129, 137, 140, 180, 182
Comiskey Park 72
Concourse Plaza Hotel 143
Connery, Bob 19–20
Connolly, Tommy 31, 72, 180

Cooke, Dusty 68
Corrigan, Red 158
Corsi, Edward 58
Coscarart, Pete 164–165
Cotillo, Salvatore A. 58
Covaleski, Stan 180
Cow Hollow District 5, 11–12
Cronin, Joe 3, 12, 119–121
Crosetti, Frank 1, 3, 103–104, 117, 123, 127–131, 133–134, 136–137, 139, 142, 144, 146, 154, 160–162, 172–173, 183
Cross, Harry 129
"Crow" 104, 134
Crowder, Alvin 119
Cuccinello, Tony 133
Cuyler, Kiki 111

Dahlgren, Babe 173
Daley, Arthur 3, 31, 154, 171
Daniel, Dan 133
"The Danish Viking" 79
Dartmouth College 122, 146
Dawson, James P. 127, 139
Dean, Dizzy 132, 161
Delehanty, Ed 107
Delmonico's 6
Demaree, Frank 113
Dempsey, Jack 44
Derks, John C. 16–17, 20–21
DeShong, Jimmy 123
Detroit University 30
Devens, Charlie 118
Devine, Joe 130
Dickey, Bill 2, 70–71, 77, 84–85, 88, 90, 98, 104, 110, 115, 118–120, 123, 129, 137, 140–141, 146, 150, 160–161, 172, 182
DiMaggio, Joe 1–3, 25, 31, 59, 33, 59, 107, 128, 130–131, 133–137, 139–140, 142–144, 146, 150–151, 154, 160–161, 172–174, 185
DiRenzo, Daniel E. 58
Doerr, Bobby 172
Dolan, Cozy 18
Donovan, Wild Bill 25
"Double X" 101, 121
Douthit, Taylor 79–80
Drebinger, John 111
Dreyfuss, Barney 90
Dugan, "Jumping Joe" 25, 28, 41, 44, 46, 51, 53, 56, 70, 77, 84, 91–92, 115
Durocher, Leo 68, 70–72, 74–76, 79, 85–88, 93, 164–165, 180

Index

Durso, Joseph 131, 136
Durst, Cedric 45, 51–52, 78–79, 81, 93
Dykes, Jimmy 85

Earnshaw, George 85, 90, 101, 106
Eastern Kentucky State Teachers College 45
Eastern League 4, 14, 68
"El Goofo" 138
Engel, Joe 100
English, Woody 111
Essick, Bill 130
Evers, Johnny 126
Ewing, Cal 8

Faber, Red 75
Falk, Bibb 57
Farley, James J. 58
Farrell, Doc 117
Fenway Park 52, 58
Ferrell, Rick 120
"Fireman" 147
Fitzsimmons, Freddie 141–142
"Five O'clock Lightning" 57, 64, 144, 150
Fletcher, Art 89, 91, 96
La Follia 58
Forbes Field 62
Fordham University 123
"The Foremost Spaghetti Farmer" 59
Foxx, Jimmie 51, 72, 85, 90, 96, 101, 105, 119–121
Frederick, Johnny 16
Frick, Ford 49
Frisch, Frank 78, 80, 120
Fuchs, Emil 126–127
Fugazy, Humbert J. 58–59
Fuji Club 8

Galan, Augie160
Gallico, Paul 38, 52, 65, 112
"The Game of the Century" 120
"The Gashouse Gang" 132
Gazzella, Mike 32–33, 47, 51, 68, 84
"The Gay Caballero" 138
"The Gay Castilian" 138
Gehrig, Lou 1–3, 24–25, 27–29, 31, 33–34, 36, 40, 43, 45–47, 51–53, 57–59, 62, 64–65, 67, 70–72, 79–81, 83, 85–87, 89–92, 95, 97, 100–101, 104, 106–113, 115, 117–118, 120–122, 125–127, 129, 135–136, 141–143, 146, 150–151, 153, 156, 160, 162, 171–173, 180–182, 184
Gehringer, Charlie 120, 125, 173
Giard, Joe 45, 48
Gold Rush 7
Golden, Harry 40
Golden Gate 6
Golden Gate Bridge
Golden Gate Natives 11
Gomez, Lefty 2–3, 93, 101, 104–105, 109–110, 118–121, 125–126, 128–129, 136–137, 140–142, 146–147, 150–152, 160–162, 171–172, 174, 182
Gooch, Johnny 61, 65
"Goofy" 105, 137
Gordon, Joe 1–2, 144–145, 147, 152, 159, 162–163
Goslin, Goose 119
Gowdy, Hank 126
Grabowski, Johnny 47, 77, 85
Graflan, Van 73
Graham, Frank 12, 147
"Grandma" 146, 160
Grange, Red 44
Grant Avenue 5
Grantham, George 62–63
Greenberg, Hank 1, 125, 132
Grimes, Burleigh 164
Grimm, Charlie 109, 111, 113, 153, 156, 161, 163
Grossfeld, Stan 55
Grove, Lefty 50–51, 72–73, 77, 85, 90, 101, 121, 181

Haas, Mule 85
Hack, Stan 155, 158, 160, 162
Hadley, Bump 137, 140–142, 145–146, 151
Hafey, Chick 3, 79, 120
Haines, Jesse 34–36, 78, 80, 180
Hall of Fame 1, 4–5, 45, 48, 79, 94, 104, 122, 137–138, 171–174, 183
Hallahan, Bill 36, 120
"The Happy Hidalgo" 138
Harbor View 10
Harlem River 49, 141
Harper, George Washington 79
Harper, John 2, 4
Harridge, Will 108, 149, 182
Harris, Bucky 108
Harris, Joe 62
Harrison, James R. 52, 68–70

Hartnett, Gabby 112, 153, 156, 158–161, 163
Heffner, Don 122, 127, 129
Heilmann, Harry 3
Heimach, Fred 74
Hendricks, Jack 17
Henrich, Tommy 144, 146, 148, 160–161
Herman, Babe 113
Herman, Billy 111, 155, 158, 173
Herrmann, Gary 17
High, Andy 79
Hill, Carmen 61, 64, 180
Hill, Jesse 129
Hoag, Myril 122–123, 127, 129, 144, 146, 152, 161
Hodapp, Johnny 95
Hollenden Hotel 32
Holly, Ed 19
Holtzman, Jerome 159
Holy Cross College 46
"The Homer in the Gloamin'" 157
Hornsby, Rogers 2, 34–38, 40–41, 62, 96, 108–109, 120, 126, 161, 180
Hotel Chase 134
Hotel Commodore 58
House of David 182
"The House That Ruth Built" 49
Howard Street Gang 12
Hoyt, Waite 2, 25, 27, 32–35, 41, 47, 51, 56, 60, 62–63, 68–70, 72–73, 76–80, 90, 92, 94–95, 171–172, 180–181, 183
Hubbell, Carl 142–143, 150–151
Hudlin, Willis 88
Hudson River 144
Huggins, Miller 23–27, 30–33, 38, 42, 45, 48–49, 51–52, 56, 58, 60, 63, 65–66, 68–73, 75–76, 79–80, 83–84, 88–89, 91–93, 96, 106, 180
Huggins Field 103, 135
Huskies 156
Huston, Cap 26, 83
Hyland, Dr. Robert F. 124

International League 4, 96, 115, 122, 165–167
International News 134
"The Iron Horse" 44, 107, 121, 123, 125, 140, 150
Italian Republican League 23, 26

Jackson, Travis 143
Jenkins, Ferguson 172

"Joe D" 146
Johnson, Ban 23, 26
Johnson, Bob 148–149
Johnson, Hank 68, 72, 77, 90
Johnson, Walter 106
Jolley, Smead 13
"Jolly Cholly" 156
"Jolting Joe" 160
Jones, Bobby 44
Jones, Sad Sam 25, 32, 174
Jorgens, Arndt 118
Judge, Joe 53
Jupiter, Harry 29, 154
Jurges, Billy 109, 111, 115, 155, 158, 162–163

Kamm, Willie 18, 57
Kampouris, Alex 165
Kelly, George 3
"The Kentucky Colonel" 44
"The Kentucky Schoolmaster" 78
Kerr, Johnny 22
Klinger, Bob 158
Knickerbocker, Billy 136
Knott, Jack 182
Koenig, Mark 1, 3, 25, 27–29, 33, 35–36, 39, 46–47, 51–52, 54–57, 62–65, 68, 70, 84–87, 91, 93–95, 109–110, 115, 117, 166, 171, 173, 179–180
Kopp, Merlin 22
Kremer, Ray 62
Krichell, Paul 19–20, 143

Lafayette College 32
LaGuardia, Fiorello H. 58
Lajoie, Napoleon 2
Landis, Kenesaw Mountain 24, 39, 42, 81, 108
Lane, H. W. 16
"Larrupin' Lou" 43, 45, 59, 77, 80, 106, 113
Lary, Lyn 76, 84, 88, 93, 100–01, 103, 117, 123
Lauria, Michael 58
Lavagetto, Cookie 133
Lazarre, Tony 16–17, 20–22
Lazzeri, Maye 11, 14, 16, 114, 143, 154, 170
Lazzeri, Tony 1–10, 12–22, 24–25, 27–31, 33–40, 42–43, 45, 48–49, 51–58, 60–63, 65–66, 68–82, 84–89, 91–95,

97–98, 100–101, 103–104, 107–109, 111, 117, 120–123, 125, 127–131, 133–141, 143–159, 162–167, 169–175, 179–184
Lazzeri, Tony, Jr. 114
League Park 33
Lee, Bill 21, 160–162
Leiber, Hank 151–152
Leman, Arthur 166–167
"Leo the Lip" 74
Lewis, Duffy 13
Liberty Bell 10
Lieb, Frederick 134
Life 133
Linn, Ed 12
Lipton, Sir Thomas 50
Literary Digest 27
Little Italy 5
Little World Series 43
Lodigiani, Dario 166
Logan, Fred 95, 97
Lombardi, Ernie 3, 12, 133–134
Louisville Slugger 45
Lowe, Bobby 107
Lyons, Ted 75

MacFayden, Danny 105, 118
Macht, Norman 27–28
Mack, Connie 18, 50, 72–74, 76, 85, 91, 96, 118, 120, 148
MacPhail, Larry 164
Mahaffey, Leroy106
Mahon, Jack 134
"The Mail Carrier" 44, 115
Malone, Pat 110, 129, 147, 140, 142
Mancuso, Francis 58
Mancuso, Gus 133
Manush, Heinie 119
Maranville, Rabbit 78, 80, 82, 126
Market Street 6, 10
"Marse Joe" 96–99, 108, 122–124, 129–130, 132, 137, 139
Martin, Billy 3
Martin, Pepper 132
Marty, Joe 158
MasterCard 113
Mathewson, Christy 126
Maybeck, Bernard 10
McCarthy, Joe 34, 45, 96–106, 108–109, 113, 115–116, 118, 122–124, 126–127, 129–130, 132, 135, 137, 139–144, 147–148, 151, 159, 161
McDonald, John 165

McGeehan, W. O. 23
McGowan, Bill 72, 80, 180
McGraw, John 27, 83, 107, 120, 145
McKechnie, Bill 78, 81, 126
McKee, Joseph V. 58
McLain, Denny 161
McNally, Dave 168
McNamee, Graham 50
Meadows, Lee 62, 64
"Meal Ticket" 150
Melton, Cliff 150–151
Merkle, Fred 170
Merriwell, Dick 52
"Merry Mortician" 56
Meusel, Bob 1–2, 25, 27, 29, 31, 38, 44, 51, 53, 60–62, 65, 71, 76–77, 79, 85, 87, 90, 92–93, 107, 137, 171, 180–181
Meusel, Irish 44
Miljus, Johnny 64–65, 180
Miller, Bing 85
Mitchell, Jackie 100–101, 181–182
Montreal Royals 166
"Monument Park" 106
Moore, Johnny 111
Moore, JoJo 110, 142
Moore, Wilcy 48, 60, 62, 64, 68, 74, 104, 118, 171, 182
Morehart, Ray 47, 51–52
Moriarity, George 75
Mullin, Willard 134
Murderers' Row 1, 42, 44, 60, 66–67, 77, 91, 109, 140
Murphy, Johnny 123, 128, 137, 140, 146–147, 151, 160–162

Nallin, Dicky 108
New York Daily News 2, 4, 112, 117, 156
New York Evening Graphic 27
New York Evening Journal 49
New York Herald-Tribune 23, 101, 170–171
New York Mirror 27
The New York Times 20, 29, 31, 49, 52–53, 57, 69, 87, 100, 103, 111, 122, 127, 135, 139, 147, 149–150, 154, 162–163, 167, 171
Newark Bears 84, 115
"Nice Guys Finish Last" 75
North Beach 5–6

Oakland Oaks 84
O'Connell, Jimmy 18

O'Doul, Lefty 13, 16, 21, 61
O'Farrell, Bob 37–38, 78–79
"Old Reliable" 146
Oldfield, Barney 10
O'Leary, Charley 70, 89
O'Neill, Steve 148, 153
Orr, Jack 100
Orwoll, Ossie 74
Ott, Mel 141, 152
Owens, Brick 80

Pacific Coast League 2, 8, 13, 18–19, 22, 24, 30, 44, 70, 84, 104, 109, 131, 167, 179, 184
Painter, Doc 95
Palace Hotel 16
Palace of Fine Arts 10
Palace Theater 56
Panama Pacific International Exposition 10
"The Paris of the Pacific" 6
Paschal, Ben 45, 78
Pearson, Monte 137, 140, 142, 146, 150, 160–162
Pegler, Westbrook 40
Pennock, Herb 2, 25, 31, 33–35, 47, 51, 60, 63, 67, 76–78, 88–89, 92, 95, 97, 102. 105, 112, 118, 122, 171, 179–180, 182
Perry, Gaylord 172
Pezzo, Francesco Stephano 18
Pfirman, Charlie 80–81
Philadelphia Inquirer 72
Philadelphia Public Ledger 72
Piedmont League 4, 168
Pipgras, George 48, 57, 63, 71, 76–79, 88, 90, 95, 97, 102, 105–106, 109–110, 112, 118, 181
Pipp, Wally 24, 47
"Pistol Pete" 164
Polo Grounds 49, 141–142
"Poosh 'Em Up" 2–4, 11, 16, 19, 21–22, 24, 27, 30–31, 33, 36, 42–43, 53, 57, 59, 65, 68, 70–71, 73–74, 76–77, 79–80, 82, 85, 90, 93, 95, 98, 103, 113, 117, 119, 131, 138, 140–141, 150, 152–153, 155, 158, 165–172, 174–175, 179, 181, 183–184
Powell, Jake 139–143, 146
"Pride of the Yankees" 113

Quinn, Johnny 149–150
Ragland, Frank 182

Raimo, Joseph 58
Randolph, Willie 2
Reagan, Ronald 41
Rec Park 13
Reese, Jimmy 19, 70, 84, 93, 97
Reiser, Pete 164
Rennie, Rud 101
Reynolds, Carl 160
Rice, Grantland 51, 65
Rice, Harry 94
Richardson, Bobby 2
Richardson, Nolen 129
Rickey, Branch 85, 115, 132
Rigler, Cy 80
Rinetti, Cesare 16
Ripken, Cal, Jr. 24
Ripple, Jimmy 142
"The Roaring Twenties" 12, 42
Robertson, Gene 67–68, 87–88
Robinson, Arthur 66
Robinson, Jackie 116, 132
Robinson, Wilbert 26, 29
Rodriguez, Alex 139
Rolfe, Red 122, 127, 137, 140, 142–143, 146, 160–161
Rolph, "Sunny Jim" 10
Roosevelt, Franklin D. 141
Root, Charlie 166, 110–113, 160
Ross, Don 166
Roth, Mark 76–77
Rotisserie Inn 16
Rowe, Schoolboy 123
Ruether, Dutch 32–33, 48, 51
Ruffing, Red 2, 93–95, 101, 105–106, 109–110, 118, 121, 128–129, 135, 137, 140–142, 146, 150, 160–162, 172
Ruppert, Colonel Jacob 17, 23–27, 49, 57–58, 82–84, 87–92, 96, 101–102, 115, 125–126, 131, 137, 143–144, 152
Ruth, Babe 1–3, 15, 21, 23–28, 30–31, 33–36, 38–40, 42, 44–47, 50–54, 56–60, 62–65, 67, 71–72, 75–85, 87–90, 92, 94–95, 97, 99–101, 104–107, 109–113, 117–118, 120–121, 123–127, 135, 137, 171–172, 180–182, 184
Ryan, Blondy 129

"Sailor Bob" 92, 96
St. Francis of Assisi Church 6
St. Paul's Church 171
St. Theresa's School 10

St. Vincent's Hospital 92
Saints Peter and Paul Church 6
Salt Lake City Bees 2, 13–17, 21–22, 30, 179, 184
Salt Lake City Tribune 16, 20, 22
Saltzgaver, Jack 103–104, 123, 127, 129, 182
San Francisco Chronicle 29, 154
San Francisco Examiner 174
San Francisco Seals 13, 17, 22, 130, 167
Sand, Heinie 18
Schoendienst, Red 172
Schumacher, Hal 120, 141–142, 150
"The Scintillator" 10
Scott, Everett 121
Seattle Indians 16–17
"Second Place Joe" 130
Seeds, Bob 142
Selkirk, George 123–124, 127, 137, 140–141, 146, 150, 160–161
Servente, Louie 170
Severeid, Hank 32
Sewell, Joe 91, 97, 104, 115, 121–122
Shaughnessy, Frank 167
Shawkey, Bob 32, 35, 48, 89, 92–94, 96
Shealy, Al 68, 74
Shellenback, Frank 179
Sherdel, Bill 34–35, 78, 80–81, 179, 181
Shibe Park 72, 138, 148, 182
Shocker, Urban 25, 31, 34, 51, 60, 68–70, 72
Simmons, Al 51, 72–74, 77, 85, 90, 94, 96, 101, 119, 181
Sing Sing Prison 54
"The Singular Senor" 138
Sisler, George 126
Slocum, Bill 117
Slocum, Frank 117
Smith, Al 150
Smith, Earl 61
Smith, Elmer 46, 141
Smith, Ken 27
Smith, Red 171
Soriano, Alfonso 2, 33
Southern Association 84, 100
Southworth, Billy 34
Speaker, Tris 32, 72–73, 181
Sport 100
The Sporting News 7, 19, 132, 134, 136
Sportsman's Park 40, 78, 80–81, 124, 179
"The Squire of Kennett Square" 122
Stengel, Casey 126

Stephenson, Riggs 110–111, 115
Stever, Max 115
Strand, Paul 17–18
Street, Gabby 101
"Subway Series" 141
Suhr, Gus 13
Sullivan Timmy 148
"The Sultan of Swat" 43, 50, 67, 123
Summers, Bill 148–150
Sundra, Steve 137
Sunset Mausoleum 171
Swift, Bill 158

Telegraph Hill 171
"The Terror of Telegraph Hill" 145
Terry, Bill 107, 141–143, 150, 165
Tettrazzini, Louisa 10
Thevenough, Tommy 40, 42
Thomas, Myles 25, 32–33, 48
Three-Eye League 14
Tiger Stadium 107
Tilden, Bill 44
Time 54
"Tony the Wop" 59
Toronto Maple Leafs 165
Trachtenberg, Leo 7, 27
Traynor, Pie 61, 64, 158
Turbeville, George 138

Uhle, George 118
United Press 53, 168
Upchurch, Woody 139

Van Atta, Russ 118
Vance, Dazzy 28–29
Vass, George 159
Veeck, Bill 172, 183
Veeck, William C. 96
Vitale, Albert H. 58
Vitt, Oscar 15–16, 21, 163

Walberg, Rube 85, 101
Walker, Dixie 118
Walker, Jimmy 24, 50
"The Walloping Wop" 59
Waner, Lloyd 61, 180
Waner, Paul 61–62, 158
Wanninger, Peewee 24
Ward, Aaron 24, 47
Ward, Arch 119–120
Warneke, Lon 110, 113
Warner Brothers 41

Watson, Thomas 10
Weiss, George 115–116
Wells, Ed 84, 90
Wera, Julie 46, 51, 70
Werber, Billy 148–149
Western League 14
Whitehead, Burgess 152, 165
Whitehill, Earl 119
Wicker, Kemp 148–149
Williams, Ted 105
Williams College 46
Wilson, Jimmie 79–80
The Winning Team 41
Woodlawn Cemetery 89
Woods, Doc 78, 87
The World 52

Wright, Glenn 61, 64
Wrigley, Phil 152–153, 156
Wrigley Field 110, 120, 155–157, 161, 163
Wuestling, Harry 94–95

"The Yankee Clipper" 161, 174
"Yankee Doodle Zany" 138
Yankee Stadium 34, 40, 45, 49–51, 54, 63, 76, 106, 121, 136–137, 145, 150, 162–163, 179
Yawkey, Tom 126
Young, Cy 8

Zachary, Tom 74, 78, 80, 88
Zimmerman, Heinie 170

www.ingramcontent.com/pod-product-compliance
Ingram Content Group UK Ltd.
Pitfield, Milton Keynes, MK11 3LW, UK
UKHW042001140426
5217IPUK00015B/922